Also by Harold T. P. Hayes

Three Levels of Time
The Last Place on Earth
Smiling Through the Apocalypse:
Esquire's History of the 60s

THE
DARK
ROMANCE OF
DIAN FOSSEY

Harold T. P. Hayes

SIMON AND SCHUSTER

NEW YORK • LONDON • TORONTO • SYDNEY • TOKYO • SINGAPORE

Simon and Schuster
Simon & Schuster Building
Rockefeller Center
1230 Avenue of the Americas
New York, New York 10020

SIMON AND SCHUSTER and colophon are registered trademarks
of Simon & Schuster Inc.

Designed by Sheree L. Goodman
Manufactured in the United States of America

1 3 5 7 9 10 8 6 4 2

Library of Congress Cataloging-in-Publication Data

Hayes, Harold.
The dark romance of Dian Fossey / Harold T. P. Hayes.
p.   cm.
Includes bibliographical references.
1. Fossey, Dian.   2. Gorilla—Rwanda.   3. Zoologists—United
States—Biography.   I. Title.
QL31.F65H39   1990
591'.092—dc20

[B]   90-34941
                                                                        CIP

ISBN 0-671-63339-2

ACKNOWLEDGMENTS

Countless people were helpful to my late husband in the writing of this book. Rather than risk omitting anyone—a sin for which I could never forgive myself—I simply wish to thank all of those who were so generous with their time, help, and support. He was deeply indebted to all of you.

For my own part, I do feel the need to give special thanks to those who were integral to the completion of this book: Ursula Obst, whose help in every area was unequalled; Candida Donadio, Harold's agent and dear friend throughout his career; Alice Mayhew, Harold's editor; George Hodgman, who contributed so much time and talent; Tom Christie, whose help as both journalist and friend were indispensable; Diana McMeekin, who gave of herself far beyond the call of duty; Cherry Alvarado, who was always there when we needed her, Ed Gierke and Jane Centofante, who helped not only in research but in countless other ways; and Dr. Wilbur Schwartz, who gave so much to both of us not only as a doctor but also as our friend.

—J.K.H.

I dedicate this book to my

beloved wife, Judy Kessler

Harold Hayes
August 8, 1988

CONTENTS

Contents

PREFACE

My husband, Harold Hayes, was a man of many passions. He loved
literature, adored music, both classical and jazz, played tennis with a
vengeance, loved good food—especially great breakfasts—thrived on
stimulating conversation, and had an unquenchable curiosity about
almost everything.

But the one thing he loved more than anything else was Africa.
From the first time he went there, in 1969, he was smitten; he
wanted to know more. So he learned. He searched, he dug, he
returned to the continent again and again. His first book, *The Last Place
on Earth*, the result of his initial fascination and concern, was published in 1976.

He took me to Africa for the first time in 1980 and I, too, got
hooked on the place, before the plane even landed. From the air I saw
wild animals roaming free—zebra, giraffe, elephant, wildebeest, and
gazelle. Somehow, it just changes you for life.

13

It was on this first trip, sitting around a campfire at the Mara River camp at Masai Mara, that I first heard of Dian Fossey. We had just finished a sumptuous dinner in the middle of the bush after a day on safari in the African sun, when a thin, quiet man sat down to join us. His name was Bob Campbell and he had spent three years with Fossey, photographing her work with the mountain gorillas in the rain forests of Rwanda for the *National Geographic* magazine. He seemed to know everything about her, and the conversation went on well into the night. I could see that Harold was mesmerized.

I didn't hear Fossey's name again until December 29, 1985. My husband was reading the *New York Times* when he came upon a tiny article buried in the paper saying that primatologist Dian Fossey had been found murdered in her cabin at Karisoke, her research camp in Rwanda. Her killer had not been found. Harold was shocked and intrigued. Ever since her favorite gorilla, Digit, was killed by poachers in December 1977, attracting worldwide publicity, Dian Fossey had been credited as the savior of the few remaining mountain gorillas in the world. Harold was desperate to know what really happened. The subject matter was familiar to him now, and he already knew many of the main characters. Over the years he had gained greatly in stature as a foremost writer on African conservation. The next day he told me that *Life* magazine had called and asked him to go to Rwanda immediately to do the story.

We had, I believe—and oddly enough—a perfect marriage. It was such an unlikely match that it could only have been made by some superior power: the son of a Southern Baptist minister from North Carolina and a Jewish girl from Seattle twenty years his junior. We loved each other deeply, we did everything together, we seldom argued, and we always treasured the time that we had. Above all, we were totally open, we talked constantly about everything, and we never lied to each other. When Harold told me about the assignment from *Life*, I was devastated. We had moved to California from New

York two years earlier and our lives were frenetic. I couldn't bear to think of his going so far away, to a place that I loved as much as he did, without me. So I told him how I felt and that he should turn down the job. I simply couldn't stand to be separated from him so long. Besides that, I was jealous.

But nothing, including me, could keep him from the Africa he loved and the work that drove him. So, in typical style, Harold resolved the problem. "Come with me," he said, as though it were the most obvious solution in the world. "Quit your job." Besides the fact that Harold could convince me of virtually anything, the temptation in this case was simply too great. So I quit my job at *Entertainment Tonight*, packed my bag, and set out to do the story with Harold in Rwanda.

It was my third trip to Africa, and by far the best. We flew first to London, where we began to meet the cast of characters in this amazing drama. After a night's rest, we set out by train to see former Karisoke researchers Ian Redmond in Bristol and Alexander Harcourt in Cambridge. When we arrived in Kigali, Rwanda's capital, the town was playing host to a suddenly-called conference of heads of state from Rwanda, Uganda, and Zaire. We were lucky to get a "class B" hotel, which provided windows with no screens and beds with no mattresses. We had been advised by an official of the United States Information Agency whom we met on the plane from Nairobi to Kigali that we would be wise to avoid eating anything but eggs in Rwanda.

The next day we drove to Ruhengeri, at the base of the mountain where Karisoke is located, over typically murderous African roads, both of us well stuffed with eggs. Harold had made the climb to Karisoke several years earlier and tried to impress upon me how difficult it was. "You're ten thousand feet up, your boots get stuck in the sticky, muddy cottonsoil so badly that your feet pop right out of them. It's so cold and damp, but you're sweating like crazy because the energy it takes to climb under these circumstances is unimaginable," he told me. Undaunted, knowing I could beat him at tennis and was still twenty years younger, I shrugged off the warnings. Within moments, I thought I would die. Gasping for breath, I slipped and slid up the hill, groping at vines sticking out of the mud to keep me from sliding all the way back where I started. But with each slippery, sloppy, tiny advance, I somehow managed to gain a little more ground than I lost. Tears filled my eyes and mosquitoes swarmed around me. But all of this became insignificant when I looked up to see a mother gorilla holding her baby and looking at me like I was crazy. It was the most thrilling moment of my life. And in that instant I understood something about the consuming obsession of Dian Fossey's life.

When we got to the top, to Karisoke, totally soaked, the woodsmen let us into a cabin to dry our clothes by the fire. We were waiting for Wayne McGuire, who would eventually be accused by the Rwandan government of Fossey's murder, but he had not yet returned from the field. When he came back, tired and wet, we chatted for several hours in his cabin, and promised him we would call his mother when we returned to the States.

Over the next month we spent time with many of the people who were integral in one way or another to Dian's life and death: besides Redmond, Harcourt, and McGuire, there were her best friend and supporter, Rosamond Carr, researchers Bill Weber and Amy Vedder, whose views of Dian were strongly opposed to Carr's, and Jean Pierre von der Becke, yet another detractor, the head of the Mountain Gorilla Project. Back in Nairobi, we lunched with Bob Campbell and his wife on the terrace of the Norfolk Hotel, a memorable meeting in which we learned the true nature of the relationship between Fossey and Campbell.

It soon became clear to both of us that this story would go far beyond the article for *Life*. (The *Life* article, along with Dian's own book, became the basis for the film *Gorillas in the Mist*. But at the time the magazine article was published and the film went into production, Harold had uncovered only a fraction of the whole story.) Harold was totally engrossed and determined to find out everything there was to discover about this fascinating and mysterious woman. He interviewed literally hundreds of people. He talked to best friends and lovers, teachers and enemies—there seemed to be no end to the people who could tell just a little more about Dian. Putting the pieces together became an unrelenting, yet tantalizing quest, and if my own involvement had not been so great, I'm sure I would have resented the fact that this woman had essentially lived with us since 1986.

The book became the highlight of Harold's life. A famous editor who had probably read as much good fiction and nonfiction as any living human being, he was constantly astounded at the richness of this story. Each time he dug up a new and more amazing piece of information, he would get a smug look on his face that I grew to understand meant, "You're really not going to believe *this*," but he would not tell me what it was until he wrote it; he always wanted to keep me in suspense.

When he was well into the writing of his book, we sat talking about it on the patio of our house, over a glass of wine. Harold said to me, "Jude, I've only lied to you once. And I have to tell you about it now." I couldn't imagine what it could be.

"*Life* didn't ask me to do this story," he confessed. "I called them and told them that I wanted to go." What a glorious way to spend the last three years of his life.

Harold Hayes died of a brain tumor on April 5, 1989, only pages away from finishing the book in the way he had planned. The respect and admiration of all those he worked so closely with in the course of this enormous undertaking are beautifully summed up in a letter that I received from Diana McMeekin, vice president of the African Wildlife Foundation in Washington, D.C., shortly after his death:

I did not know Harold as well as I would have wished—with a handful of pleasant exceptions our contact was almost exclusively by telephone and letter. We met in 1981 when he was researching an article for *Life* magazine, but I learned of his passing last week with profound sadness. So many of those whose lives he touched throughout his illustrious career have lost a valued friend.

The illusion of having known him longer is due in part to having known of him and admired his work for several years. I have said when asked, and volunteered when not, that *The Last Place on Earth* is the single finest piece of writing ever done about the realities of conservation in Africa. I have told Harold often that his book saved me from many a stray bullet when I first began to work in East Africa, and that I re-read it frequently for renewed inspiration and guidance. Each time the reading brought not only valuable information, but also unfailing pleasure for the craft and intelligence which he exercised so skillfully. A century from now, if there is still an earth left to conserve and people charged with the will to do so, *The Last Place on Earth* will still be read and valued.

Harold's love of language, both written and verbal, made him a joy to read and listen to. But a lot of good writers and a multitude of good talkers have come out of the South. What set Harold apart was his respect for language and for the integrity of the facts it could be employed to convey. No contemporary writer of whom I'm aware was as dedicated to the search for information's roots as he. His disciplined determination to find out all there was to know before allowing himself the luxury of telling, elevated him to a class of one. We have lost not only the man but all the knowledge he would have led us to.

Only a few weeks before Harold died—his intense interest and total immersion in this subject undiminished—we were watching some videotapes about gorillas that he had been collecting when he came across a quote by the philosopher Henry Beston that struck him deeply. It said: "We need another and a wiser and perhaps a more mystical concept of animals. For the animal shall not be measured by man. They are not brethren. They are not underlings. They are other nations caught with ourselves in the net of life and time; fellow prisoners of the splendor and travail of birth."

"That," Harold told me, "is really what this book is about."

Judith Kessler Hayes
Los Angeles, California
April, 1989

THE
DARK
ROMANCE OF
DIAN FOSSEY

You can outdistance that which is running
after you but not what is running inside you.

—*Rwandan proverb*

1

A MURDER IN RWANDA

The soft trade winds that blow in from the Indian Ocean across the tops of Rwanda's Virunga volcanos are responsible for much of the gloom and discomfort at Dian Fossey's Karisoke Centre for Mountain Gorilla Research. The warm equatorial air condenses there, enshrouding Karisoke, high in the Virungas, with mist and rain. But the moisture also provides a long-term gain. Rwanda's volcanos mark the far western shelf of the Great Rift Valley, a cresting point of the continental divide. Water flowing off them to the east runs into the Nile, and to the west into the Congo. The discomforts of Karisoke are part of the process that sustains the two mighty rivers of Africa, which in turn sustain most of the life on the continent.

Visitors to Karisoke, however, quickly lose sight of the rain's benefits. Even when it isn't raining, the days are dark, and the steep trails around the camp are difficult to maneuver. In the rain, they are hopeless.

•   •   •

Wayne McGuire, one of Dian Fossey's student researchers, was tired of it all. He cursed the weather as he watched the slow but purposeful movements of the gorillas in Group 5 and muttered to himself about Fossey's foul mood. Christmas was too big a deal for her. McGuire didn't think she was any more religious than he was, but she was hung up on the holiday. First she had planned this big Christmas party for everybody; then she postponed it until New Year's Eve because she had guests from the States coming up. But instead of just letting it ride until then, she had kept right on getting ready, decorating her cabin, wrapping presents and, like a closet Scrooge, hating it all, every step of the way.

Several days back, watching her decorate the Christmas tree in her cabin, and hoping to warm her up, McGuire had ventured an opening.

"Oh, you've got a Christmas tree," he said. "How nice."

"McGuire," she said, "why don't you get out of my life?"

McGuire had been at Karisoke since July and that fact showed in his appearance. His face was almost obscured by hair, dark locks of it spilling out of his trucker's cap and merging with a full-grown woodsman's beard. He was a big man. With his heavy rain gear he bulked to the size of a halfback. He looked like nobody's scapegoat, too rugged, certainly, for any woman to pick on. But when he thought of Fossey, his face gathered into a scowl.

She always called him by his last name. Nobody had called him by his last name since he was a kid at the YMCA in Hoboken. But he had let it pass, as he had let many things pass since coming there the previous summer. Fossey had got on his case the first week, studiously ignoring him at first, then testing him by sending him into Zaire to look for lone silverbacks. Then she rode him continually about the time he got lost overnight. And he just took it. McGuire had promised himself he would go with the flow.

Oohhmmm-aahhhh-ohhmmmmm . . . half moaning, half belching,

26

McGuire made the sound all the researchers had learned from Fossey, who had learned it from the gorillas. He wanted to reassure the members of Group 5 that he was still there, sitting quietly and minding his own business. They were starting to settle down for a siesta. To see better, he shifted his weight in the wet brambles, moving carefully. The last thing he was going to do was take these animals for granted, especially Pablo, the fiesty blackback who had a cute tendency to grab you by the collar and run off with you. Pablo was at least four times stronger than he, and McGuire had learned not to resist when Pablo grabbed him.

The center of attention now, however, was not Pablo but a great silverback named Ziz, who weighed in at four hundred pounds or so. Stretching out on his belly, he looked like a monstrously huge drowsing dog. McGuire could never get quite used to the terrifying size of the silverback; his forearms were the size of a sumo wrestler's thighs, his hands were like catcher's mitts. When he yawned you could see canines the size of a lion's. Ziz ran things in Group 5. When infants hurled themselves at him, he would endure the transgression without reaction. But when the infants began to pick on each other, Ziz glared sternly and the commotion stopped instantly. In no other species of great ape does the principal male concern himself so protectively with the welfare of the young. This, in a nutshell, was the whole reason that Wayne McGuire, on December 26, 1985, was sitting in wet brambles on top of a volcano in Africa. His research for his Ph.D. dissertation in anthropology was centered on male parental care in the mountain gorilla community, a subject that could be investigated nowhere else. With diligence, persistence, and not a lot of money, McGuire had worked his way through college and graduate school, earning a master's degree. Now his further advancement depended on Dian Fossey. It had taken him four years just to get her consent to come to Karisoke. *Four years!* He wasn't about to blow it. If Fossey wanted him to get lost while she decorated her Christmas tree, he would get lost.

27

He had stayed clear of her until the night before, Christmas night, when she had insisted that he and Joseph, the Rwandese biology student in camp, come to her cabin for Christmas dinner. Knowing what he did about her crazy shifts in mood, he should have expected the inevitable—the swift and total collapse of her dinner party. Joseph was the first to get the treatment. His faculty adviser at Rwanda's small university had sent up a request for some rain gear, saying he fully intended to pay for it. But Fossey lit into Joseph for the man's presumption, implying he wanted the stuff for nothing. "You *don't* ask people to give away things at Christmas," she had yelled, her eyes burning. "You *don't do that!*"

Fossey looked like hell, and with plenty of reasons. Locked up in her cabin all the time, she seldom saw the light of day. And beyond that, beyond the boozing, the chronic emphysema stoked by three packs of cigarettes a day, the recurring pneumonia, and the insomnia, she just didn't care. She made an effort to pull herself together when guests came up. Otherwise, she didn't try. "God, I haven't taken a bath in four days," she once said to McGuire, and she smelled like it, too. But when she got crazy, it wasn't her appearance that struck McGuire, it was the force of her wrath. Anything could happen then. He had seen her get pissed off at park officials down in Kigali, whom she suspected of trying to take over her camp. She was going to stockpile kerosene to torch the place, she said. Nobody doubted she was capable of it.

When Fossey started railing against Joseph's adviser, McGuire and Joseph had responded as the students usually did. They did nothing; they called it the Gandhi response. They just sat there waiting for her to exhaust her fury. Fossey ranted and raged, screaming and yelling about how miserable Joseph's professor was. And then she shrieked at the cook, making the Africans so nervous they started dropping things. By that time she was screaming and yelling that the dinner was cold.

Trying to shake the memory, McGuire gathered up his gear and eased back out of the gorillas' resting site. Making his way back toward the camp, he skidded and slid from brier patch to bramble bush. The rain and the muck were endless, the mud so deep in places you could sink up to your thighs. The longer you stayed, the worse it became. Nothing much you could do about that. But it was also almost unbearably lonely—and some of that was Fossey's fault. The person who runs a field station sets its style. Fossey's Karisoke Research Centre—she insisted on the British spelling—was hermitic. She stayed in her cabin all day and all night, and expected the researchers to stay in theirs when they weren't in the field. They all ate their meals alone. If they wanted to say something to somebody, they sent a note. McGuire didn't know any language but his own, and English was the fourth preferred language in Rwanda. He couldn't even talk with the staff.

McGuire realized he had spent too much time on the mountain. Going "bushy" was Fossey's word for it. Back in the States, his faculty adviser had predicted that could happen. You should make it a point of going down every two weeks, his adviser had warned. If you don't, you will start to change without knowing it. Fossey didn't want to go down at all anymore. If it only took seven weeks to make him bushy, what must it be like for a woman who'd been up there almost eighteen years?

McGuire let himself into his cabin. Trying not to think about the giant rats under the floor, he fixed himself a cup of hot tea and fell into an exhausted sleep.

At 5:45 the next morning, McGuire was awakened by Kenyaragana, Dian's houseman, shouting outside his door. "Dian *kufa kufa*," he yelled. *Kufa* was one of the few Swahili words McGuire could understand. It meant "dead."

Pulling on his clothes as he ran, McGuire covered the path to Fossey's cabin in minutes. Everything inside the house was a mess. Drawers were pulled out. Shattered glass littered the floor. Fossey was lying on her back in bed in her long johns, completely still.

Moving closer, he could see that her face had been split open. Still frozen to her features was the agony of that moment of death, a splintered expression of horror. McGuire went to her side and felt for her pulse. Her body was cold, her arm stiff.

Later that day Kathleen Austen, duty officer at the American Embassy in Kigali, decided that she had better go over to national park headquarters, the Office Rwandais du Tourisme et des Parcs Nationaux (ORTPN) at Kinigi, where there was radio communication to Karisoke. She wanted to confirm an earlier message received by the embassy that Dian Fossey was dead, possibly murdered. With the post of ambassador vacant and everyone else gone for the weekend, Austen was, at that moment, the principal representative of the United States in Rwanda.

A woman in her late thirties, brisk and impatient, Austen seemed equal to any executive challenge. When confirmation of Dian Fossey's murder arrived at ORTPN, Austen knew at once she would have to go up the mountain. But she didn't know what would be expected of her once she was there. This was the murder of an American citizen on foreign soil and the victim was an internationally famous scientist. The murder was sure to attract world scrutiny. What laws applied? What protocol? What should she expect from the host country? She had never even been up to Karisoke.

But she knew someone who had: Amy Vedder. A primatologist affiliated with the New York Zoological Society, Vedder was in trim good shape from chasing apes up and down Rwanda's hills. She and her husband, a USAID program researcher named Bill Weber, were old Rwanda hands. Back in the seventies, just out of the Peace Corps, they had worked as research assistants to Fossey at Karisoke, and then stayed on in Rwanda. Vedder could speak French and Swahili; she was known and liked by most of the Africans on Fossey's staff, and to Austen's good fortune, she had dropped by ORTPN just as Austen herself had walked in. Austen asked Vedder if she would go up the mountain with her. She expected to stay overnight.

Despite the obvious urgency of the situation, Vedder took a moment to think it over. She had never seen a dead person, and she didn't welcome the opportunity. She was nursing her infant son and hadn't been parted from him for more than a few hours at a time. Both were reasons enough for saying no. Furthermore, Vedder abhorred Fossey, and vice versa. On selected occasions Fossey, with great enthusiasm, had referred to Vedder as "the Cunt." But, given the dire circumstances, and her concern for the mountain gorillas left without Fossey's protective presence, Vedder turned the baby over to her husband and accompanied Austen to the base station at Visoke. From there they made the two-hour climb to Fossey's camp.

By the time they arrived it was nearly dark. Vedder spotted Neymeye, one of Karisoke's most skilled trackers, a man in his early thirties who had worked for Fossey since he was sixteen. He had tracked for Vedder some years earlier. She saw he was upset and went over to him, embracing him in Rwandese fashion with a hug on both sides and a kiss on the cheek. An unusual gesture for a white to make toward a Rwandan, Vedder's embrace did not escape the notice of the guards who watched the women as they approached Fossey's cabin. Inside the cabin, kerosene lamps burned and several dozen people milled about. The mood was subdued; the talk was soft. At the dining table, an investigator was questioning one of the members of Fossey's African staff. Two typists recorded his answers.

Vedder knew Wayne McGuire better than Austen did. She had met him in August when he first came to Rwanda. She thought McGuire looked a little shaky, but basically okay, in control of himself. She hoped that Austen would be just as stoic. Though Austen was not here to conduct an investigation (officially she was present only to confirm Fossey's death), she was obliged to view the body and review the circumstances of the murder. The Rwandese officials gathered about her. They asked Dr. Philippe Bertrand, the French surgeon from the Ruhengeri hospital, to examine the body, which he did as Austen looked on. Since the cause of death—a crushing blow to the head—was apparent, he saw no reason to perform an autopsy.

31

A quick inspection was made of the house and its contents. A blood-stained panga, or machete, presumably the murder weapon, was found under Fossey's bed and there was a gun on the floor. A hole cut from the outside through the tin wall of Fossey's bedroom was evidently the intruder's point of entry. Nothing of value was missing. Rwandese and American money were found in a dresser drawer.

By 7:30 it was over. Fossey's cabin was locked. Guards were posted around the camp. Jean Pierre von der Becke, head of a conservation agency known as the Mountain Gorilla Project, the Rwandese officials, and Dr. Bertrand headed back down the mountain. Austen and Vedder decided to stay in the cabin closest to Fossey's for the night, and for a while McGuire joined them. All three urgently needed to talk about what had happened. Much of it was still unclear. There were only shards and fragments, random details, scattered around one indisputable fact: in the early morning hours of December 27, 1985, Dian Fossey was brutally murdered.

Later memories of the murder scene would inevitably vary with each observer. Wayne McGuire remembered more than Kathleen Austen and Amy Vedder because he was there throughout the day. His account of finding the body was consistent with what Austen had heard from others. She herself particularly remembered the Christmas tree. The holiday had passed, but the presents, all tagged under the tree, hadn't been opened.

McGuire remembered an empty quart bottle of Primus beer in the top drawer of Fossey's desk, and on top of the desk, a half-empty bottle of Johnny Walker scotch. He thought that Fossey might have been in a drunken stupor and, when she heard her wall being cut open, tried to load her pistol, but before she could do this, she was struck in the back of the head and, rolling over, was hit in the face. The doctor had said her death was not instantaneous. Her body was bruised, McGuire said, as if the killer had hit it to see if she was still alive. But Austen remembered no significant bruises on the body.

McGuire said that Fossey held human hair in her right fist. Austen remembered hair in both Fossey's fists. Vedder remembered Dr. Bertrand saying to Austen that he was 95 percent sure the hair was Fossey's, that it was European hair, but if she wanted to be certain it could be analyzed. Later, when Austen announced she had taken samples of the hair for this purpose, Vedder was shocked at the implication: McGuire was the only white person in the camp at the time of the murder. McGuire said nothing.

Who had murdered Dian Fossey? And why?

Neither Austen nor McGuire nor Vedder, who had known her longest, was qualified to deal with these questions. Fossey's many enemies predated the three of them. Poachers, cattle herders, park officials, Western conservationists, members of her staff, a couple dozen researchers—the parade of possible suspects extended far back into the past. In pursuit of her singular goal, the protection of the endangered mountain gorilla, Fossey had shot at her enemies, kidnapped their children, whipped them about the genitals, smeared them with ape dung, killed their cattle, burned their property, and sent them to jail. Anyone who dared to threaten her gorillas, or even to challenge her methods, set her off, and the force of her malevolence was difficult to imagine.

She was not unaware of her excesses in this respect, and sometimes even joked about it. In 1977, she remarked to an old friend that the eruption of a volcano in the Virungas, just a few miles north of Karisoke, could be traced directly to the displeasure of Dian Fossey. It was her temper exploding, and it had caused a sympathetic reaction from Mount Nyiragongo, who was her sister. Fossey raising her voice in anger had caused her sister to belch up 80,000 cubic meters of lava, flowing at the rate of 100 kilometers an hour into the streets of Goma.

But if Fossey was so aware of the fierceness of her passion, how could she seem so blithely indifferent to its consequences? She lived in a setting far removed from legal restraints or police protection. She was easy prey for revenge. And she was no fool. She understood the risks of the life she had chosen since her first months in Zaire, in 1967. Clearly, had it not been for her gorillas, she wouldn't have tempted fate—wouldn't now be dead. So it was also an indisputable fact that Dian Fossey had died for her gorillas.

The morning of Dian Fossey's funeral, Tuesday, December 31, was beautiful. Glistening bright green against the rich black soil of the potato field, the tangled vine wall of the looming rain forest appeared almost benign, inviting.

About fifty people gathered around Kathleen Austen's Toyota, waiting—quite a number for such a climb, but at least half of them were porters, hired to carry the coffin up the mountain to Karisoke. The mourners included three members of the U.S. Embassy in Kigali; the Reverend Elton Wallace, who would conduct the service, and his wife; and Rosamond Carr, Dian's oldest and best friend in Rwanda. Silver-haired, slender, and with a regal bearing, Mrs. Carr was seventy-four. She hadn't made the climb to Karisoke in eight years and needed every bit of her strength to make it even at her own pace. She started up the trail early.

The Wallaces, who had never climbed the mountain, left with her. The Reverend Wallace, formerly of St. Helena, California, and now of the Seventh-day Adventist University in Gisenyi, struggled up the muddy path, slipping and skidding, attempting to keep both his body in balance and his mind on the ball. He wondered what he would say about the deceased. His neighbor Rosamond Carr had asked him to conduct the service, but he hadn't known Dian Fossey, except by reputation. Nor had he had time to prepare the kind of funeral service he felt she deserved. He had decided on the scriptures, but a fitting eulogy continued to elude him. He would include some reference to Fossey's defense of her beloved gorillas, maybe a call for others to come to their aid. But what else? He still lacked a theme.

Rosamond Carr, walking next to Wallace, stopped to catch her breath as they approached the meadow's edge at Karisoke. Yes, it was just as she remembered it: the tall mossy Hagenias encircling the wild grass meadow, the clear pure little stream, the vaulting lobelias and the orchids growing wild. It was eighteen years since she had first come there to visit Dian Fossey. All Fossey had then were three tents, one for herself, another for storage, and a small pup tent for guests. Carr could still remember their dinner that night—mushroom soup and a cold chicken she had brought up. They had sat laughing and talking, smoke from the fire bringing tears to their eyes all through the evening. In the middle of the night Carr had been awakened by an elephant wandering close to her tent, and as she lay there frightened and apprehensive, she had marveled at Fossey, typing away by the light of a kerosene lamp, oblivious to this gargantuan distraction.

While awaiting the arrival of the mourners, the Wallaces and Mrs. Carr walked across the meadow to Fossey's cabin. Looking through the windows into the dark dining room, they wondered anew at the awful tragedy.

Wallace circled the cabin and came upon the grave site. He saw that Fossey's resting place was to be among the gorillas who had died there before, with Mwelu and Uncle Bert and the other giant primates the world had come to know through her National Geographic films and her book. Fossey had fashioned this graveyard just for her gorillas; a wooden cross bearing the animal's name stood at the head of each grave. She would rest beside the gorilla she had named Digit, whose death at the hands of poachers had caught the world's interest and brought help to her tiny beleaguered forces.

Quite suddenly, just as the coffin bearers arrived at the edge of the meadow, the message Wallace was seeking came to him. He rehearsed it in his mind as the coffin was carried to the site, where the gravediggers were still at work.

Many brought flowers to place on the coffin: yellow lilies, a single red rose, and some of the plants gorillas favored—thistles, Galium vines, and blackberries. As the gravediggers worked on, the mourners waited, a curious assemblage.

Looking slightly dazed and confused—he had thought Wallace a Catholic priest, and Fossey a Jew—Wayne McGuire held a color postcard of Fossey sitting among her gorillas. Amy Vedder had come back for reasons that were still complicated and troubling to her. She didn't believe in God, but if she had, she would have held no illusions about the ultimate disposition of Fossey's soul. Still, since she was the one former researcher left in Rwanda who *could* come up, she was there to show some gesture of respect. Standing with her colleagues from the embassy, her face tight and unrevealing, Kathleen Austen was there because it was required of her. She was discharging her duty as representative of the United States and now, thank God, it was almost over.

Crowding in on all of them were the Africans—five or six for each European. They had carried Fossey's coffin on their backs, and it was their earth into which the Reverend Wallace was about to consign her. Would they be there if they didn't have to be? What might they be thinking about this woman who had bent their laws to her will, insisting on her higher right to chase and physically abuse their countrymen?

In this somber gathering under the wet black Hagenia trees, as the mourners waited hushed and reflective while the diggers toiled, Rosamond Carr wept quietly. If no one else knew or cared much about Fossey's past, Rosamond Carr knew and cared very much. She knew of Fossey's troubled childhood and of the horrid times in the Congo when just to be white was to risk your life. She knew of Fossey's indomitable persistence in trampling through these alien rain forests, and of the desperate love affair that had crushed everything inside her but her will to stay on. She knew of Fossey's tenderness for those she cared for, and she cherished her friend's matchless integrity.

The Reverend Wallace raised his eyes and looked around him, indicating the service was about to begin. First he read the selection of verses he had chosen, and next he offered some of the personal remembrances about Fossey that he had received from Mrs. Carr. Then he delivered his eulogy.

"Last week," he said, "the world did honor to a long-ago event that changed its history more than any other, the coming if its Lord to earth fashioned as a man, born in a manger. We see at our feet a parable of that magnificent condescension: Dian Fossey, born to a home of comfort and privilege she left by her choice to live among a race facing extinction. It was not to be an easy life; nor would she be widely praised. How often she may have been tempted to give it up and return to her own. But she deemed it worth the sacrifice. And when evil men conspired to take her life she has come to be buried with those among whom she has lived and among whom she has died. . . . I weep again," Wallace said, "not for Dian. There was a completeness about her life beyond sorrow. But for my Lord. . . ."

As the casket was slowly lowered into the ground, Rosamond Carr turned away. "I can't bear this anymore," she said to no one, except to herself and the friend who was not there.

Then, in a moment of rare perception, Wallace offered a benediction that even the skeptical Dian Fossey might have respected:

"And if you think the distance that Christ came to take the likeness of man is not so great as that from man to gorilla, then you don't know men or gorillas, or God."

2

SEEDS OF
CHOICE

An underrated form of personal communication is that section of any newspaper or magazine known as the classifieds. For those occasional readers looking to satisfy some unrealized need, some opportunity they may hope for, the classifieds offer a wealth of second chances and new starts. They hold out the lure of infinite possibility, a dice roll on the future. And for some gamblers, those tiny lines of print may prove to be a turning point or crossroads.

In 1954, a graduating senior at San Jose State College in California, Dian Fossey was interning at local hospitals to earn her certification as an occupational therapist, her second-best choice for a lifetime career. What she had wanted most was to work with animals, but her grades in science in her first two years at the University of California at Davis were too low to qualify her for veterinary school. And so, since she was also drawn to children, especially helpless children, she had changed both her residence and her curriculum. For her last two years she enrolled at San Jose, where she could learn how to teach crafts to crippled patients, preferably children. Now, with the end of her internship in sight, Fossey was looking for a job.

She didn't ask for much. She had no desire to stay in California, and hoped to get as far away as she could. She wanted to find a place where she could be near animals, horses in particular. She had no driving compulsion to see the world, or to make a lot of money. There was no lover to hold her back. Scanning the classified section of the *American Journal of Occupational Therapy*, she found an ad for an occupational therapist at Kosair Crippled Children's Hospital in Louisville, Kentucky. Louisville seemed to her like the dead center of the United States. It was far enough away from home, and she was certain there would be more horses there than anywhere else. Louisville would be fine. Why not?

In the same year, in the less agreeable climate of London—he would recall it as a particularly cold and wet day in November—Walter Baumgartel wandered off Cockspur Street and into the reading room of a Barclay's Bank. He had taken an idle notion to glance through newspapers of the various countries of the Commonwealth (a task which would have occupied more of his time in 1954 than it would today). He browsed with no particular purpose, but the papers stirred a vague longing in him.

Baumgartel, who was almost old enough to be Dian Fossey's father, was thinking of making a move. An established wanderer, he had flown for the South African air force as an aerial photographer, run a book business in Johannesburg, performed as an actor, and traveled on his own impulse through most of the big game parks in East Africa. Now at loose ends in London, scanning stories from distant places, he realized he wanted to return to the most beautiful and exciting place he'd ever been. The logotype of the *East African Standard*, a newspaper published in Nairobi, caught his eye. Turning to the classifieds, he was drawn in by an ad that read, "Partner wanted for hotel project in western Uganda . . . located at the borders of Uganda,

Rwanda and the Belgian Congo, at the foot of Virunga Volcanos, near Gorilla Sanctuary."

By responding to their respective classifieds, Fossey and Baumgartel were taking the first steps toward the path that would draw them together years later on the Kisoro lava plain beneath Uganda's Mountains of the Moon.

To the people who would come to know him and love him, Baumgartel did not look like anybody's idea of a romantic. He was short and chunky in a squared-off kind of way, like a Swiss woodcarving, and he had a thick Viennese strudel accent. And yet he had opened an adventure for himself with a casual skimming of the *East African Standard*, and he set out on it now with no less exuberance than a nineteenth-century explorer searching for the source of the Nile.

He sailed on a German cargo ship bound for the seaport of Mombasa, Kenya, on the Indian Ocean. From there he would slowly make his way to Kisoro, Uganda. In Nairobi, three hundred miles inland, he bought himself a secondhand Hillman Minx and headed over the Kenyan highlands to Kampala, the Ugandan capital, and from there in a southwesterly direction to the western edge of the Rift Valley, a delicate chain of mountains and lakes connecting, however tenuously, the Horn of Africa to the rest of the continent.

It is a geographical fact that three of the most prominent lakes along the Rift belong to Uganda. But the influence of the British was unmistakable, the lakes were named Albert, George, and Edward. Having colonized this country and put it on the civilized map, the British were still very much in charge. For any European just passing through—or, like Baumgartel, thinking of going into business there— the Crown's presence seemed an assurance of permanent stability. Though all this was abruptly to change—Lake Edward, for example, would soon be renamed Lake Idi Amin—Baumgartel had no reason to question the security of his future in his new country at the time.

When he arrived at the Kanabe Gap at 8,000 feet, what he saw laid out before him made him a very happy man.

Beyond Kisoro, through the breaking clouds, rose one of the most impressive sights on the continent: the eight Virungas, stretching westward from Uganda into Rwanda and on into the Congo. The most ancient of these great volcanos was half a million years old and the most recently formed were still active. Their scalding lava could cook the fish down in Lake Kivu, a hundred miles to the south.

The Virungas marked the continental divide, a terrestrial line beyond which the lights went out and the mystery began. Behind Baumgartel were the rolling hills and grassland plains, the sunny savanna of East Africa reaching back to the Indian Ocean, the land of Eden. Just ahead, on the far side of the Virungas, was the Congo basin—the steaming, fetid jungle which shut out the sun so that more than two-thirds of the continent, all the way to the Atlantic, lay in darkness.

In that part of Africa, in the Virungas and lands to the west, were the exotic images of Baumgartel's dreams: the tiny Pygmies of the forest, the giant Watutsi and their lyre-horned cattle; the dangerous gold smugglers lurking in the ports of Lake Kivu; the weavers of spells of witchcraft and magic; and most wondrous of all, still hidden from civilization—the continent's rarest and most secret treasure—the giant ape few people had ever seen, the mountain gorilla, which lived only in the Virungas.

These possibilities thrilled the heart of Walter Baumgartel as the verdant country seduced his senses. The air was sweet—a heady mixture of smoke, freshly turned earth, and the fragrance of flowers—and just below him, through the mist still clinging from the early morning rains, the rolling hills glistened in the white sun. In this magical corner of Uganda, everything was green and growing. Clusters of tiny farms hugged the contours of the foothills, every inch of their lava soil under cultivation. Shoots and stalks almost burst from the earth—peas and beans, potatoes and corn, bananas and pineapples. Wild things—feretia, lilacs, wild elder, African tulips—grew where the cultivated land left off. Handsome people streamed along the sides of the road. Baumgartel's spirits soared. He eagerly traveled on to Kisoro, to the site of the inn he had seen advertised.

For the seasoned traveler, the great country inns of East Africa are considered worthy destinations in themselves. Built from cut stone and African hardwoods, they offered British colonials the amenities they felt they had earned for enduring hardships in a strange place— overstuffed furniture gathered about vast open hearths, spacious dining rooms with attentive service, bathtubs deep enough to float in, and bars cozy as a Mayfair pub. At the inn in Kabala, just up the road from Kisoro, guests dressed for dinner. There was a golf course and playing fields for tennis, badminton, and croquet. Baumgartel soon discovered that his inn had little in common with the inn at Kabala. Although located, as advertised, at the intersection of the borders of Uganda, Rwanda, and the Belgian Congo, "Traveller's Rest"—the irony of the name made his teeth hurt—was a decrepit one-room wooden building with three adobe outer huts furnished only with double-decker bunks. There were no guests. Awaiting him in this seedy way station were a stack of unpaid bills and an Irish proprietor who expected Baumgartel to bail him out.

Heroically resisting the urge to move on, Baumgartel accepted the challenge, buying out his partner and laboring to put the place in some semblance of order. He refurbished the buildings, installed a toilet, planted a lawn, a vegetable garden, a flower bed, and an herb patch. He coaxed bougainvillea up the outside walls. In seven months he turned his wretched investment into a marginally comfortable little inn, though he had to resign himself to a provender that would never be considered much better than bad. Finally he was able to turn his attention to that part of the classified ad that had attracted him to Kisoro first and foremost—the mountain gorillas of the Virungas.

Baumgartel knew little about these animals, but no one, including the most informed of Western zoologists, did at that time. Though the mountain gorilla species had been known to exist since the days of Hanno, who explored the coast of Africa in 400 B.C., few had been captured or closely observed. Most of what was known came from observation of the subspecies designated as lowland gorillas. The mountain gorilla—a separate subspecies named *Gorilla gorilla beringei* after Oscar von Beringe, the German hunter who first shot one—was the largest, the most powerful, and the least known of all the great apes. In 1903, von Beringue's carcass allowed scientists to establish the taxonomy of the animal for the first time. At the time Baumgartel came to Uganda, there were none in captivity (nor are there now). Most of the very few stalwarts who had actually seen them alive had done so through the sights of high-powered rifles. There was not even a photographic record of the mountain gorilla. From the myths of his own culture and from the stories of locals who lived among them, Baumgartel learned that the most powerful of all animals was the least disposed toward human visitors. Nevertheless, he vowed to see them.

An immediate problem for him was how to get there. Mount Muhavura, seven miles away, was the closest of the Virungas peaks to Kisoro, accessible only by a deep-rutted lava-bed road which merged into a barely visible grass track. Baumgartel's secondhand car would never make it. For a man who had to put business first, it was out of the question to walk that distance to the foot of the mountain, climb its slopes, and still expect to be back by the dinner hour. Baumgartel turned to his cook, who had a bicycle.

Sensitive to his standing among the Africans with whom he now worked, he had hesitated to ask, anxious not to give the wrong impression. And then, since there really was no other way, Baumgartel went riding off to Muhavura to see what he could of the greatest of the great apes. On his cook's bicycle.

When Dian Fossey came there, Louisville was just beginning to make the transition from a large town to a small city. While certain traditional values—a deep reverence for God, strong whiskey, mild tobacco, and fine horses—remained unchanged, Louisville was waking up after an extended period of somnambulance. There were few harbingers in the Louisville of 1955 of the civil rights disturbances that would soon sweep through the South. All was calm. Even as it grew, Louisville remained under the benevolent influence of older families who had established themselves generations earlier, and among whom there was still a palpable sense of gentility and *noblesse oblige*.

The Kosair Crippled Children's Hospital was an admirable example of such benevolence. Discreetly disguised as an English manor house and set back on a rolling green shaded by pin oaks and flowering dogwoods, Kosair was supported by local businessmen and maintained without charge to the parents of the patients who were brought there, many of them the children of impoverished families from the mountains of eastern Kentucky. Most of these children were the victims of polio—an infirmity especially disheartening for those who suffered from it in 1955. The Salk vaccine, which was just then becoming available, and which would sharply reduce the disease around the world, could do nothing for those already afflicted, like the young patients in residence at Kosair.

In the field of orthopedics the job of occupational therapist, or O.T., was in 1955, as it is now, somewhat anomalous. Little medical training was required, but a qualified applicant had to have nine months of clinical training and a full college degree. An O.T. helped patients use their crippled muscles to make useful things, like baskets and pocketbooks, and constructed simple braces for the manipulation of essential tools, like a knife and fork. The pay was poor and the future limited; in orthopedics, O.T. was a dead-end job. Consequently, when Anna Quinn, the administrative superintendent at Kosair, was looking to fill a vacancy, there were more opportunities for beginning O.T.'s around the country than qualified applicants. Quinn knew of no one in Louisville who might be interested, and so she had placed the ad in the *American Journal of Occupational Therapy*.

That is how Dian Fossey arrived to join Kosair's small staff of seventeen—two doctors, five nurses, and ten aides.

Fossey was extremely shy and made no attempt to impose herself on others, but she had a resoluteness about certain things, which brooked no challenge. For one thing, she wanted to live alone in a place of her own choosing, well away from everybody else. In the local paper she found an offering of a cottage on a large estate ten miles out of town, the property of a local lawyer named George Long whose family had held it since antebellum days. Long resided in the main house, a large white neoclassical structure with tall doors and windows. An extravagant verandah encircled the entire place. But though four hundred acres of the property were still intact, there was some evidence that the Long estate was going to seed: the ersatz Greek statuary in the formal gardens had crumbled and moss had formed on the rock walls of the swimming pool. Nevertheless, near the main house, but still far enough away for privacy, was exactly the sort of accommodation Fossey was seeking: a cottage the Long family had called the "Washhouse," an outbuilding where servants had laundered the clothes of George Long's ancestors. Long had fixed the place up, dividing it into a small living room, dinette, bedroom, kitchen, and bath. It was a quarter of a mile from the main road.

Long is an affable redhead, a confirmed bachelor now taking on a bit of a belly. "On one cold rainy night, she came to my house and asked to see it," he recalls. He was disposed toward her until he learned she was single. "I told her I would show it to her, but I was looking for a couple."

Fossey said she would take it.

"I told her I really couldn't rent it to her. It would be irresponsible for me to do so. The place was too remote for a lady by herself."

Fossey said it was exactly what she was looking for, and if she couldn't have it, she would leave Louisville and return to California. Long was unmoved. He said he didn't feel comfortable accommodating her.

The next day, Long received a call from Anna Quinn, who was very concerned. "She said Dian wasn't kidding. She really would quit her job at Kosair if I didn't rent the cottage to her. She said the position Dian held had been very hard to fill. She hoped I might be persuaded to change my mind."

Fossey moved into Long's cottage and lived there ten years, moving on (to an even more remote house) only when she returned from a vacation to discover that Long had put a mobile home for his two aged aunts behind the cottage.

Long's cottage proved ideal—not just because of its privacy. Along the highway leading to the property was a convenient place to set loose unwanted dogs, and Fossey soon became accustomed to watching out for them and taking them home. At Kosair, she collected scraps from lunch trays to feed her strays.

For this reason and others which seemed a little eccentric, the staff at Kosair never knew quite what to make of Fossey. She had no boyfriend among the young interns, no outside social life as far as anyone could tell, and she showed little interest in making small talk. When the nurses gathered over coffee to gossip, she would walk away. The consensus was that Fossey liked animals better than people.

For one whose physical stature assured she could hardly be missed, Fossey was surprisingly anonymous. A doctor named Richard Welch was there four months before he became aware of her presence. Fossey clearly lacked the personal fastidiousness of the other nurses. "She was not the pinnacle of neatness," Welch recalls. "Her dress was wrinkled, her hair straight and long. She wasn't unwashed but she wasn't completely washed, either. I'm pretty straight, and frankly, I thought she was off the wall."

But appearances aside, Fossey was more than competent. Her affection for children was unforced, and she could talk with them easily. Training them to deal with their warped limbs and wasted flesh, she was tough-minded and demanding, less yielding than the nurses, with whom she sometimes quarreled. She couldn't tolerate their tendency to indulge their young patients. Some of the children disliked her, others loved her, some looked at her with grudging respect, others with near idolatry.

Norma Kelley was thirteen when Fossey came to Kosair. She had been there longer than almost anyone else. To her Fossey was exquisite—she looked just like Jackie Kennedy, she recalls—dark and beautiful but distant; her voice was hushed, tentative. She had a certain softness that showed when you caught her off guard. Fossey was the sort of person who wouldn't seek out a friendship—she would stand back and let you decide whether that's what *you* wanted, whether to be a friend or just somebody else.

Kelley had been in and out of Kosair since she was one year old. The surgeons told her she would never walk again, but they had kept trying, operating on her legs in 1956, twice in 1959, and again in 1960. In 1961 yet another operation was performed, and this time it was miraculously successful, freeing Kelley from her braces and her long residence at Kosair. She was nineteen now, and so attached to the institution that had nurtured her that she decided she wanted to work there. In April 1962, just after a job in the office came open, she traveled with her mother to Frankfort to take the civil service examination necessary to qualify. And then a terrible thing happened to her.

"Two miles out of Frankfort," Kelley recalls, "my mother lost control of the car. We broke down a concrete telephone pole and then went into a utility pole. I was sitting in the center, in the middle of the seat, and that's where we hit." In the emergency room at the Frankfort hospital, her mother had the presence of mind to have her sent back to Kosair, because of her past history of surgery there. "I remember going in. I remember seeing all those faces, the shock everybody felt. I had to be taken into surgery twice because I was going into shock and they couldn't fix everything the first time. Every time I opened my eyes Miss Fossey was standing by my bed and saying, 'Why her? Why couldn't it have been me?'"

"I don't remember a lot of the first two weeks except that I wasn't allowed to have a mirror, and all of the time, Miss Fossey was there. My jaws were broken and I had to eat baby food. She fed me, made me eat to keep up my strength."

Fossey kept encouraging her. You can do it, she told Kelley, I know you can do it. You've done everything else, you can do this. "She was always there," Kelley says, "and later, when I had to go back to my braces, I think it hurt her more than me in a way. They said I would never walk again, and it broke her heart.

"But I did walk again. And I went on to marry and have two sons."

3

FAMILY AFFAIRS

As he crept along behind Reuben, his guide, whose creaking shoes and froggy whisper broadcast their presence, Walter Baumgartel realized once again that he knew next to nothing about gorillas. His heart was pounding, and his mouth had turned dry. He was unarmed. Once they found one, what then? What if it should charge? What should he do? The conventional wisdom varied with the animal. With a charging rhino, you were supposed to wait as long as you dared and then leap to the side, hoping his momentum would carry him past you—and then you ran. But should you run from a charging gorilla, or what? Baumgartel wasn't sure. A gorilla was not a rhinoceros. It had arms and legs, like a man, and people said it had the strength of ten men!

What did he know about anything in the Virungas, for that matter—about any of the other inhabitants of those mountains? There were said to be elephants up there, buffalo, leopard, giant rats—and hyenas so hungry they took bites out of living things.

Baumgartel realized he had arranged for himself a very strange holiday. Even the process of getting there—skidding across lichen and crawling on his hands and knees through nettle thickets—had been a gross abuse of his constitution. His breath had left him hours ago, and it still hadn't returned.

Suddenly from the bamboo grove on their right came a heavy crashing sound. Both men froze. Baumgartel could see black flashes through the bamboo. The animals were moving slowly. There were three of them—two large animals and an infant. Could it be? He was expecting red-eyed monsters, and what he saw before him was—a family! Entranced, more beguiled than frightened, Baumgartel remained motionless, watching something he could never have imagined.

Seeing Reuben, the male swiftly moved off into the bush at their left and disappeared, followed immediately by the female. But the infant stopped to stare at them, became confused, and turned back toward the bamboo grove. Dashing back across the opening, the female grabbed the infant, swatted its bottom, and pulled it after her to rejoin the male. Then they were gone.

Baumgartel found himself oddly moved by what he had seen, and it was all he could think about as he slipped and skidded back down the mountain, retrieved his bicycle, and pedaled the seven jolting miles back to Traveller's Rest.

Over brandy that night, and for quite a few nights to come, Baumgartel found his thoughts moving back and forth from the demanding problems of running his little inn to the sweetly primeval family outing he had seen up on Muhavura. Through a most improbable series of coincidences he had been privileged to see something few others ever had. That little family scene had seemed astonishingly humanlike. And an Italian just back from building a road in the Congo had told him about another episode. As the men worked with their tractors, a family of gorillas had come out of the forest and stood at the edge to watch—for half an hour!

Baumgartel had the wit to appreciate the enormity of the opportunity. These were the most spectacular animals on earth, living as they had for hundreds of thousands of years. For *millions* perhaps. But who knew how long they could survive. Though the British had joined with the Belgians to establish a contiguous reserve across the forests of the Virungas to protect the gorillas, you didn't have to be a demographer to see that their future was sharply limited. World War II and God's missionaries had forever changed the face of Africa by introducing hygiene. While the human birth rate was as high as it had ever been, the death rate had dropped sharply. Everywhere, but especially here in the central highlands, there were too many people for the land available to feed them. For the gorillas of Muhavura, already taking up too much of this rich black lava soil, it was only a matter of time.

Baumgartel had to admit the future of Muhavura's gorillas was less than promising, like his own. He was in Uganda to make a living—he wasn't about to fool himself on that. If Traveller's Rest didn't make it, he would just have to pack up and head back to godforsaken civilization, an alternative that made him wince. Then slowly it dawned on him that his concerns for the future of the gorillas of Mount Muhavura and the future of Traveller's Rest need not be mutually exclusive. Why shouldn't Traveller's Rest come to be known as the one place in the world where people could see the last of the mountain gorillas? Was there any other place that could make that claim? There was not. Why shouldn't they come there? *Gorillaland!* He liked the sound of that. He would become the host for the gorillas, their sponsor—more than that, their protector. He would save them, they would save him.

But how should he go about it? To afford them any protection at all, he had to know something about them—how many there were, the extent of their range, how they organized themselves. These were questions no one could answer, since no one had made any systematic effort to observe them. Somebody ought to get up there on that mountain, Baumgartel decided. He couldn't do it, if he was going to keep his place going. Who, then?

Baumgartel hadn't the slightest idea. Even if he had known someone with the proper background (and he couldn't imagine what that might be), he had nothing to offer but his emotional support. Financially he was strapped himself, although he supposed he might manage free room and board at the inn, if that would help.

In the soft glow of his kerosene lamp, Baumgartel brooded. He needed some advice—but whose? Now the boldness that had brought him to Uganda again came into play. Without benefit of an introduction, Baumgartel decided he would write the one man he could think of who might share his concern for the gorilla, a man who had gained an international reputation as a zoologist, anatomist, archaeologist, anthropologist, and paleontologist. Baumgartel carefully composed a letter to Louis Leakey, in Nairobi.

In November 1955, after two months at the Kosair Crippled Children's Hospital, Dian Fossey had made a friend of a young secretary named Mary White Henry, with whom she shared an office. Anybody who later came to know Fossey at all would find it unusual that she had managed this so quickly. Mary believed it was mostly because she didn't push it. While the rest of the staff viewed Dian as aloof and maybe a little snooty, Mary had read her differently. She decided Dian was just shy, and so she didn't push to get too close.

But the two young women were drawn to each other by virtue of a similarity in background which others at Kosair didn't share. Dian was bookish and polite, college educated. Her formal manner bespoke obvious cultivation. She didn't talk about any of this to Mary. She didn't have to; Mary was unusually observant. The second daughter of the late M. J. Henry, a general surgeon at St. Joseph's Hospital and the respected head of one of the older families in Louisville, Mary had gone east to Manhattanville College of the Sacred Heart, and she was a member of the Junior League. There the similarities came to an end, however. Mary, who was dramatically attractive with auburn hair and pale skin, was outgoing, popular with boys, and of average height (she came up only to Dian's shoulder). Still, because they regarded the only other girl in their office as "country," Mary and Dian were drawn together. Soon Mary invited Dian to lunch at her home, a comfortable fieldstone colonial set back among the oaks on Summit Avenue, just a mile or so from the hospital.

Lunch at the Henrys' entranced Dian; the family was unlike any she had ever known. While the fare was modest (sliced tomatoes and peanut butter sandwiches) and served in the breakfast nook help-yourself style, the ambience was Hellzapoppin, a noisy stream of friends, relatives, and itinerants. Because the Henrys were Catholic, many of their guests were, too, and all of them were more exuberant than Dian would have imagined Catholics could be. Those closest to the Church were often the most colorful: Father MacPherson brought his bagpipes to play; and down from Gethsemane Abbey came a Frenchman named François, who had been imported to teach the silent Trappist monks how to sing Gregorian chant. People dashed in and out of this midday festival like the rotating cast in a summer stock comedy. Which is why, Mary cheerfully explained to Dian, the Henrys referred to their house as the Henry Hotel.

The spirit of the place could be traced to a single individual, a small, gray-haired woman with big eyes and a prominent nose who would become more important to Dian than anyone else in Louisville. This was Gaynee Henry, the mother of Mary and her older sister Betty, surrogate mother of the extended Henry family. One of her great-nieces recalls the special warmth everyone, especially children, felt in her presence. "We had an ivory chess set, and she looked just like one of the pawns, an ancient Chinese peasant in long robes. Children are afraid of wrinkles and age, but they weren't of her. It wasn't how she looked but the way she made you *feel*." Though she came from a family of some standing in the community (her father had been a distiller of sour mash bourbon), Gaynee Henry had no social pretenses. She collected people, especially oddities, and particularly relished people who traveled. "A rolling stone gathers polish," she liked to remind her daughters.

Without being oppressive about it, or trying to impose it on others, or watering it down with sentimentality, Gaynee Henry had found what she needed for herself in her Catholicism, including the strength to sustain some sadness in her life. She had lost two children, and her beloved husband, Joe, who had been fatally stricken while attending Mass the previous June. Her Catholicism was also the basis for the happiness in her life. "Our mother was a saint," Betty says. "She was never judgmental, but she somehow let you know if you weren't doing the right thing. Her daughters were never left in doubt, nor was Dian when she later came to know her." Gaynee Henry, it was obvious, was the kind of mother Dian Fossey had always wanted for herself.

Kitty Price, Dian's mother, was something of a mystery to Mary Henry, a mystery which only deepened with Dian's reluctance to discuss any part of her past. If she had friends back in California, she didn't say so, and she hardly mentioned her parents at all. In those few instances when the subject was unavoidable, she referred to Kitty as "the mother," as though she had become an abstraction. If Dian wanted to talk about her, Mary figured, she would. But she did not.

When Mary left Kosair and took a job downtown with American Express, Dian came to the Henrys' just as often so that she could be with Gaynee. Mary and Betty soon came to regard Dian as "Mother's other daughter." To all the Henrys it became increasingly apparent that Dian's deepening affection for Gaynee derived from some displacement in her own life.

But as the years passed Dian did come to let down her guard just a bit, gradually confiding a few things. By the time Dian left Louisville, Mary knew that Dian deeply resented her mother and stepfather. She had had an unhappy childhood. She had been starved for affection, and she still was. She could barely talk about these feelings. Even with Mary, she spoke haltingly, as if it were a struggle to tear the bits and pieces of memory from her mind.

In 1977, when she was forty-five years old, Fossey told a friend that she was so terrified at the prospect of going home to Atherton that she was taking along a can of Mace as protection. A few years later she confided to another friend that she did not feel physically safe in the Price household unless she slept with a pistol under her pillow. She abhorred her stepfather and complained bitterly about him all her life. In the late 1970s, when she seemed on the verge of physical and emotional collapse and her colleagues tried to place her on the staff of an American university, the possibility of a post at Berkeley arose. She said this was out of the question because it would oblige her to live in the same state as her stepfather, Richard Price.

And yet Dian continued to correspond with the Prices and to visit their home throughout her life. Two months before her death she was seen by a San Jose sorority sister strolling with her mother into the Atherton post office. Those who knew both Kitty and Dian have no doubt of Kitty's love for Dian; and Kitty herself indignantly maintains that Dian always adored Richard Price.

Whatever the truth of their relationship, it imposed a burden on Dian for the rest of her life. There can be little doubt that Dian Fossey had been an unhappy child.

Dian's unhappiness began when her father and mother were divorced. Dian was three years old. The dissolution of her marriage was an occasion of great bitterness to Kitty, and she took the position from then on that Dian's father, George Fossey III, was dead.

And for all practical purposes, so far as Dian was concerned, he was. She wouldn't see him again until she was thirty-three years old.

Without a father, she had to look solely to her mother for emotional support, but she saw little of her, for Kitty had to work. When Dian was small Kitty was a fashion model for clothing stores. According to a gossip columnist on the *San Francisco Chronicle*, she was the most beautiful model in the city. In these years Dian was often left with Kitty's sister, her Aunt Flossie, and her uncle Bert Chapin, whom she would later remember with great affection. (She named two gorillas after them.) She believed they had more to do with raising her than her mother. When Dian was five, Kitty married Price, an ambitious entrepreneur whose aspirations would carry over into his social life, and Kitty shared his desire for prominence in the community. Tall, well turned out, imperious and demanding, Price doted on his beautiful wife, but he was not naturally drawn to small children, and he had some stern views on how they should be raised. "They are little adults," he once said, but he didn't feel they should be included in the adult world. Although Kitty would sometimes have lunch with Dian in the kitchen, Dian was not allowed to join the Prices at dinner until she was ten years old.

Already uncertain of her value to anyone else, Dian withdrew all the more into herself. She later said she had always loved animals but as a child she was allowed only to have a goldfish. (This simply wasn't true, Kitty says. She had a bird, too, and a dog, and she was given riding lessons from the time she was six.)

As Price became successful in his business affairs, the quality of their lives improved. Dian didn't have to work her way through school. Price sent her to college, and in her last two years she could afford to stable her own horse and drive her own car. Her mother had cocktail parties for Dian's sorority friends at their house in Atherton. But none of this came to count for much to Dian as she grew older.

What she chose to remember was the deprivation of her past. Once, she told Mary, she was present in the house when Price threatened her mother. "I found you in the gutter, and I can always put you back there," he warned her. Dian hated Price, and she never forgave her mother for marrying him.

There were other grievances, too. The beautiful mother was overly concerned about her daughter's appearance. Dian was very tall for her age and Kitty took her to a doctor to find out if anything could be done about it. "Look," the doctor said after the examination, "she's just *big*."

By the time she was fourteen, Dian was six foot one. Her freakish height made Kitty uncomfortable—this was some years before great heights would become fashionable—and it mortified Dian. She was not only taller than everyone her age, she was taller than her parents. And she wasn't pretty—or so she believed. Actually, with thick black hair, dark eyebrows, hazel eyes, and a tentative smile, she was quite pretty. Her small bones and delicate features contrasted strikingly with her height. At San Jose her sorority sisters regarded her as beautiful. But Dian didn't see herself that way.

How much her mother might have done to assuage her discomfort over her hated size is an open question. Later in her life, in the 1970s, one of Fossey's closest friends was Bettie Crigler, the wife of the American ambassador to Rwanda. Crigler looked startlingly like Fossey, and was almost as tall. Their backgrounds were also similar. Bettie, too, had a stepfather but he, in marked contrast to Richard Price, had worked to reassure his daughter about her height. "Even though I was a head and a half taller than anyone in my class," she says, "he kept telling me it was wonderful I was so tall; that I should stand straight; and that he would give me modeling lessons. But I think Mrs. Price made Dian feel she was too big, too awkward, that she was no great beauty, and that she wouldn't be received well in good company."

At a vulnerable age Dian developed a negative sense of herself. Her mother was a petite blonde, but all Dian inherited from Kitty were her features, and the prominent nose, which was Kitty's least attractive feature. Dian believed herself to be the victim of a cruel biological joke. She was a grotesquely tall brunette who desperately wanted to be an average-sized blonde. And too early in her life, she learned she would have to cope with her problems all by herself. She eventually did, and mother and daughter grew apart over the years.

In her school years Dian invested much of her time and interest in horses. She was remembered at Lowell High School as a member of the riding club, and she continued this avid interest at college. When she wasn't in class or studying, she spent most of her time out riding.

Indeed it may be that the horses saved her, for she was able to invest in them the emotion she would otherwise have had to dam up in herself. In that sense, her love of horses carried her through adolescence and into young womanhood, got her past the bumpiest parts of the ordeal of living inside a body that was too large and within a family she didn't like.

She kept a horse at San Jose, and when she moved to Louisville she left it in the care of her college roommate and her boyfriend, who would later marry. Bud and Patty Hjelm of Menlo Park would become her last contacts with the California world she had left behind.

By the time she reached Louisville, she was just as starved for affection as she had ever been.

Gaynee Henry helped fill Dian's need for affection. Everything about Gaynee captivated Dian—including her religion. After an evening at the movies with Mary, Dian would sometimes spend the night at the Henrys', a silent but interested witness to the family recitation of the rosary, a custom observed nightly since a time when Dr. Henry's mother had lived with the family a generation earlier. And inevitably she grew to share the Henrys' powerful attachment to a Boston Irish priest who was a great influence on the family. Joe Flanagan had been a Jesuit priest and taught philosophy at Boston University until he joined the Order of the Cistercians of the Stricter Observance, or more familiarly, the Trappist monks, at Gethsemane Abbey near the Henrys' home. The vow of silence was an unusually severe restriction for the loquacious Father Raymond (as he became known), who liked to pepper his conversation, when he was allowed to speak, with mild profanities ("Hell, girl! That's just damn nonsense!"). In 1949 Dr. Henry had operated successfully on Father Raymond for stomach cancer, and Father Raymond and his family—the rest of the Flanagans back in Cape Cod—had become close to the Henrys. When Father Raymond was allowed to have visitors at the Abbey, the Henrys came to see him, relaying his messages to the outside world.

Happily shepherding Father Raymond's guests from the airport at any hour of the day or night, Dian soon became fascinated with the theology of this vigorous, athletic, cocky, intellectual priest. If she had doubts, he was happy to slap them down. Once she asked him how he could prove God exists, and why he allowed the suffering of the children at Kosair. She also sought out a Protestant minister and asked him the same questions. She preferred Father Raymond's version.

Eventually Dian decided to convert to Catholicism. At St. Gabriel's parish near the Washhouse in Fern Creek, she took instruction from a priest named Father Emrich, who remembers only one thing about her—that she criticized him for not being well read. At her baptism, Mary White Henry became her godmother, and she took the names Gaynee and Raymond at her confirmation. For the rest of her stay in Louisville, she worked at being as reverent and faithful to God as her beloved Henry family.

As she drew closer to the Henrys, to Father Raymond, and to the Church, Dian became even further removed from her family in Atherton. Rebelling against their aspirations to social standing, Dian committed herself to good works, to caring for others and alleviating suffering if she could. She had no patience for the sort of people her parents admired.

Beyond her newly acquired religious devotion, Dian had other impulses that moved her, additional energy to burn. In her long hours alone at the Washhouse she set some creative goals for herself. Her aspirations were high. She was certain she could do anything she set her mind to; and she believed there were some things she should be doing whether she liked them or not. She hated opera, for example, but she studied it because she thought she should. She decided she ought to know how to play the piano, and she took lessons for several years. When she decided she would learn creative writing, she enrolled in a correspondence course with the Famous Writers School.

Although she was always on the go, anyone who observed her closely could see that Dian was alone, and though she never complained, she was lonely. Sometimes on the weekends she would join the crowd around George Long's swimming pool, but she never paired off with anyone. Long liked her, and so did the others who came there; she was quiet and reserved but she had a good sense of humor. Still, no one got to know her very well, and to all outward appearances, she was a single woman, growing older, quite alone, and going nowhere.

This could hardly be said of her best friend. Mary Henry was also single but she dated regularly, and her job at a travel agency helped make it possible for her to go abroad. Since Dian had come to know her, Mary had been to Paris, Amsterdam, and Saigon. With her mother's encouragement she set off at every opportunity, even traveling to Africa to see the family of a tobacco farmer in Salisbury, Rhodesia, named Franz Joseph Forrester. The Forresters were part Austrian, part Irish, all Catholic, and wholly delightful. Friends of Father Raymond, they dropped in at the Henry Hotel from time to time and always extended reciprocal invitations to Mary and Dian, any time either or both of them took a mind to see Africa.

In 1960, Mary decided to take them up on the invitation. She flew off to Rhodesia and was shown a smashing time by Franz and Peg Forrester's sons. Dian was as impressed as everyone else at the Henry Hotel by Mary's adventure, and she was captivated by the animals Mary had photographed. But Africa was out of the question for her, an unimaginable luxury on her salary of $5,300 a year, the most she could ever expect to make as an O.T. It would take her entire year's salary to go. Where would she get that kind of money? Richard Price had it, of course, but she would die before she asked him for a dime. Like so many other things, this was a dream Dian had to put out of her mind. For three years, she thought no more about it.

But on a quiet day in 1963, the possibility came up again and in an odd and unexpected way. Filling some empty time at the Washhouse, she baked herself a pecan pie. As she cut the pie into quarters, she found this mindless task was forcing her into a reckoning. Life was passing her by. Could she truthfully say she was meeting her own high expectations for herself? She wanted a family, and now she had one. But it was not her own. She had always followed someone else's direction or example. She knew she had a lot to give. But could she say her children at the hospital and her stray dogs were enough, that they allowed her to give as *much* as she had? She had always wanted children. And what about marriage? She was thirty-one years old. No one asked her out for dates, and no one seemed likely to. She wouldn't have gone anyway, unless the man was taller than she—and how many did that leave?

If men were out, then sex was out. This apparently troubled her more than she let on. She was a healthy young woman who, from most accounts, seemed to want and need a man's tenderness and affection. But most of her friends, including Mary Henry, assumed she was a virgin. Others suspected that some event in the past had complicated Dian's feelings about sex. Whatever the truth was, there is no indication that Dian Fossey had sexual or romantic attachments during her time in Louisville. All she had was her job, which she had known all along was a dead end.

She was now locked into her life in Louisville, and unless she did something drastic, she had done about as much as she would ever do. Quite suddenly, she decided to change all that. She didn't know where she might find the money, but she would go to Africa. What did she have to lose? She would roll the dice again.

4

THE BLACK MAN
WITH A WHITE
FACE

Along Uhuru Road in Nairobi, at the entrance to the National Museum of Kenya, stands a bronze statue of a man that seems a sort of joke on the whole idea of public monuments. Dressed in baggy coveralls, the man is wearing no socks and the state of his shoes is a disgrace: the laces are gone and the tongues are hanging out. He is not sitting on a horse or even standing on a pedestal. He is surrounded by none of the customary props—no flag, weapon, or scroll. The man is sitting on the ground, hunched forward the way old men sit. He holds a rock in his hand.

As it happens, the man honored in this unusual fashion is faithfully captured in one of his most characteristic moments. But this alone is not what is so arresting about the statue. Even to those who know nothing about him, it is evident that this man is Caucasian, his facial features sharply chiseled. He is unmistakably white. Since 1960—when 300 million Africans had finally achieved independence from the European nations that had colonized them—this may well be the only statue on the entire continent raised by black men to a white man.

As far as Louis Leakey himself was concerned, he was and always had been African. Born in Kenya to British missionaries, Leakey was raised among the tribe his parents sought to convert, the Kikuyus, today the majority people of Kenya. As an adolescent he was initiated into the tribe, and as an adult he was accorded the full privileges of a tribal elder. He considered Kikuyu his first and best language; he dreamed in it; and at Cambridge, where he was required to show mastery in a language other than English in order to qualify for his doctorate, he chose Kikuyu. (Since there was no one else who knew enough of it to test him, he was permitted to test himself. He gave himself a first.) To a chief of the Kikuyu people he was "the black man with a white face." Could the statue of Louis Leakey come to life, the man would consider himself no less African than the school-children strolling past him into the museum he had headed for the last third of his life.

But it is the searching look in the statue's eyes that begins to suggest the importance of Louis Leakey to all races of the human species. He was our preeminent prehistorian, renowned for the fossil evidence discovered by himself and his family.

By 1924, when Leakey was at Cambridge, evolutionary science had established that man was more closely related to the great ape than to any other animal. Just from the similarity of the basic physiology of the two species, this was evident. Many other long-held assumptions were now known to be in error, however. Earlier, it was believed that man became separated from the apes by virtue of his large and complex brain, and that this divergence occurred some 500,000 years ago, in Asia. That same year, an anatomist named Raymond Dart announced the discovery in South Africa of a prehuman skull he believed to be more than a million years old. Strangely, the face of the skull suggested that of a man but the size of the brain was similar to an ape's. At the time no one paid any attention to Dart, and when Leakey left Cambridge to search for human origins, he was advised to go to Asia. But Charles Darwin had believed man was born in Africa, because that's where chimpanzees and gorillas were, the two animals closest to man. And so Leakey returned to Africa.

By the time of Leakey's death in 1972, the broad outline of human evolution had begun to emerge. Man began to separate from the great apes not 500,000 years ago but some 4 million years ago—perhaps even earlier—in a long and gradual continuum. The cause was not our large, powerful brain, however. Four million years ago our brain—as Dart's skull had suggested fifty years earlier—was not much different from the ape's. Our potential for humanness lay below the belt, in our hip sockets. When we began to walk upright, our brains grew larger and more complex. "This unique ability," wrote Mary Leakey, Louis's wife, "freed the hands for myriad possibilities— carrying, tool making, intricate manipulation. From this single development, in fact, stems all modern technology. Somewhat oversimplified, the formula holds that this new freedom of limbs posed a challenge. The brain expanded to meet it. And mankind was born."

In 1956, when Walter Baumgartel sought Louis Leakey's help in finding someone to underwrite a study of the gorillas of Muhavura, much human evolutionary history still lay hidden among the fossil clues in the African earth. When Leakey was not out scraping in the desert dirt with a metal pick trying to get at them, he was running the Kenya museum. He was a very busy man, and had problems of his own. He was determined to be the leader in his field but his headquarters were thousands of miles from the major Western intellectual centers. Unerringly, however, Baumgartel had gone straight to one of Leakey's major concerns, the state of the great ape in modern times. Leakey was certain that the apes held important clues to the behavior of our earliest ancestors, and he wanted to see them studied in the few remaining patches of prehistoric wilderness where they still survived. No scientific institution of means—no museum, zoological society, or university—had made the slightest effort to study these precious animals. Leakey was undaunted; if need be, he was prepared to undertake such studies himself. But where would he find the time? Or the money?

When he heard from Baumgartel, Leakey had no idea who the fellow might be. And while he had some reservations about the purity of Baumgartel's motives—the man was planning treks so that his paying guests could see the gorillas—Leakey knew an opportunity when he saw one. He wrote Baumgartel that he would do what he could to find someone to go to Kisoro. If he were a younger man, he said, he would go there himself.

Leakey's candidate surprised Baumgartel a few weeks later at the door of Traveller's Rest. Leakey had sent a twenty-two-year-old woman, Rosalie Osborn, originally from Scotland. Osborn had no scientific experience except a brief stint of working on a Leakey dig, searching for fossils. But she was strong and healthy, and prepared to do whatever was required, although she would prefer not to cook. Between cooking and, say, mixing concrete, she preferred the latter.

Who was he to quibble? Surely Louis Leakey knew what he was doing. Baumgartel assigned Reuben and two trackers to Osborn and prepared to send her up the mountain, where she would spend the better part of four months in what they both expected to be a year-long study. Baumgartel was happy. Already, people were beginning to come there, and for exactly the right reasons. Because this was Gorillaland.

Over brandy after dinner, Baumgartel was pleased to entertain his guests as resident expert on gorilla lore. There was record of at least one man having been killed by the gorillas. When they did kill, they apparently showed some pleasure in redistributing their victim's bones. Baumgartel told the story of Captain Oscar von Beringe, after whom the animals were named. An official of the Tanganyika railway who came to Africa for mountain climbing, he shot two of the gorillas, one of which was examined by a taxonomist back in Berlin named Matschie. This, in 1903, was the first official record of this subspecies.

Baumgartel also knew the wonderfully romantic tale of the American Carl Akeley, who led an expedition to hunt specimens for the American Museum of Natural History in New York. Akeley shot five of the animals—you could see them now in the African room of the museum—but was stricken by what he had done. In 1922, he persuaded King Albert of Belgium to set aside the Congo part of the Virungas as a national park to protect the gorillas (the British followed suit on the Ugandan side in 1929). In 1926, Akeley was drawn back to Africa to see the gorillas again, but fell desperately ill in the course of the safari. Should he not recover, he told his wife, it was his wish to be buried in Kabara Meadow on the saddle between Karisimbi and Mikeno, the most beautiful place on earth. His body was buried there, under a simple headstone, on the Congo side of the Virungas.

Once Osborn had begun her work, stealthily tracking the gorillas—a pioneer compiling a record no one else thus far had sought to make—Baumgartel came to admire her inordinately. She went up the mountain on the average of two days out of three, uncomplaining and fearless. She didn't get too close, but who could blame her. Unfortunately, she tended to accept the conclusions of Baumgartel's guide Reuben. For example, Reuben told her that the occasional lone male they encountered had probably been excluded from the family circle by his pregnant mate. But why wouldn't Osborn believe him? By now Reuben knew more about gorillas than anyone alive. Baumgartel was impressed by Osborn's habit of making meticulous notes on her observations. He was convinced her record would one day become historic; it was already of much interest to everyone who came to Kisoro, including most recently a Western reporter who stopped by.

The reporter was so impressed by Osborn that he wrote her up for his paper back in Scotland.

And so it was understandable that Baumgartel's vision for Traveller's Rest continued to expand. Perhaps Traveller's Rest would become a center not only for adventurous travelers but for scientists as well. A place for a really serious, first-class scientific expedition to observe the mountain gorilla. If Louis Leakey had thought enough of his plan to send Osborn to help him, certainly other scientists would come too? Of course, he'd have to spend some money on the place. The hotel was still a losing proposition; he'd have to find an investor. But it was not an impossibility, not by a long shot. And what a reward it would be for the scientific community. Baumgartel decided there were some other people he ought to write, people very highly placed.

But then a wrench was thrown into his plan. Believing her daughter to be working with Louis Leakey in the safety of Nairobi, Osborn's mother back in Scotland opened her paper one morning to find an account of Rosalie's exciting adventures among the wild mountain gorillas of the Virungas in Central Africa. Mrs. Osborn sent word to her daughter to come down from the mountain instantly. Exit Rosalie Osborn.

Louis Leakey never had enough money to do all the things he wanted and was forced to dig into his own meager resources to make ends meet. But his biggest problem was time. Local and international scientists, conservationists, tourists, people just passing through—Leakey could resist few of them. He was too accessible, especially in light of the endless variety of projects he wanted to explore and the inevitable need for fund-raising. His health was also precarious. He smoked too much and, at fifty-four, had a history of malaria, bilharzia, and epilepsy. But he stubbornly persisted. He believed that accessibility fostered unexpected opportunity.

For example, if his door hadn't been open to strangers he might have missed the unannounced arrival of Jane Goodall, a British woman from

Bournemouth who sought him out because she wanted to work with wild animals. He had hired Goodall as a secretary, and already he was scheming how to get her set up in Tanganyika to study the chimpanzee, one of the three species of great apes Leakey wanted to see studied.

At other times Leakey had to agree he carried accessibility too far; Walter Baumgartel was a case in point. Without consulting Leakey, Baumgartel had taken it upon himself to hire a woman out of South Africa to carry on Rosalie Osborn's research, a journalist named Jill Donisthorpe. Beyond that, Leakey had no idea who she was, but he was worried that Baumgartel's meddling might upset his efforts to obtain funds for a truly scientific, long-range gorilla study.

Leakey had written for support to Sir Solly Zuckerman, a leading authority on primates and a scientist highly placed in the British establishment. In turn, Zuckerman had enthusiastically endorsed Leakey's proposal to Harold Coolidge, who was in a position to provide the means for an extended study. Coolidge, then president of the National Academy of Sciences, had gone to Africa in the 1920s precisely for the purpose of refining the taxonomy of the mountain gorilla. Leakey was confident of his interest. Everything had been falling neatly into place until Baumgartel, this amateur—this hotel-keeper who wanted nothing more than to use the gorillas to draw customers—had put himself squarely in the middle. Because Baumgartel had access to the gorillas, he wanted to run the whole show.

On Jill Donisthorpe's first day in Kisoro, Baumgartel blithely tried to leap over a lily bed but misjudged the distance and broke his leg. Donisthorpe, strong as a buffalo, left immediately for Muhavura anyway. Between February and September of 1957, she spent 122 days on the mountain, encountering gorillas forty-one times.

While Leakey was writing Baumgartel stiff letters of rebuke (accusing him of being in it only for the money), Donisthorpe was risking her life for a scientific establishment that hardly knew she was there. Once she was lost on the mountain for three days, without food—without even a match! But Donisthorpe did things no one had ever done before. She identified the food the animals ate (twenty-three plants), their habitation (at 8,000 to 12,000 feet), their smell (like a mixture of human sweat, manure, and charred wood), their sounds (roars, barks, screams, toots, and murmurs) and their response to humans.

This last was easily the most extraordinary of her achievements. So far as Baumgartel knew, Donisthorpe was the first person ever to get close enough to a male gorilla to draw his charge, and then, without a weapon of any kind to defend herself, to stand her ground and see what happened. *Unimaginable*! Baumgartel had never got over the fear that came from simply being in the presence of these animals. With courage and total self-possession, Donisthorpe had drawn the charges twice, within twenty yards, and come back to report it was the gorilla that had turned away.

So far as Baumgartel was concerned, this was news of a major kind. Forced into close contact with a human, the most fierce primate on earth wouldn't tear the human's head off, but would turn away. Who before had known this? Certainly not those hunters who simply killed the animal when they got close enough to shoot.

Despite his pleasure at Donisthorpe's progress, Baumgartel had no money to fund her. He had told Leakey this and asked for some. Then he had written Zuckerman, too. Between them they had raised £100. This was not enough, and Baumgartel told them so. He suggested they try the wealthy American Leighton Wilkie, who was known to fund worthy schemes in Africa. He added that if they didn't get adequate help to him by August 1, he would consider himself free of obligation to either of them and turn to Raymond Dart in South Africa, who recently had expressed great admiration for his work with Donisthorpe. Already chilly, Leakey's letters now turned frigid.

With Baumgartel's deadline before him, Leakey realized he had underestimated the man. Here was this innkeeper playing him off against Raymond Dart, who, since his discovery of a prehuman skull known as the Taung Baby, was in the front rank of their field. Dart was Leakey's major competition for private funding from Leighton Wilkie. How could Baumgartel have known of *him?*" Wilkie was a very wealthy man who believed the first tools were responsible for civilization, an assumption that pleased him since he manufactured modern tools back in Illinois. One day Wilkie had walked in off the street to Leakey's office. Leakey fished a fossil molar from his desk drawer and proceeded to tell the entranced Wilkie the story of its evolution. Leighton Wilkie became a benefactor of Louis Leakey. Thus he had come to fund Leakey in Kenya in his search for stone tools, and now as well Raymond Dart in South Africa in his search for bone tools.

Leakey went through the roof at Baumgartel's presumptuousness. But the tone of the letter he wrote back to Baumgartel was detached and impersonal. He informed him that any approach to Wilkie was completely out of the question. (The truth was, Leakey had Wilkie in mind for the Jane Goodall project.) He was confident an appropriate expedition would soon be organized, but in the meantime certain rules of procedure must be followed, and these things took time. Leakey would see what he could do to find a little more money for Donisthorpe, whom Leakey hoped Baumgartel would persuade to stay as long as possible. But Leakey stressed that it was to no one's advantage for competing expeditions to be organized, and he was certain Raymond Dart wouldn't want to become involved in such a competition. Scientists did not usually do that sort of thing.

Leakey now wrote a careful, detailed proposal for a two-year survey, by a two-man team, of the Virungas gorillas. He sent this, together with the reports of Osborn and Donisthorpe, to Zuckerman, who forwarded it on to Coolidge. After a preliminary funding authorization, a proposal to study the mountain gorilla was sent by Coolidge to an ornithologist at the University of Wisconsin named

71

John Emlen. One day after class—this was still in 1957—Emlen asked a promising young graduate student, a German immigrant named George Schaller, if he would like to go to Africa with him and study gorillas in the field. Schaller said yes, he would be very much interested in doing that.

5

··

LAST CHANCE

As long as she was going to do this, Dian Fossey decided, she might as well do it right. She was not going to be a part of one of those awful prepackaged tourist groups, with their cameras and canvas hats. She would go first class, and she would stay there long enough to *see* something. Leaving the hard part—where the money would come from—until last, she started her research, concluding:

1. She would stay for seven weeks.

2. She would visit Kenya first of all, and then anywhere else she might see the most wild animals.

3. She would hire her own guide with his own vehicle, so that she would be free to move about as she liked.

To accomplish all this she would have to borrow $8,000, the equivalent of a year and a half of her salary. Without resources, without collateral of any kind, hoping to borrow the money for a reason any bank officer would regard as frivolous, she realized what

73

a poor risk she was. However, she found a savings and loan willing to make the loan on harsh terms: she must put up sufficient collateral to cover a default; pay 18 percent interest; and pay it off within three years. Hating to ask anything from anybody, Fossey turned to the person she hated least to ask, and that was Mary White Henry, who, without a second's pause, signed over securities left her by her father.

With the money in hand, Fossey took her time getting ready. She bought herself some good boots and a lot of insect spray, got the necessary vaccinations and visas, and took Swahili lessons from a Kikuyu studying at the University of Kentucky. Rather than book through a tourist agency, she decided to fly straight to Nairobi and from there proceed to what she understood to be the most luxurious lodge in Kenya, the Mount Kenya Safari Club near Nanyuki. It was a first-class place to start from. She would find her guide there. On the way back she would take the Forresters up on their invitation to visit them at their farm in Rhodesia.

The Forresters were the most conspicuous example of Gaynee Henry's admiration for world travelers, for the urbanity and sophistication that come from firsthand familiarity with distant places. Franz Joseph Forrester was an Austrian count, a cousin of the Lichtensteins and a descendant of the Hapsburgs. Escaping from the Nazis with a price on his head, he had settled in Rhodesia, where he trained British troops in World War II. Then he had established a tobacco farm. Peg Forrester was Irish, the daughter of the late Michael Hartney, lord mayor of Limerick. Peg's sister was a nun whose financial acumen would one day see her to the office of treasurer of the Sisters of the Holy Cross. This was Sister Gerald, at Notre Dame, the link between the Forresters in Rhodesia and Father Raymond and the Henrys in Kentucky. When Forrester decided he wanted to explore the possibility of growing Kentucky burley leaf on his farm, Sister Gerald had written to Father Raymond, who replied: Why, of course. Send Forrester on down. He can stay at the Henrys'.

Forrester was a tall, strapping man, and so were all three of his sons, Michael, Alexie, and Robert, or "Pookie." Father Raymond remembers showing Dian a photograph of the brothers, with Alexie standing in the middle. She pointed at him and said, "That's my boy." Alexie had a round face like his father and his mother's strawberry-blond coloring. He ran the family's farms outside of Salisbury, overseeing two hundred African field hands. Like any young African settler in those days, he knew how to handle himself in an emergency.

Not the least that could be said of Alexie, in describing him to Dian, was that he was six feet six inches tall. If the two of them stood side by side, Alexie would be almost a head taller than Dian. To the hopeful matchmaker at the Henry Hotel, the fact that he was seven years younger than Dian did not strike them as inappropriate. "You weren't aware of those boys' age," Mary says. "They were so much more sophisticated than their American contemporaries."

In Rhodesia, Alexie had also learned something of Dian. His brother Pookie had come back from a visit with the Henrys raving about her, and Father Raymond had written him of Dian's impending visit. He wrote of what a lovely young woman she was. Alexie was putting in his crops at that moment, and when he wrote back to Father Raymond, he had only one question about Dian Fossey: "Can she plow?"

"Africa is like an infection," the German conservationist Bernhard Grzimek used to say, with more enthusiasm that precision. "Once bitten, you never recover." Visiting the continent for the first time, most people have little idea of what to expect either of the place or of the people. Going home, they may return with their misperceptions undisturbed. But they will know they have been touched by something.

75

Most flights departing from European capitals leave late in the evening and arrive in Nairobi the next morning around eight. The weather is nearly always good, and so the flight is smooth and uneventful, soporific for even the most apprehensive of flyers. But to sleep past dawn on one's first flight across the Horn of Africa is to miss a breathtaking experience. Gliding high over copper slabs of sand and rock you can begin to see what was once an animal-filled grassland plain, stretching out across the eastern part of the continent. Clouds cast their shadows onto the higher shelves of the wasteland; the copper bleaches to ochre under the rising white light of the African sun. Soon thin lines of pale green and gray appear. These trace lines of scrub brush are broken occasionally by the faintest suggestion of water. Brightening, deepening, and widening, the trace lines grow into amorphous patches which ultimately converge into the modern African savanna. On these near-desert grasslands reside most of Africa's surviving varieties of wildlife: lion and elephant, hippopotamus, water buffalo, wild dog and cheetah, crocodile and monkey. At about the time the wheels are let down, you are well over these grasslands, and as you near the Nairobi airport, if you look closely, you can see wildebeest and gazelle racing across them.

From Nairobi, Dian Fossey proceeded directly to what she supposed to be the quintessential African lodge, the Mount Kenya Safari Club. This turned out to be not what she had in mind. Not only was there a swimming pool but it was a *heated* swimming pool; and the management had imported tropical birds to heighten the effect of an exotic resort. This was hardly the Africa she had come to see. Determined to waste as little time as possible, she learned the actor William Holden was in residence, sought him out, and told him she was looking for a white hunter to take her on a private safari through East Africa. Was there someone he might recommend?

Holden said he knew a man down the mountain in Nanyuki who he thought might be suitable. He had his own vehicle and camping supplies, sometimes worked at the club between safaris, carving wood signs and doing odd jobs, and probably could use the work. His name was John Alexander.

Though she hadn't specified her man as to type, Fossey's concept of a "white hunter" necessarily would have been based on fictions she had picked up back home from books and movies—a rugged, adventurous sort, British probably, able to shoot straight and hold his own against charging animals. Romantic possibilities would not be excluded; she was more than open to them. They were long overdue.

With certain minor exceptions, John Alexander was close to what she had in mind. He was forty-one and recently divorced. A former warden of the Abedare National Park, he knew well the behavior of most wild animals; he was a member of the East African Professional Hunters Association; he was florid-faced from the African sun; and, with hair slicked down so tightly it seemed nailed in place, he was extremely British. He was also six feet one inch tall. He knew that Fossey wanted a guide, not a hunter. He could accommodate her in that regard, but in others, he was lacking. Though he could still stir a response in some of the women he had known (in Nairobi he was known to brag a little too much about such things), he was not otherwise available. Alexander had recently become engaged to a seventeen-year-old girl whom he was wild about.

Alexander lives now, twenty-five years later, on the outskirts of Nairobi, where he is still in the safari business. He is well aware he was the first person to have anything to do with Dian Fossey in Africa, but he is not pleased with the memory. Rather, Alexander would put himself at the head of any list of the enemies Fossey made over the years. While she should have been everlastingly grateful to him for introducing her to her destiny ("She owed it to me, her whole ultimate life's work!"), he contends she took advantage of him.

She lied, she cheated, and she discredited him with two people who were very important in wildlife circles, Alan and Joan Root. But the most outrageous part of it was that the woman accused him of trying to seduce her, when the truth was *she* had tried to seduce *him*.

At the Mount Kenya Safari Club, Alexander met with Fossey to set out an itinerary. He proposed they follow what was known among locals as the "milk run," their sardonic shorthand for the thousand-mile loop that carried the visitor through most of the major aggregations of wild animals in East Africa, which is to say the most left on the continent. This of course was exactly what Fossey had come for. Since she had been wise enough to allow time for a real game run, she could travel at her own pace, moving from one lodge to the next along the route, and occasionally, when the mood struck her, putting up in a tent out in the bush.

Heading southwest out of Nairobi and moving in a clockwise direction, they would go into the scrub desert country of Tsavo, then drop down to the edge of Maasai Steppe in northern Tanganyika. This would enable Fossey to see Manyara, Ngorongoro, and the Serengeti Plain. Then, Alexander explained, they would come out through the northern corridor of the Serengeti into the Mara River country, and through southwest Kenya back up to Nairobi. Depending on how much she wanted to see, this could take two weeks or ten. Most of the roads of course were terrible, so pitted in places that the ruts were knee-deep, and virtually impassable when wet. Making a hundred miles a day would be pushing it.

But for a first-timer like Fossey, the milk run was definitely the best way to see most of what there was here. In Tsavo alone, there were some 20,000 elephants, and thousands upon thousands of rhinos. The elephants blew raw Tsavo dirt through their trunks over their backs, turning them as orange as the desert. At Manyara there was a large saline lake which the huge flocks of flamingos literally turned pink, and the lions of Manyara could be seen climbing trees to escape the tsetse fly. The Ngorongoro Crater was a hollow-coned volcano holding within its rim a menagerie of almost all the African fauna, all of it existing in balance. Elephants take the grass, lions take the gazelles, and hyenas and vultures take anything left.

Just beyond Ngorongoro to the west is the Olduvai Gorge, the prehistoric lake bed where Louis and Mary Leakey found fossils of the earliest man. Alexander knew Leakey and he told Fossey that perhaps they might see the famous man himself, working his digs. Then, just a few miles farther on, they would arrive at the Serengeti Plain. Its hundred of thousands of plains game—zebra, giraffe, wildebeest, gazelle—were the crowning experience of any trip to Africa.

Alexander agreed to keep his price as low as she could afford, with Fossey agreeing to pay part in advance and the balance upon completion of their trip. Alexander said it would take him half a day to get his equipment organized. They planned to leave the next day, as quickly as he could get ready.

While he was working down at his place in Nanyuki, packing up his trailer and so on, Fossey called, Alexander says, and their conversation, which he is certain he remembers clearly, went like this:

"How many men are you bringing?"

"Three."

"Can't you cook?"

"Well, yes, I can."

"Why don't you leave the men behind and we'll just go together?"

"Okay," Alexander said not thinking much about it at the time. "If you want it that way, if you don't mind my cooking."

And so off they went, just the two of them, following the route Alexander had proposed, which fulfilled every bit of the promise. They saw the elephants and rhinos of Tsavo, the pink flamingos and tree-dwelling lions of Manyara; and they climbed up through the coffee farms of Tanganyika to the crest of the Ngorongoro caldera where they could look down over the crater rim into the peaceable

kingdom below. Though it was part of the high adventure of following the milk run, the road was, as Alexander had predicted, bone-
jarringly rough. Together they bounced along in Alexander's Land
Rover.

An admirable vehicle in every other way, the Land Rover is not
designed for physical comfort. The front seat is hard-bottomed, narrow, and confining. Even when the vehicle is at rest, bodily contact
between passengers is hard to avoid; in motion, it is inevitable. Sitting
next to Alexander, her head bumping against the roof and her shoulder jostling his as they plowed across the pitted tracks of East
Africa—riding out in this fashion each day from early morning to just
before dusk—Fossey found herself physically as close to John Alexander, her Great White Hunter, as she had ever been to any man.

However, she said little to him, so little, in fact, that Alexander
thought her just a bit neurotic. She was moody. Obviously she didn't
like to talk. Also, she smoked incessantly, and he couldn't help
noticing she sipped whiskey as they went along. Although no one
back in Louisville remembers Fossey as drinking anything more than
the occasional cocktail, Alexander is as certain of her tippling as he is
of her smoking. But he drew no conclusions about any of this. It was
no business of his. Things went along well enough between them,
until they came to Louis Leakey's place at Olduvai Gorge. Suddenly,
Fossey seemed oddly ambivalent toward him. She seemed unable to
decide whether she liked him or not.

In her book, *Gorillas in the Mist*, Fossey begins her life story at this
point. It is as if for her, everything started at Olduvai Gorge.

> Two of the main goals of my first African trip were to visit the
> mountain gorillas of Mt. Mikeno in the Congo and to meet Louis and
> Mary Leakey at Olduvai Gorge in Tanzania. Both wishes came true.
> How vividly I can recall Dr. Leakey's sparkling interest in hearing that
> I was on my way to visit briefly the gorillas at Kabara in the Congolese
> sector of the Virungas Mountains, where George Schaller had worked
> a few years previously. Dr. Leakey spoke to me most enthusiastically

about Jane Goodall's excellent field work with the chimpanzees at the Gombe Stream Research Center in Tanzania, then only in its third year, and he stressed the importance of long-range field studies with the great apes. I believe it was at this time the seed was planted in my head, even if unconsciously, that I would someday return to Africa to study the gorillas of the mountains.

There are discrepancies between Fossey's memory and the accounts of others who were involved.

Mary Henry does not remember Fossey mentioning either the Leakeys or the Virunga gorillas before she left for Africa. She was going to see wild animals and the Forresters, as Mary herself had done. In those days, no established tourist circuit included gorilla-viewing. John Alexander says it was his idea to stop off to see the Leakey digs at Olduvai, between Ngorongoro and Serengeti; it was something he recommended to all his clients. In planning their safari back at the Mount Kenya Safari Club, Alexander says, there had been no mention of including gorillas. He had never been to see them before; he had no notion of how to go about seeing them. Their plan was simply to follow the milk run, proceeding from Serengeti into the Mara in southwest Kenya and then returning to Nairobi.

Fossey's version of her meeting with Leakey is emblematic of the poignant, near-heroic efforts she would later make to reconstruct those parts of her life that were not consistent with her larger vision of herself. The proof is in an article which she wrote for the *Louisville Courier Journal* shortly after returning home. Describing her African trip, she said she had seen Leakey but he had no time for her. He was suffering from a bout of emphysema. They didn't talk about anything at all. He posed with Alexander for her camera, and then pointed the way to the digs and retired to his quarters. According to Mary Leakey, sitting twenty-five years later in her small office at the National Museum in Nairobi, puffing on her cigar with amused detachment, Louis Leakey had nothing to do with Dian

Fossey when she first came to Olduvai Gorge. She was just another tourist stopping by.

In *Gorillas in the Mist*, Fossey recounted a journey farther down into the Olduvai to see the recently excavated fossils of a prehistoric giraffe. During the trip she lost her footing and cracked her ankle. Her injury was so sharply painful, she said, that she threw up on the giraffe fossils. Back in camp, Mary Leakey served her lemon squash and concurred with her "driver" (in Fossey's book Alexander is unnamed) that a visit to the gorillas of Kabara would be ill-advised. Neither Mary Leakey nor the driver understood the extent of her resolve, Fossey wrote. The accident simply increased her determination to go on, as she had all along intended, and see the gorillas anyway.

In those days Mary Leakey was quick to make mincemeat out of anyone talking nonsense, even if the nonsense came from her distinguished husband. She did not hesitate to correct Louis in the presence of others if the subject happened to be something she knew anything about, which was a good deal. Having begun as his protégée (she was Leakey's second wife), Mary was now close to becoming his peer. The discovery four years earlier of *Zinjanthropus*, a prehuman skull dating back 1,750,000 years, was hers. She had found it at Olduvai. This discovery brought media attention from the *National Geographic* and others and opened a new rich vein of funding for Louis's endless projects. But Mary Leakey had never really shared Louis's interest in the great apes.

This was to become evident in later years when Louis Leakey and Dian Fossey would become closely associated. For now, suffice it to say that Fossey's version does not coincide with Mary Leakey's. Mary Leakey remembers that Fossey did fall; there was some question as to whether her boot should be removed because the swelling might later prevent her from putting it back on. But she remembers nothing about Fossey throwing up on the giraffe fossils, or about her determination to see gorillas. What she does remember quite clearly is the way Fossey was hanging on to Alexander. She was all over him, Mary Leakey says, but when Fossey was alone with her, she referred to him as "that dreadful Alexander." Mary Leakey had thought this rather odd.

Fossey's next step, the Serengeti Plain, is a carpet of grass extending several thousand square miles. Embedded in volcanic ash thrown down millennia ago, the grasses of the Serengeti are sustained by seasonal rains, progressive grazing, and the droppings of its animal residents. To the stranger suddenly coming upon it, the Serengeti does not seem quite real. Hundred of thousands of animals—gazelle, eland, giraffe—graze together peaceably. The air is soft; there is no noise; the light is brilliantly clear. More than four hundred species of birds fly over the Serengeti, and when the rare rains fall, flowers blossom overnight. It seems too perfectly ordered, too peaceful, given the fact that the plain is home to the greatest aggregation of hooved animals to be found anywhere on earth. During their seasonal migration they literally swarm around the visitor's vehicle, and one proceeds slowly and with great caution. Even the predators of these peaceful flocks—the lions, hyenas, and vultures—are overwhelmed and tend to keep out of sight.

But more than anything else, it is the sense of openness, of grass reaching to the horizon, that so reassures the observer. It is a world apart, like no other. The visitor to Serengeti will never come upon a more peaceful scene. Even the local people conspire to maintain the illusion. Having been exploited by colonialism as much as Africans anywhere else, and so wretchedly poor as to cause the most frugal tourist to feel wealthy by comparison, the people in this part of East Africa receive foreigners with a warmth and deference that is too genuine to be mocking, as though it is their sole purpose in life to preserve the Serengeti's tranquillity. If there are those among them with other things on their mind, as surely there must be, they manage, like the predators, to stay out of sight.

It was in this Edenseque setting that Fossey heard about the most spectacular animal in all of Africa, the mountain gorilla. Before coming to Serengeti she had never heard of the mountain gorilla; John Alexander is certain of this. He says he introduced her to the man who first told her about these animals. This was a diminutive biologist wearing khaki shorts and knee socks, a Belgian of histrionic gesture, with flashing eyes, a depressing past, and an uncertain future. His name was Jacques Veschuren.

According to Alexander, Veschuren told Fossey that the mountain gorilla was the most impressive of all primates, of all three great apes. But, sadly, this most amazing of all African creatures was probably nearing extinction. A recent study by his American friend George Schaller, he said, indicated that the gorillas lived mainly in the vicinity of the Virunga volcanos—in the Congo, about a five-day drive from the Serengeti. Because the borders of three countries ran down the center of this mountain range—the Congo on the west, Rwanda on the southeast, and Uganda on the north—the animals did not fall exclusively under the jurisdiction of any one country. They moved back and forth across the borders. Most of them were believed to be on the Congo side, around Mount Mikeno. That was certainly the best place for a tourist to try for a sighting. Veschuren himself had seen them there.

Mikeno fell within Albert National Park, where Veschuren had served as scientific director until the trouble that came with independence in 1960. After a series of unsavory episodes convinced him he was no longer welcome, Veschuren had left. In one of these episodes, drunken soldiers had held a pistol in his face while he debated with them for two hours the issue of whether they should kill him.

Neither Fossey nor Alexander, nor anyone else in East Africa (including Veschuren, who had been out of there since 1960), had any reliable way of knowing just how bad things had become in the west, especially in the vicinity of the Virungas, which was the leading

84

edge of the dark part of Africa. In Rwanda the Bahutu and Watutsi peoples were killing each other in the hundreds of thousands in a genocidal tribal war that to this day remains unreported. In the Congo, from 1960 until 1969, when the killing finally stopped, the estimated dead would reach half a million. In the early 1960s white Belgians like Veschuren who were crazy enough to stay on made highly visible targets—especially the women—for murder or rape. In the Congo, deference no longer was paid to anyone.

But Fossey decided that she had to see the gorillas. She told Alexander to take her to Mount Mikeno in the Congo. She would regret it for the rest of her life if she didn't at least attempt to see the most spectacular animal in all of Africa. Veschuren wrote a note for them to present to the park officials—if they could find any. When he left the job, the park directorship had been turned over to a twenty-three-year-old agronomy student named Anicet Mburanumwe. There was no way of knowing for certain that tourists could get in, Veschuren said, although unless they were stopped at the border they might very well assume they would have no problem. The thing to do was to make their way to park headquarters, going through Uganda, and to proceed on from there.

Well, all right then, Alexander had said, if Fossey was so sure that was what she wanted to do. Although her ankle was still a problem, she should know better than anyone else whether she could manage. For his part, he had heard all sorts of problems you could run into there. For one, the Congolese military had a nasty habit of appropriating your vehicle. If they were going to run this risk, they would have to return to Nairobi so he could insure his Land Rover, an extra charge Fossey would have to pay. Veschuren had suggested she take a movie camera to photograph the gorillas, and Alexander had a Bolex back there he could rent to her. They would have to get film, too, and Nairobi was the only place for that. But quite frankly, Alexander said, he was nervous about going out for the first time to see gorillas. They were animals he knew nothing about. He decided he had better pick up a pistol (whether it was allowed in the park or not) and some firecrackers to scare them off if they should charge.

Because of this detour, it was the late afternoon of October 16 by the time Fossey and Alexander pulled into Traveller's Rest in Kisoro. They were greeted warmly by the lodge's estimable proprietor, Walter Baumgartel.

6

THE KING OF GORILLALAND

Now in the eighth year of his reign, the King of Gorillaland was in his late sixties, with snow-white hair, regal bags under his eyes, and an imperial waistline. He kept a stein of brandy stationed at his elbow and a Pygmy outside the lodge to attend new arrivals. All around him were the accoutrements of his kingship—photographs of gorillas, a gorilla skull on the bar, a gorilla death mask on the wall—and his African staff treated him as if he were royalty. When Baumgartel left even just to go to the market, they lined the drive waving him off with tears in their eyes. *"Kaweri, bwana,"* they cried. "Hurry back safely!"

So what if his friends liked to kid him about his extravagant claims for himself? (Alan Root was merciless, right down to the accent: "I am der kink uff Gorillaland!") But just as readily did Baumgartel join in making fun of himself. With the unquenchable high spirits of a fat man who finds fat men funny, Baumgartel welcomed the badinage.

He liked nothing better than long evenings with his legions of good friends, who now hailed from all over East Africa. Coming from anywhere else, especially from the Congo, they made a beeline for Traveller's Rest. Despite the dingy sheets, the oil lamps, and the stringy chicken, it was a safe place, an oasis in this unpredictable part of the world.

On the night of Dian Fossey's arrival, Baumgartel savored the sun slipping behind the mountain and the deep folds of mauve which fell over the hills. He felt good in spite of the difficulties mounting around him. Over the border the Congo was still falling to pieces—three thousand Belgian refugees had come out this way not so long ago. And Uganda without the British was hardly the Uganda it used to be.

When a Land Rover pulled up in the car park, Baumgartel turned his attention back to business. Rushing out to greet his guests with Falstaffian hospitality, he pumped the hands of the tall, shy young woman from Kentucky and her Kenyan tour guide. Fossey told him she had come to see the gorillas.

Then she had come to the right place, Baumgartel said—although, regrettably, there were no gorillas any longer up on Muhavura, his own domain, where he himself had first seen them. But he would get her to where she wanted to go. In the meantime, they would have their dinner and drinks, over which he would provide his new friends with his own introduction to gorilla watching. His table had become famous, less for its cuisine than this house speciality. Did they know Bob Ardrey's splendid new book on human origins, *African Genesis*, Baumgartel inquired. Bob had brought the manuscript with him when he came here, just before it was published. In Kisoro, as Bob had written—and to quote him exactly—"is a hotel called Traveller's Rest, dedicated to madmen and scientists. While no literature may yet exist on gorilla ways, at the hotel dining room and nowhere else in the world one can at least hear gorilla gossip."

Through dinner and late into the evening, Baumgartel told them what he knew. It was a dark and thrilling history, filled with false starts and forgotten names, half-truths and superstitions. Baumgartel told them of the magic vested by the Africans in the mountain gorilla: its sexual organs were believed to assure human potency. He bemoaned the killing of these poor beasts. For *no* good reason! Farmers trying to clear land, cattle people seeking new pasturage; the gorillas died over trivial concerns. Once villagers had stoned six of them, only God knows why. Would it never end? Baumgartel sipped his brandy and changed his mood.

Madmen and scientists! Yes, really. Bob Ardrey had it exactly right, although it was not always easy to tell one from the other. There was a Dane who had come there to study gorilla night nests, finding them so comfortable he couldn't help falling asleep himself. One genius wanted to tie cowbells around the apes' necks so he could keep track of them. But Fossey and Alexander should look through the guest register for themselves. There they would find the names of Sir Julian Huxley (the geneticist whose grandfather had defended Charles Darwin against Bishop Wilburforce), Raymond Dart, the South African paleontologist (he had insisted Baumgartel make him a salad from the plants the gorillas ate), Harold Coolidge of the National Academy of Sciences, Leighton Wilkie, the wealthy American who had funded Louis Leakey so that he could send Jane Goodall to the Gombe Stream Reserve to study the other African great ape, the chimpanzee.

Ah, yes, Louis Leakey. Baumgartel had provided him every opportunity to use Traveller's Rest as a base for a major expedition, but Leakey had seen it all slip from his hands. Leakey, Baumgartel said, had written Solly Zuckerman in England and Harold Coolidge in the U.S., and eventually the Americans had become interested. But they themselves took it on. The National Science Foundation and the New York Zoological Society had sent out John Emlen and George Schaller, so well funded they were able to bring their wives!

But who could deny the breathtaking zeal of these two men? Or the brilliant intensity and dogged commitment of young George Schaller? For the first six months they had surveyed by vehicle and on foot an area of 15,000 square miles. Schaller had even hiked into cannibal country. Emlen and Schaller estimated the existence of some 5,000 to 15,000 gorillas. But most of these were the smaller lowland gorillas. Of the giant mountain gorillas there were only 400-odd, and these were all in the vicinity of the Virungas.

After their initial survey, the Emlens had gone home, and the Schallers had set up a base camp in the Kabara Meadow on Mount Mikeno—where Carl Akeley was buried, where Fossey and Alexander would be going. Though he had lived there for just under a year, Schaller was incredible. He had worked among the gorillas, on one occasion literally sleeping among them. He had accumulated 466 hours of direct observation, and kept meticulous records. Everyone was awaiting his formal study, which was due out later that year.

But in the summer of 1960, after Schaller had been up on the mountain for eight months, the Congo went crazy with very little notice. Schaller, Baumgartel reported, got his wife out. Then several months later, when the drunken soldiers almost killed Jacques Veschuren, Schaller and Veschuren left the country together. Veschuren eventually wound up on the Serengeti Plain.

Surfeited with Baumgartel's enthusiastic but seemingly endless monologue, Fossey and Alexander asked him how to get to the gorillas. They told Baumgartel that Veschuren had given them a note for the park headquarters people, although he wasn't clear about who might be in charge. He said they might be able to spend the night there before they started the climb up Mount Mikeno. At the village of Kibumba, they should hire porters.

Exactly right, Baumgartel said. Only in the Congo could they be certain to see gorillas in the time they had allotted. They should take the road across the border leading to Rumangabo and plan to stay there, if possible. What conditions might be at any moment in the eastern Congo was hard to say, but for now it seemed quiet enough. Fossey and Alexander would want to proceed with caution, however.

To their good fortune, they would find two very close friends of his, a splendid young couple, Joan and Alan Root, in the Kabara Meadow. The Roots had been up there the better part of a month. Joan had been coming out there on photographic safaris, assisting her father, Edmund Thorpe, since 1959. In 1960, Alan had come through with Bernhard Grzimek, the German conservationist, both of them getting the hell out of the Congo just ahead of some crazy soldiers. In 1960, Joan and Alan had got married and had become one of the best wildlife film teams in Africa. They were now making a film of the gorillas for Grzimek.

Come to think of it, Baumgartel had a note he wanted to get to the Roots. He gave it to them to deliver and wished them a good journey.

7

······································

THE SHOCK OF SAMENESS

What had happened to Albert National Park and its wild animals since Jacques Veschuren's departure was anyone's guess, although it was known that twenty-three rangers had been killed by marauding soldiers. Tourists didn't come that way much anymore. A couple of years back Bernhard Grzimek had gone in to advise the president of breakaway Kivu province on how to get tourism going again in the park. But before Grzimek could get to see him, the president—having suddenly become the ex-president when the central government regained control in 1962—was paraded through the streets in a cage, his teeth knocked out and his moustache torn from his face.

Nevertheless, apart from Alexander having to surrender his passport to the border police to assure his exit, he and Fossey crossed into the Congo without incident. They arrived at park headquarters in Rumangabo late on October 17. Veschuren's note did not get them a bungalow, as they had hoped, but a room stacked with beer crates in one of the park buildings. The room smelled like a beer hall, but Alexander was used to making do in worse circumstances. As it was his responsibility to look after his client, he set about arranging suitable sleeping spaces.

"I started to stack the beer crates down the middle of the room so that Dian could sleep near the wall on the far side," he recalls, "and I would sleep near the door on this side. And while I was stacking the beer crates—" Alexander pauses. "And don't think I hold this against Dian. As a completely normal man I would have been delighted under ordinary circumstances. But suddenly she said to me, 'John Alexander, you're a damn fool.'

" 'Why?' I said.

" 'Here we've been three weeks on safari,' she said. 'We could have shacked up together and had a hell of a good time.'

"And I recall exactly what my reaction was," Alexander says. "I said, 'Dian, I am very honored by your proposal, but I happen to be engaged to a very lovely girl I am in love with, and am just not available. I am sorry for you and I am sorry for me . . . under other circumstances, I can assure you I would have welcomed your idea very much.' "

Fossey said he was making a mistake. " 'What makes you think sex has anything to do with love?' " Alexander recalls her saying to him.

And so that had been that, insofar as Alexander was concerned. They had retired on either side of the beer crates he had stacked together. But he didn't mind admitting he had felt damned uncomfortable about it all. Now it was clear why she had told him to leave his men behind. "She wanted me to play around. As I say, normally I would have gone along. But—and while it's a bore to have to say it—I haven't done this sort of thing on my safaris."

The next morning Fossey and Alexander rolled up their sleeping bags, cleared out of the beer hall, and headed into the adventure still awaiting them, the climb up Mount Mikeno in hopes of seeing gorillas. Anicet Mburanumwe, the young park director, assigned two armed rangers to accompany them, and at Kibumba, the small village at the foot of the mountain, they hired eleven porters to carry up their gear (40 pounds a man, for 42 cents each). Fossey's ankle was still tightly bandaged, and it hurt, and even without the effort required for high-altitude hiking her wind was not what it should be. After the first few minutes in the bush she was gasping for breath. So, taking it as easy as possible, they slowly followed the porters, resting often. They climbed up through bamboo groves, over elephant trails, along the edge of a canyon wall two hundred feet high (Fossey suffered from acrophobia but she wasn't about to let Alexander know that), and under the dark Hagenia trees until, after six very long, very taxing hours, they came to an opening on this dark mountain. At last, the sunlight streamed through.

Kabara Meadow was a natural clearing so diminutive in scale that it was really little more than a glade. But it was as lovely as they had been told to expect. For one thing, they could finally see where they were—high on the mountain at an altitude of over 10,000 feet. Off to the east the peak of Mount Karisimbi rose even higher out of the alpine forest on the Rwanda side of the range. There were wildflowers growing among the meadow grasses, and near the forest edge a small pool. On the far side of the clearing was Carl Akeley's grave. Closer by was a small wooden cabin with a tin roof, the back half of it burned away. In front of the cabin, staring back at them with an expression of polite dismay, stood Joan and Alan Root.

Blond, bespectacled, looking like siblings, the Roots were pleasing to look at. Both were twenty-six, five years younger than Fossey. They were dressed rummage-bin informal, as though at a backyard barbecue rather than deep in the Congo wilderness. Joan kept her golden hair up under a baseball cap. There was a sense of harmony about the Roots, as if they belonged to each other and to nothing or no one else. (In time, they would become the closest friends Fossey had in Africa. Their friendship would weather many difficult moments. At one point, Fossey spent a night with Alan Root and Joan found out. But the friendship survived, and Joan and Alan Root went on to shelter Fossey after a crushing love affair that almost destroyed her.)

But right now, the Roots were pissed. That was the only word for it. They had been led to believe by the park officials that they would have the mountain to themselves. No one had ever attempted to make a film record of the mountain gorilla. They had been there for a month, attempting to do so. Not only did they have to find these elusive animals, they had somehow to film them before they ran. What they assuredly did not need were tourists in their hair. And especially that day.

The night before, Alan and their tracker Sanweckwe had crouched for hours in the wet bushes of the Bushitsi escarpment watching helplessly as sixty poachers carved up an elephant. They were worried their presence would be detected by the poachers' dogs, but they couldn't get out. By the time they did, it was after midnight, and a worried Joan had tried to guide them down with a pressure lamp. But the night was so black and the forest so dense that the lamp couldn't be seen. Stumbling along behind Sanweckwe, whose tracking skill was all he had, Alan had stuck phosphorescent fungus to the back of Sanweckwe's belt so he could follow him. Wet, cold, exhausted, they had finally made it back to the meadow at three in the morning. For the first time since they had come there—for the first time in a month—Joan and Alan had decided to sleep in. "Had a rest," Alan entered in that day's journal. "Of all people, John Alexander turned up with a woman to see gorillas."

After they had shaken hands, politely but coolly, Alan Root suggested that Alexander might want to put their tents up behind the cabin. Fossey gave Root the note from Baumgartel, which was received and read without comment. Alexander sensed the awkwardness of the situation but didn't know how to get around it. He didn't know Root well but he knew him well enough to realize their presence wasn't welcome. But it hadn't been his idea to come there.

When Alexander had asked the obvious question—where were the gorillas?—Root told him they were back in the direction he and Fossey had come from. And then the Roots had gone on about their business.

That night, Alexander says, Fossey did it again. "Dian came into my tent and more or less said, 'Come on, get cracking.' I felt very sorry for her. I think I did put my arms around her. But then I said, 'You know, we can't do it because of my girl at home.' " Fossey returned to her tent.

By the next day, both were aware they were pariahs in the promised land. But there was something else in the air, too. Fossey was now dealing differently with Alexander. In her mind, he was no longer the Great White Hunter, but just the Great White. She despised him. Preparing to go out with their two armed rangers, who quite obviously knew little about what they were doing, Alexander oiled his revolver—a precaution that was observed by the Roots with some disgust. They believed that animals had more to fear from humans that the other way around. With no guidance from the Roots, Fossey, Alexander, and the two rangers spent the day aimlessly clambering about the mountainside below Kabara. They saw nothing.

Fossey decided to take matters into her own hands. Alexander was useless to her there. But the Roots knew where the gorillas were and knew how to find them. If she was to see gorillas at all, which was what she had come for, it would be through the benevolence of the Roots, whom she already greatly admired. They were like no other people she had ever known. They seemed to love animals as much as she did, and she guessed they wanted to spend their lives among them there in the African wilderness. They did the sort of things she herself longed to do, and with the skill and precision she admired in people who knew how to do things right. The next day she stayed in camp.

She decided to do everything in her power to change the way things were going. First she collected as many flowers as she could find—St.-John-of-the-Cross, wild orchids, and violets—and strung them along the guy lines of her tent. From logs lying about she fashioned a tea table. For chairs she collected lava rocks and covered them with soft moss. When the Roots came back at the end of their day of photographing the gorillas, Fossey invited them to tea. Alexander was not invited.

By now, the Roots had got a good look at this persistent American woman and they didn't quite know what to make of her. She had no business being up there. Kabara Meadow was no place for tourists, and Alexander should certainly have known that. She was obviously not fit—she had a discernible wheeze, she smoked heavily, and her ankle needed attention. Despite all this, they could see she had grit, and so they had accepted the invitation to tea.

The wheeze the Roots heard may have been deliberately exaggerated. Sick or well, Fossey had an unusual voice. It was low and husky, and she had become expert at playing it like a beautifully bowed viola. Haltingly sometimes, rushing breathlessly over her words at others, she used it in flagrant defiance of her great stature. Even well into middle age, she could sound like a bewildered young girl—small, vulnerable, defenseless.

At tea with the Roots, Fossey explained how she had come to be there. Ever since she had read the books of Carl Akeley, she said, she had been desperate to see mountain gorillas, to come to Kabara to find them. She had borrowed money to do so, but once in Africa the best she could do for a guide was this man Alexander. She had cracked her ankle in Olduvai Gorge but she had told him to bring her on here anyway, even though she realized he was out of his element. The man was frightened of gorillas. He had brought a gun up here, and firecrackers to throw at them to scare them away. But that wasn't the worst of it.

Hesitantly, sounding very vulnerable, she told how Alexander had tried to seduce her. She didn't like talking about this but she didn't know what else to do. She had to tell someone. She had had a devil of a time keeping him off. He had come into her tent just the night before last. . . .

And now (*sotto voce*) it looked as though she wouldn't see the gorillas after all. The rangers didn't know how to track them, and neither did Alexander. They spent the whole day yesterday climbing about the mountainside. They had found nothing, and she was certain they never would, if they kept going about it that way. And in just a few more days, she would have to start back home. . . .

Twenty-five years later, John Alexander is still sore. He says he told Joan Root, who has hardly spoken to him since, that he suspected Fossey of lying about him. He is certain that is why Alan Root has always avoided him.

Joan responded that when Fossey came to Kabara in 1963 she was a fairly recent convert to Catholicism. Had Fossey told him that? she asked.

No, Alexander replied.

"And, according to her best friend at the time, she had not had any romantic affairs. Her friend believed her to be a virgin. In view of this it seems remarkable she would have made sexual advances," Joan told him.

Alexander stands by his version of events. "I'll look anybody in the eye and tell them exactly this," he says. "I know it's not usual for a woman to make the advances, but I got the feeling Dian was very neurotic."

Joan Root says that today she is "not so sure" about Fossey's story. "Of course, in 1963, I believed what Dian told us," she says. And perhaps that was part of the reason why, after tea, Joan and Alan Root said they would be pleased to take Fossey out with them the next day to see the gorillas.

Seeing wild gorillas is a transcendent experience, a discovery of such intensity that each visitor remembers the moment in the most personal terms. Perhaps no small part of it is the fact that one confronts the gorillas in person, not from inside a Land Rover as is often the case with other animals. Meeting the gorillas is a one-on-one experience, and in the dense bush of the Virungas there is no place to run, no way to break free of the entrapping vegetation which the gorilla, if so inclined, can glide through in an instant.

So one must be prepared not just to look, but to watch and be watched. Behind the gigantic, high-crested skull lies a brain with similarities to its human counterpart; in the infant gorilla, the lateral folds of the brain are almost indistinguishable from the human's. But the nose is very different, like a misplaced cauliflower ear, and the jaws are savagely powerful. These differences, however, do not seem enough. In the gorilla's eyes, one senses and shares the shock of recognition. This animal is not an alien species; it is some*one* else.

When the writer Alan Moorehead, historian of the Nile, saw his first wild gorilla he later spent pages trying to capture the singularity of that experience. But at the time all he could manage were the words, "Oh my God, how wonderful!"

Fossey didn't do much better than Moorehead. As she followed behind Joan and Alan Root, her first contact with the gorillas was their smell—the odor of the barnyard mixed with human sweat. When she heard them scream, the hair tingled on the back of her neck. Then Sanweckwe cut a window in the bush with his panga and the Roots pushed her forward so she could see them for the first time. She was never the same again.

8

....

THE
COLONIALIST

Before she even left East Africa for Rhodesia and her visit to the Forresters, Fossey had a big fight with Alexander. Leaving the Congo, they had had a long, dangerous delay at the border post, finally managing to retrieve Alexander's passport by bribing guards with the last of her cigarettes and his beer. Returning through Uganda to northern Kenya, the tension between them nearing the boiling point ("Hell hath no fury . . ." Alexander later opined), they arrived in Nairobi on the first of November, where, as was his duty to his client, Alexander saw Fossey safely checked into a hotel. There they fell into a violent dispute over the additional money he maintained she now owed him. Alexander ticked off the surcharges: the extra mileage from going into the Congo, the cost of insuring his vehicle, the rental fee for his Bolex, the purchase of sixteen rolls of film; all of it coming to an additional $710.

Outrageous, Fossey complained later in a letter to Joan and Alan

Root. That damnable Alexander had tried to rob her. She had told him she would not pay him another penny. Yes, she would, Alexander had replied, or he would have her airline ticket impounded. He would be around the next morning to pick up the money she owed him, or else. She had never felt so alone in all her life, Dian told the Roots. But by the time Alexander returned the next morning, she had left town, having talked her way onto an earlier flight departing for Salisbury.

In the first three articles she later wrote for the Louisville paper about her adventure, Fossey said she had returned from her Africa safari with her dreams realized in every way but one. Next time, she said, she would be sure to go without the Great White. So embittered were her subsequent references to Alexander—and so ambiguous was her sexual life in the years to come—that the question of what really happened between them deserves some scrutiny.

Mary White Henry, now Mrs. Donald Grobmyer of Boca Raton, Florida, stands firm as a character witness for her friend, whom she loved like a sister. But, like Joan Root, she is inclined to believe Alexander—with some reservations.

"First of all," Mary says, "nothing should be made of Dian telling Alexander not to bring along his African assistants. That was Dian just trying to save money! I don't know about the drinking. She didn't drink that way in Louisville. But all that smoking simply meant she was nervous. Dian always smoked a lot, but when she chain-smoked, she was *very* nervous.

"And I wouldn't say her behavior was neurotic, either. I would say she behaved the way she did because she was an individualist who set her own standards. She knocked herself out to live up to what she expected of herself—not what others expected of her. She was extremely shy, and some of this was simply her shyness. When Dian was uncomfortable in her surroundings she could be very abrupt.

"In Louisville Dian certainly wouldn't have acted with *any* man the way Alexander says she did with him. She had never necked or petted as so many girls of our generation did in those days. Not that I'm aware of. [Here it must be noted that a confidant from much later in Dian's life is certain she was not a virgin in those days. Says Anita McClellan: "I submit to you Dian was introduced to sex early and in the most unsavory way imaginable."] You could tell this about her— in mixed company she could talk a good game, but there was no experience behind it. If she had tried to act as sexual aggressor in those days, you can be certain the word would have traveled very quickly.

"Remember these things happened to Dian after she got to Africa. John Alexander was across that ocean! There is something different about Africa. It changes your outlook. The moon and the stars, and the open skies, sitting on a mountainside . . . And remember that in those days American girls with Dian's background were stupidly naïve. Traveling alone they *expected* things to happen. Foreign men were supposed to make advances. I can hear her saying to Alexander—more of it talk than anything else: 'When are you going to do what you're supposed to do?' In effect: 'What's with you that you're not living up to what everyone expects you to do? How come? Why not with me?'

"And then, just as readily, I can see her turning around and telling the Roots exactly the opposite of what had really happened, doing this to protect herself. She had to make herself look good, and if a man like Alexander already had a reputation, I can see Dian taking advantage of it. It is even conceivable she could have twisted events in her mind to convince herself he had made the advances. Because that is what she expected him to do.

"As to their fight over what he says she owed him, if Dian thought Alexander had cheated her, I wouldn't be in the least bit surprised about her reaction."

Fossey discovered that Salisbury, Rhodesia, was comparable to Louisville—too large to be provincial, too small to be impersonal.

There were skyscrapers, restaurants, tree-lined boulevards, and when Peg Forrester brought her guest to her family's sprawling house in the suburbs, it was as though Fossey had returned at last to the bosom of the Henry family—the African branch at least. Having just come from the best of her safari (the gorillas) and the worst (the Great White), she found the Forrester's Salisbury a perfect conclusion to her adventure, both familiar and exotic. Beyond the obvious, however—the disparities between two families separated by culture and an ocean—there were some noticeable differences from life in Louisville.

Gaynee Henry had two black domestics. The Forresters had four— plus two hundred farm workers. Blacks constituted a large majority of the Rhodesian population, yet they were forbidden by law to own preferred farmlands or to work at skilled labor. In consequence, domestic help was plentiful and cheap.

The Forresters were less sensitive toward their black help than the Henrys; they took subservience for granted. In Rhodesia in 1963, black rights were for the future—the very distant future. The Henrys were more self-conscious about such things, tending to identify personally with their black servants. When the Forresters visited Louisville, the Henry sisters recall, their mother had worried about this difference in their outlook. "We had a cook and a man to serve," Betty says, "but they treated them like so much furniture."

To Fossey, there was a more obvious and immediate difference in the Forresters' life in Rhodesia, one which suited her preferences. Everything about the Forrester household suggested large masculine bodies. Gaynee Henry's children were women, and the interior of her Summit Avenue house reflected as much. Peg Forrester's children were men, not one of them less than six foot three. Chairs were oversized, well stuffed, and solidly constructed to accommodate big frames. Already as disposed toward this loving and outgoing Catholic family as anyone else in the Henry Hotel, Fossey was comfortable amid such furnishings and pleased to be among such masculine men.

And what striking, rugged men! Franz Forrester was a farmer, and his boys worked the land, a task by American standards more reminiscent of the nineteenth century than the twentieth. With wild animals and unpredictable African neighbors, a farm in Rhodesia was frontier country, and the Forrester boys had been raised as pioneers. But they were also aristocratic in bearing, British in demeanor, yet exuberant and outgoing. If they seemed imperious, Mary Henry had once said, that was because they *were* imperious. They were among the last remnants of the era of African colonialism.

Soon after Fossey arrived, Peg Forrester took her to Mteroshanga, the family's tobacco and cattle farm outside the city, to meet her middle son, Alexie, the one Fossey had picked out in Father Raymond's photograph. Alexie climbed down from his tractor to greet them, and for once in her life, Fossey looked up instead of down. Father Raymond described the scene:

"The two just stood there and looked at each other. Finally Dian broke the silence, saying,

" 'I can plow.'

" 'There's the machine,' said Alexie."

A year later, Forrester told Father Raymond how his interest in Fossey had been kindled. "That girl plowed that entire field. The only trouble was that, as she finished the last furrow, she hit a rock and broke the plow. Little did I care! The field was ready for discing, and I had seen a *real* woman!"

Forrester came to the United States soon thereafter for two reasons: to go to college and to marry Dian Fossey.

Or so Father Raymond says.

There are several versions of the Fossey/Forrester affair, but everyone who saw it develop agrees that Fossey was completely thrown by it. Few of the friends she would make later would ever hear from her about it, and it was given no space in her autobiography. Her last three years in Louisville—from her return in November 1963 until

December 1966, when she went back to Africa—are covered in less than a page. Forrester, like the hapless Alexander, warrants no mention.

Forrester arrived in the United States in September 1964 to attend Notre Dame University in South Bend, Indiana. But he didn't see Fossey until Thanksgiving, a year after they had first met. By that time Fossey, still enthralled with the life she had seen, had drifted back into the placidity of her Louisville routine. She remained Gaynee Henry's loving Other Daughter and she was now virtually the only one around: Mary spent most of her time with Don Grobmyer, whom she would soon marry; and Betty, with her husband and four children, was living in another part of town. Fossey was working at Kosair, going to Mass daily, looking after her stray dogs, and trying to write magazine articles about her grand and desperate adventure. She had cut out eating lunches and other expendable items, giving up half of her salary as part of her three-year plan to pay for her trip.

Forrester, who had entered Notre Dame through the assistance of his aunt Maura, a Catholic nun now known as Sister Gerald, was cutting corners himself. A scholarship student, he made his living expenses as a night watchman and construction worker. To cut down on rent he slept in a funeral parlor. Three hundred miles from South Bend, Louisville seemed a long way away.

Just after Christmas, during Forrester's second visit to the Henry Hotel, it became obvious to everyone that he and Fossey had fallen in love. They were a striking pair. "A handsomer couple would be hard to find," wrote the enthusiastic Father Raymond. "Each stood at about six feet, two inches; each was endowed by God with exceptionally good looks; each was magnificently built." Before his second visit was over, in early 1965, they decided in a burst of impetuosity to marry. And the sooner the better.

Today, Alexie Forrester is an investment banker in London, where he lives with his wife and five children. He speaks his mind quickly and with conviction, as though he knows precisely where he stands on whatever question is put to him. He talks of Dian Fossey as though he can't quite imagine what he was thinking of when he got so involved with her, but certain aspects of the attraction do come clear. She threw herself into her commitments, he says, never doing anything by half. She was dedicated to the problems of handicapped children and the dispossessed. While she showed respect for people she admired, she still relied completely on herself. These things he could say for her. Her will was indomitable.

Despite the fact that he saw her only occasionally, Forrester saw more of Fossey than she had previously let others see. By the time they came together she had also found her father, with whom she had established an uneasy reunion. Exactly how this came about Forrester has no idea. One day George Fossey was simply back in his daughter's life. Forrester says Fossey saw her father three times—in Chicago, New York, and San Francisco. He was mysterious. When he walked out of Dian's life he had simply disappeared, and it was only through her initiative that they had got together after so many years. The man evidently had some problems, Forrester says, which she didn't know how to handle. "She related to him on two separate planes, almost schizophrenically. On the one hand, he could do no wrong. He was a wonderful man, misunderstood—the usual nonsense. On the other, when she saw the reality of how she'd been treated by him, she didn't like it at all." Forrester didn't know what to make of it, either. He respected her privacy in the matter, and let it go at that.

"We knew we wanted to marry in 1965," he says, "but we didn't discuss it with anyone until 1966. By then everyone was aware of it. I went out to California to see her stepfather, whom I wanted formally to advise that I wanted to marry her when I completed my studies. When I met with him, he pooh-poohed the whole idea of my staying in college at all. He suggested it was a waste of time, and that I should come join him in his business right away. It was there for me to take over. We should get married and I should run things. I felt completely overpowered by that. It wasn't what I'd had in mind at all.

"He tried to provide for the rest of my stay in the university, and I refused this, too. There was a bit of a conflict going there. I insisted on staying on and finishing my university, and I said to Dian, why don't you just go on and do something for a year? It was my suggestion she go to Dr. Leakey in the first place. I had another year before I graduated, so we weren't going to get married until then anyway."

9

SISTER GERALD'S VERSION

All who know Sister Gerald acknowledge her competence in the management of her order's fiscal accounts, that secular domain where piety has no claim. Through the recommendations of Ernst & Ernst, one of the nation's largest accounting firms, she has also become a member of various boards of directors. She is as firm in her opinions as her nephew (whom she adores), and she is always ready to advise anyone, close relative or stranger, on temporal concerns. On the subject of the Fossey/Forrester affair, she knows exactly where she stood and how she came to her opinion.

"I visited Rhodesia in July 1964," she says, "and while I was there Alexie drove me around to the mission. I asked him if he'd ever thought of the priesthood. Alexie said, 'I have thought about the priesthood, and seriously, but my first choice would be marriage. And if I met a girl who helped me to achieve what God made me for, which was eternity in heaven, then I would want to marry her. But I haven't met her.'"

Two months later Forrester came to the United States to go to Notre Dame. After Christmas he wrote Sister Gerald that he was going to marry Dian Fossey.

Reminding him that he was only twenty-four, Sister Gerald said that if he really loved her, he would continue his studies so he could support a wife. He was only a freshman, and graduation was a long row ahead.

Yes, Alexie wrote back, on reflection he realized it would be irresponsible to marry somebody he couldn't support and go through life without a university education. He would put marriage off until he graduated. He continued to visit Fossey during his vacations.

In late 1966, more than a year later, Forrester visited Sister Gerald at St. Mary's College at Notre Dame. She remembers their discussion well.

" 'Aunt Maura,' he said, 'I've got some surprising news for you. I'm going to marry Dian.'

" 'Congratulations,' I said.

" 'I thought you'd give me an argument.'

"Why," Sister Gerald responded. She told him that he was now two years older and that she was sure he had worked out how he could finish school and support a wife.

Forrester said he had, but wondered if Sister Gerald could help Dian find an occupational therapy position at St. Joseph's Hospital in Louisville. She said she'd try.

Sister Gerald had one concern, however. "You're working at night, you're in class in the daytime," she said. "Dian will be working in the daytime as an occupational therapist. Have you figured out how you'll ever see her?"

Forrester said he had never thought of that. He asked Sister Gerald if she would be willing to talk to Dian about it. She agreed.

"As it happened—this seemed providential to me—I was going the next day to consult with the Sisters of Nazareth at Nazareth College in Kentucky," Sister Gerald says. "Dian came out to Nazareth, and I sat down and talked with her. She was very taken aback by what I had to say.

" 'Dian,' I said, 'my concern is, if Alexie marries, he'll never graduate. It's an impossible solution to be able to support you and be on that kind of schedule' " She also expressed a second concern: the seven-year age difference. " 'For instance,' I said, 'when he's thirty-five, you'll be forty-two. In a country where it's very difficult to maintain integrity in marriage, I'd be less than honest if I didn't say I have a concern about that, also.'

"Dian replied, 'I will see to it that he finishes at Notre Dame.'

"And this is the pivotal point of the whole story, by the way. I said, 'And what if God sent a child by the end of the first year and Alexie didn't have a job?'

" 'We would have a baby-sitter to take care of the child,' she said.

"I kissed her good-bye and I said, 'Don't forget, Dian. I'll be as supportive as I can possibly be.' "

"When I got back, Alexie came to see me. He wanted to know what had happened. I said, 'I told her I was concerned that the two of you wouldn't have a normal married life if you married before graduation. I expressed my concern to Dian that you would never finish if you married, and she said to me, "I'll see to it that he does." ' "

" 'I did not like that, Alexie,' I said, 'because already she's superior to you educationally. She's superior to you chronologically, and the fact that she says she will see to it that you do finish—I don't see a partnership there. I see an ownership there. And that concerns me. And when I asked if a child should come before graduation, and she said she would put the child out to be cared for by a baby-sitter, I left it at that and pledged my support.'

"So, he said, 'I'm still going to marry her.'

"Much to my amazement, I later got a letter from Alexie. 'Nothing you said influenced me against marrying Dian,' he said, 'except one thought—that two people could be selfish enough to enter into marriage, bring a child to birth and not be able to take care of that child. That stopped me dead. So I have decided that unless we are selfish, we should be able to postpone the marriage until I have a job and we'll be able to take whatever children God sends us.' "

•   •   •

Misinformation abounds, misunderstandings persist. As far as the families were concerned, the marriage had seemed imminent. The Prices had flown to Louisville and met the Henrys, and the Forresters had gone to San Francisco, bringing along Sister Gerald, to meet the Prices. On the surface, things had seemed just fine. Kitty Price was thrilled at the prospect of her daughter marrying into the European aristocracy, although somehow she got it in her head that Dian had converted to Catholicism solely in order to do so. Dian evidently didn't try to set her straight.

When the idea of the marriage began to come unraveled, Dian let Kitty believe the Forresters disapproved because Kitty was divorced, a bit of misinformation Sister Gerald personally found appalling. ("I don't believe the child of divorced people should ever be penalized. That would be very un-Christian.") In any case, the wedding of Dian and Alexie was postponed till a more convenient time, until Alexie finished Notre Dame in 1968. Forrester himself saw no particular reason why anyone should make much of a fuss about it, nor does he today.

And so, no one did, except Dian. Kitty Price says that Dian was devastated. She clearly believed the marriage would never take place. She went into hysterics and disappeared for two weeks.

"I saw how exact Thomas Aquinas was when he said that grace builds on nature," Father Raymond wrote of Fossey at this time. "Dian had much before she came into the Catholic Church. She received much more from that Church, and it all became manifest in what must be called character, in that arresting sense which bespeaks integrity, fidelity, loyalty, dependability, sincerity and limpid honesty."

Whatever radiance she may have projected to Father Raymond, she didn't see it in herself. She felt she had an eleven-year hangover. She was no further ahead than when she had started. She worked at a job that offered no advancement, where her experience led her nowhere. She was forced to struggle for her subsistence more than ever before, required to give over half her salary to meet the terms of her $8,000 loan. She had even lost the Washhouse (having fled after George Long put his aging aunts in the mobile home in her backyard) and was living in an even more remote farmhouse with neither heat nor running water. She had her privacy, her dogs, and very little else.

Even the memory of her great adventure was receding into the past. All she had to remind her were stories about Joan and Alan Root in the *Saturday Evening Post* and the *National Geographic*. The Roots were leading lives of adventure in the very place where she wanted to be. But there was no way she could get back. Africa was in her past.

Worst of all, she was no closer to marriage than she had ever been. Her engagement to Forrester had been postponed twice. She was furious and humiliated. And now, in the last weeks of March 1966, she had, like Job, developed boils.

Arriving in Louisville the first weekend in April 1966, Louis Leakey was more exalted than ever, although somewhat the worse for wear. The world's most esteemed expert in paleoanthropology was winding up his career by shifting his pace from a frantic sprint to a mad dash. He was getting older; his hip sockets were ossifying from arthritis, he limped and he wheezed. Yet, like a hyperkinetic child, Louis Leakey, sixty-three now, would run until he dropped. Once he told Jane Goodall's mother, Vanne, his closest companion outside Africa, that he never expected to die. The way he said it, it was almost possible to believe he wasn't kidding. He had no time for it; he had too many irons in the fire.

Over the years Leakey had used his enormous prestige to establish one more ambitious project after another, a dozen or so of them spread over several continents. He had started digs in Tanzania, Kenya, Israel, Ethiopia, and Southern California. He presided over an assortment of primate studies, including a breeding center to supply monkeys for medical research. (Around 20,000 monkeys a year were needed, and it was Leakey's intention to protect the wild stock.) Jane Goodall's chimpanzee studies had been his idea. He had raised the money and sent her to the Gombe Stream Reserve, where she was becoming world-famous. He was director of the new Centre for Prehistory Studies in Nairobi, and more recently he had undertaken the establishment of a department of osteology there, warehousing the skeletons of Africa fauna.

But what he had done was nowhere close to what he still wanted to do. He believed tuberculosis might be cured with zebra fat; that human reproduction could be regulated by diet (as it was in monkeys); that the Sahara could be irrigated with sea water, restoring the verdancy that was there before the Ice Age. And he wanted the other two species of great ape studied, the orangutan and the mountain gorilla. While he was impressed with George Schaller's study in 1960, he wasn't impressed enough to leave it at that. He believed a researcher ought to be willing to conduct observations in the field as long as need be, certainly longer than Schaller's 466 hours. He wanted the mountain gorilla studied properly, as Goodall was studying the chimpanzee. That is to say, his way.

Leakey had little patience with the growing tendency of modern science to insist upon statistical quantification of each and every phenomenon observed. He was an old-fashioned empiricist. At various times, to prove some of his theories about early man, he had charged, naked and unarmed, a pack of hyenas to scavenge their kill, and chipped out a stone ax in order to skin a dead animal, then chewed off a chunk of the carcass and ate it. Having begun his career as a pariah, he had attained that station all scientists dream of but few achieve. He was a public figure. By 1966, Leakey had become ringmaster of his own circus.

But running the show his way involved funding it. If there was something he wanted done, he had long ago learned it was up to him to find the money to do it. While some large foundations and private benefactors, like Leighton Wilkie, were favorably disposed toward him, there was never enough money to do all that he wanted to at any one time. And so Leakey spent a lot of time on the road, fund-raising. In the spring of 1966, he was going as fast as modern conveyances could move him, foraging for funds in the sort of tightly scheduled expedition that would lead to his collapse, from pure physical exhaustion, on a runway at O'Hare Airport less than a year later.

But, arriving in Louisville that April, he gave no mind to such things. He simply could not afford to let himself feel as tired as he deserved to be. The next day, he would have a bite of breakfast and be on his way.

Dr. Fred Coy has a warm place in his heart for Dian Fossey. When Coy's son was small, the boy fell against a cellar door and severed a nerve in his armpit. Over the years Fossey worked tirelessly with him in an effort to help him regain the use of his arm. In time, she became as close to the Coy family as she would to any of her associates at Kosair, where Coy was an orthopedist. One day Coy saw a notice that Louis Leakey would be speaking at the University of Louisville, and knowing of Fossey's interest in him, made a point of telling her. The lecture was scheduled for Sunday, April 3, at 8:00 P.M.

Despite her boils (a staph infection so virulent the hospital had suggested she stay home until she recovered), Fossey resolved to seize the moment. She would show Leakey a drawing she had made of *Zinjanthropus*, and the three articles she had published in the *Louisville Courier Journal*. One article was the account of the first part of her trip, riding out among the animals of East Africa. One described the fossil discoveries at Olduvai Gorge and contained everything she had read about Dr. Leakey's research into early man. And the third was about her experience seeing the mountain gorillas on Mount Mikeno, an article entitled "I Photographed the Mountain Gorilla."

While this was true enough, the photographs of gorillas used to illustrate the article were not hers. Her photographs had turned out to be overexposed. When the newspaper editor discovered she had some gorilla photographs he could use—photographs sent her by the Roots as a memento of her trip—he said he wanted them. Though Fossey had written the Roots asking their permission, the published article showed no one's name under any of the photographs, the first-person title thus suggesting that all the photographs were Fossey's.

On the night of April 3, with her drawing and clippings, Fossey sat in the back of Bigelow Hall at the University of Louisville, sharing the excitement of hearing Leakey tell the story of the earliest man. "His talk ended at eleven," she would recall many years later, to the writer Victor Cox, "and there he is standing in a line, letting people come talk to him. He was due to leave at something like nine in the morning. And I had my hot little palms filled with articles about Africa, and about Dr. Leakey himself, and I had drawn a picture of *Zinjanthropus*.

"So he looked at these articles. The one about Olduvai he wasn't interested in. The one about the animals of Africa he wasn't interested in. And then he saw the one about gorillas, and he said,

" 'You take these pictures?'

"I said yes."

"He said, 'Well, I want to talk with you.' "

10

....

AMAZING GRACE

In *Gorillas in the Mist*, Fossey's version of her meeting with Leakey is brief, perfunctory, and vague. She writes that after her articles and photographs had come to Leakey's attention (she doesn't say how), he invited her to become his "gorilla girl." Because she would be working in such a remote area, far from any medical facility, he recommended she have her appendix out before her departure. Often through the years, as a sort of rueful joke on them both, she told of having her appendix removed, only to receive a letter from Leakey implying he had just been testing her resolve.

Fossey began to revise the story of her meeting with Leakey early on, as if she were already weaving a myth around herself. On December 6, 1966, before she left for Africa, she was interviewed by Linda Koch of the *Fresno Bee*. Koch's article included this account of Fossey's association with Leakey:

The article found its way to Africa and was seen by Dr. Leakey. Last April, while on a tour of the U.S., Dr. Leakey was lecturing at the University of [Louisville]. Remembering Miss Fossey's obvious interest in his adopted country, Dr. Leakey held a two-day concentrated interview with the occupational therapist.

"He turned me inside out," she recalled. "And when he was through I think he knew everything about me."

There is little question that Fossey's *Louisville Courier Journal* article about mountain gorillas helped reveal her remarkable attributes to Louis Leakey. First of all, unlike any other tourist venturing to East Africa in those days, she had managed on her own to get to where the gorillas were. Secondly, she had seen the gorillas and, in spite of her term-paper prose, had managed to evoke the quality of that experience. And, most impressively, she had the pictures to prove it.

The next morning, she had breakfast with Leakey at Stouffer's Inn. She left half an hour later exhilarated at the prospect before her. Leakey told her he had been looking for someone like Jane Goodall to study the mountain gorilla. He was not at all put off by Fossey's lack of qualifications, or the fact that she was, at thirty-four, a little long in the tooth for such an assignment. But she should have a preemptive appendectomy. Mary Leakey had suffered an attack of appendicitis in the bush, as had one of his assistants, who almost died before receiving medical treatment.

Leakey was a formidable conversationalist about whatever he cared to discuss and he tended to smother his audience with enthusiasm. That morning, Leakey was at his best. But nothing indicates that Leakey, at that moment, had any real intention of sweeping Fossey off to Africa. He was well known for his unorthodox selection of protégés, and he did prefer untrained women for his primate studies. Women, he argued, were more patient, more sensitive to mother-infant relations, and less likely to arouse aggression in males. He liked them untrained because trained scientists tended to see too much.

Though Fossey was eager, Leakey did not sign her up that night in Louisville. What he did was put her on hold.

Back in Nairobi, Leakey tried to check Fossey out with Alan Root, whom he knew very well. Alan was, as a matter of fact, in the safari business with Leakey's son Richard. They had set up the partnership to support Alan's interest in wildlife photography and Richard's interest in fossil exploration. Indeed, Louis Leakey had tried to persuade Alan Root to make a film record of Jane Goodall's work at Gombe Stream. On April 26, he wrote to Root asking whether he thought Fossey would be up to the sustained effort required for an intensive study of the gorilla. In other words, would she have any chance of matching Goodall's work with chimpanzees? Unfortunately, Alan and Joan Root were in Australia, and Leakey's query went unanswered.

On May 5, having heard nothing further, Fossey wrote Leakey, anxious to sustain his interest. She had read both of Schaller's books, she said, and was memorizing a Swahili text, but she hadn't given notice at the hospital nor had her appendix removed. She was looking forward to further word.

On May 17, Leakey wrote back to say he had made some preliminary inquiries but it would take some time before he had anything more definite to say. He made no mention of her proposed appendectomy.

On June 8, a sort of chess game began. Fossey opened play with a negative option. She acknowledged no hesitancy on Leakey's part. Instead, she announced her intention to have her appendix out in three weeks unless she heard otherwise from Leakey.

On June 15, Leakey—wary—responded with a gambit of his own. His plan was to pay all her expenses for the trip out, as well as a return ticket; the cost of one or more African staff; and a small salary. But first he had to raise the money; he hoped to do so by applying to the National Geographic in her behalf. If successful, she could look forward to additional income from the sale of her articles and photographs to the *National Geographic*, from lectures, and from any books she might write. Moreover, the National Geographic might very well assign a filmmaker to cover her study. In the meantime, Fossey should send him a detailed statement of her background, together with a written account of her experience with the gorillas in 1963. As for her negative option, he responded with negative ambiguity: "I would suggest that you don't have your appendix out until we know more, although, frankly, I am not sure that is good advice. It is always a good thing to get rid of it while it is healthy."

On June 20, Fossey put him in check. Her appendectomy was scheduled for the following Tuesday, June 28. If Leakey wished her to cancel the operation, he should cable her immediately. Collect.

On July 1, Leakey overturned his king. He made no further reference to her appendectomy but said he would do everything he could to raise the necessary money and get the expedition organized.

Fossey, recovering from her operation at the Henrys' house, was thrilled. There was no longer any question in her mind that she was going to Africa to study mountain gorillas for Louis Leakey and the *National Geographic* magazine. Although Leakey had promised nothing specifically, had no commitment from the National Geographic Society, and had no more money for her "study" than when he came to Louisville, Fossey gave her notice at Kosair with high heart and few regrets. She packed several trunks and put them in storage. One contained the books of Catholic theology she had read and discussed with Father Raymond. One was filled with her craft works and some drawings and paintings she had made. Another held housewares.

If Alexie Forrester figured in her life at this point, she didn't mention it, though he said they were still planning for the future. "The plan was, she would finish what she was doing in Africa," he says. "That would take another year, a year and a half, and then she would come back. Meanwhile, I would get my degree and become involved in some sort of career."

Everyone at the Henry Hotel was happy for Fossey. Beloved to them all, their adopted daughter had finally gotten the big break she had always deserved. They prepared for her departure at the end of July, when she would return to Atherton, driving cross-country in her old Saab to spend some time with her parents before Dr. Leakey sent for her. Always the special favorite of the Henry nephews and nieces, she became the center of a fuss over who would have the honor of driving with her. There was room for only one. Gaynee Henry, then seventy-seven, had settled it by deciding that she would go, and when the day came, the women merrily waved good-bye as they drove off to the west. "The cooling system in her car wasn't working," Betty Schwartzel remembers, "and when they came to the Great Plains they had to keep the heater on to prevent the radiator from boiling over. They had a wonderful time!"

Leakey continued to hedge his bets. He wrote to Fossey in California that the permission from the Congolese authorities for her to work in Kabara had not come. Until it did, he said, there was little reason for him to seek funding. On September 1, after she had spent a bleak month with her unenthusiastic parents, Fossey wrote to Leakey again. She made it clear that she hoped to leave for Africa sooner rather than later. All right, Leakey wrote back; he had submitted his grant proposals to the National Geographic even though he still had heard nothing from the Congo officials.

Almost two months passed. Fossey was beginning to wonder who had finessed whom. Politely but pointedly, she wrote to Leakey on October 24 reminding him she had quit her job of eleven years, cutting off her only source of income. She had given up her home and friends she loved. Was she going to Africa to study gorillas or not?

He was doing everything it was possible to do, Leakey reassured her, although he still lacked permission from the Congo. And the National Geographic said it had never received his grant applications. He would have to apply for her all over again. By November 1, he said, he was certain he would be able to think of something.

120

On November 3, definitely in a pinch, Leakey wrote Leighton Wilkie, his former benefactor in the United States:

You will, I am sure, remember that many years ago you afforded me invaluable help in the way of a grant, to enable me to get the Chimpanzee Research, by Jane Goodall, started.

As you are doubtless aware, she has made a magnificent job of her research, and at the moment, is writing up her scientific results in the form of several books. She has also published a number of scientific papers, as well as two popular articles which have appeared in the *National Geographic* magazine.

I am sure that you are aware of some of the results, either through the *National Geographic* magazine articles, or through the television film that was shown last year in the States, and when her first book is published, we shall send a copy to you at once. You will, therefore, be aware that Jane has established that chimpanzees, under entirely wild and natural conditions, regularly make and use primitive tools. Indeed, as a result of this discovery by her, anthropologists have been forced to abandon the old definition of man as "the primate that makes tools to certain and regular pattern."

Knowing your interest in primitive tools and tool-making, as well as in Early Man, I am writing to ask whether you would like to receive two or three examples of these exceedingly primitive tools that chimpanzees make [Leakey does not say what they are], since we now have some available.

I am also wondering whether you would be willing to help me launch a similar piece of research in respect to the Mountain Gorilla. As you are aware, it is always the initial launching of a research scheme of this sort that is so difficult. Once it has got underway, and has been shown to be a successful project, the considerably greater funds that are required to maintain the research can usually be obtained with less difficultly.

You presumably know of the study of the Mountain Gorilla by George Schaller. Personally I feel it was magnificent as far as it went, but it was very incomplete. For some time now, therefore, I have been looking for a suitable research worker to continue where Schaller left off, and in view of the greater patience of women, I have been looking for a suitable girl to do the job, and follow Jane's example.

I have, now, found what I believe to be an indubitably suitable candidate, and I am anxious to get her launched into the field to study Mountain Gorillas as soon as possible, and I am wondering whether you will be willing to help us with a grant in aid. If you are willing to consider doing so, I will send you more information, and you could also perhaps meet the girl in question, as she is an American, and is still in the States.

Wilkie came through with $3,000, enough to assure Fossey that Leakey's extravagant plans were not as capricious as she had begun to think. She would indeed have the opportunity to start her life over again.

On Monday, December 19, 1966, she left the United States, more or less for good.

11

A REAL MAN

At Heathrow Airport in London, waiting to board her flight, Joan Root heard herself paged over the loudspeaker. It was a telephone call from Alan, making sure she had gotten to the airport on time. Neither of them would have been very surprised if she hadn't. The Roots' schedule, which had kept them away from home for seven months, was threatening to swamp them. As part of their safari business with Richard Leakey, they were to meet sixteen Americans in three weeks at the airport in Entebbe, Uganda, for a six-week safari. Other projects included a film on the hippos and crocodiles living in a volcanic spring outside Tsavo; a plan to trap bongos, the endangered white-striped antelopes, for zoo breeding; and a film of George Schaller's new lion study in the Serengeti. The schedule at the moment was for Alan to wrap things up at their film office in London while Joan headed out to prepare for the Entebbe safari. Just as she finished the call with Alan, Joan turned to find Dian Fossey standing behind her.

"Dian!" she said. "What're *you* doing here?"

"I'm off to study the gorillas," Fossey announced, only half-expecting Root to believe that she was headed to Nairobi, too. But it turned out they were on the same flight. As usual Fossey ran on, telling Root what a wreck she was. Last time it was a bum ankle. This time she had asthma and a cold and fever on top of it. But never mind; she had more important news. She told Root of her incredible luck: she was going to become Louis Leakey's "gorilla girl." Leakey was going to send her back to the Kabara Meadow with Joan and Alan.

Root was more astonished than she let on. Unpredictable events had come to be the norm in her life, but she found the prospect of Dian Fossey as a serious field researcher on mountain gorillas difficult to absorb. Still, she responded to the news with the enthusiasm Fossey had every right to expect from her.

When their flight was called, they discovered they were seated far apart. They would talk again in the morning. Throughout the long overnight flight to Nairobi, Root dozed intermittently, wondering betweentimes what had come over Louis Leakey.

Fossey was clearly unfit. Three years earlier in Kabara, she had been wheezing from her bad lungs, and she seemed no better now. She was too fragile for the Virungas—and too naïve. On the mountain she had told Joan and Alan of her love for dogs and horses. But loving domestic animals had very little to do with working among wild animals of any kind, especially gorillas, who weren't looking for love from humans. Root worried over Fossey's romantic impulses: Africa wasn't what Fossey thought it was. She was an American tourist. How could she be expected to cope? Any list of the skills she lacked would just be endless.

She knew nothing of the local languages—neither Swahili, the lingua franca of East Africa and the Congo, nor French, which was spoken from the Virungas westward, including Kabara and the Albert National Park headquarters down the mountain.

She knew nothing of the mountain rain forest, nothing about the wet, clinging vegetation, the constant mud; the steep slopes, the hidden ravines; the endless rain and fog, the periodic hailstorms; wet clothes and wet tents that never dried. She had never even lived in a tent.

She knew nothing of the local people—the Bahutu, the Watutsi, the Batwa—who had lived in the Virungas for more than four hundred years. She had never worked with Africans anywhere. If she was like other Westerners Root knew—and there was no reason to assume she was not—she would at first try too hard to make up for the fact that she was white and they were not. This would confuse the Africans, who wouldn't know how to respond. When the Africans took advantage of Westerners' effusiveness, not knowing when they had gone too far, the Westerners became embittered and resentful, and then reacted too strongly the *other* way, viewing the Africans as savages. Root had seen this happen all too often with foundation people and U.N. officials.

Root was most worried about Fossey's ignorance of the political battles that had plagued the Congo since independence. No one knew how bad things were now, but there were always roadblocks and drunken soldiers looking to make trouble. Leaving the country not long after their meeting with Fossey in 1963, Joan and Alan had barely escaped imprisonment. At the last minute, Alan had been forced to strike a guard and run down a road barricade. The Roots had left their passports behind. Later, an Indian trader told them that the Congolese, carrying machine guns, had followed them in an old Ford.

It wasn't Joan Root's nature to second-guess Louis Leakey. People like the Roots appreciated his unorthodox ways, and women of ambition, like Joan, cheered his success with Jane Goodall, who had helped prove his point about the natural superiority of women as primate researchers.

But she knew that Goodall had worked in Leakey's office for a year

125

and had studied animal behavior in London for another year before she had gone into the wilderness. Goodall had also taken her mother along when she finally ventured into the bush. Fossey, it seemed, was prepared to proceed directly from Kentucky to the Congo.

Their plane landed seven hours late. Leakey had sent his secretary to collect Fossey, and before they parted, Joan Root invited her to come to her house at Lake Naivasha for Christmas, which was fast approaching. Not knowing what Leakey had planned for her, Fossey promised to let her know.

Later, when Alan Root arrived from London, he found a letter from Leakey dated December 15, well before Fossey had even left the U.S. "Dear Alan," it read. "I am sure that you will remember some time ago meeting Miss Dian Fossey at Kabara, when she was looking at gorilla.

"She will be shortly returning to this country on her way to do three years research on gorillas, along the lines of Jane Goodall's research on chimpanzees. I am wondering whether by any chance you would be willing to accompany her to Kabara."

Coughing and sniffling, feverish from the excitement and her cold, Fossey saw Nairobi as if she had never really seen it before, as though it were her first day of school. She wanted to spend Christmas with the Roots. She was convinced they were the best thing that had ever happened to her, and nothing would ever change her mind about that. But Leakey had other plans. He wanted her to have some field orientation. He had to be sure that she was properly equipped, and that she was in good enough physical condition to go into the Congo. (He also needed to get some more financial backing, but that was his problem, not hers.) Leakey said he thought it best if she spent Christmas with Jane Goodall and her husband, Hugo von Laiwick, who were going up to Lake Baringo on the northern frontier. It was hot and dry there and she could get over her cold.

It was so hot there even the lizards were sweating, and the camp was a hundred miles from the nearest town. Fossey found it all strange and awkward. She didn't get to know Goodall very well. All they had to celebrate Christmas was a paper tree and some balloons to hang from their VW camper. Fossey had wrapped their presents in Kleenex and strands of grass.

Back in Nairobi, Fossey visited the Leakeys' home. "Oh, so you're the one who is going to out-Schaller Schaller?" Mary Leakey said, with a wicked gleam in her eye. Fossey would never forget that, but she had other things to think about. Everything seemed to be coming together. With Leighton Wilkie's money Louis Leakey had bought her a secondhand Land Rover, which he test-drove himself, sending pedestrians and motorists scattering in all directions.

Somebody suggested she go down to Serengeti and talk with George Schaller about his year in Kabara, but Leakey nixed that. He said he didn't want to prejudice her study. Instead, he sent her to Gombe with Goodall in a small charter plane. She stayed there two days and was not all that impressed with what Goodall was doing. Goodall had forty electric feeder boxes—filled with banana bait—to draw the chimpanzees out of the woods to a central place where she could observe them. Fossey was sure there must be a way to observe wild animals without baiting them.

A week after her arrival in Africa, Fossey was back in Nairobi again. Leakey had arranged for Alan Root to take her to Kabara. They planned to leave in five days; that would allow Alan time to get her set up in the Congo before meeting Joan back in Uganda for the safari. Leakey sent Fossey out to Nairobi National Park to learn how to drive her Land Rover. One of Leakey's Africans, who spoke no English, accompanied her. When she failed to double-clutch or stalled in a warthog hole, he yelled at her in Swahili. She had to look up his words in her Swahili glossary.

Dr. Leakey wanted her to get her Ph.D., like Jane Goodall. He said that he had written W. H. Thorpe, the famous ethologist at Cambridge, about her. Things were moving fast. Fossey hardly knew how to keep up with all that was happening to her. Clearly, marriage to Alexie Forrester was no longer in her life plan, but she had no time to think about it.

Joan Root took her shopping—Fossey had a list a mile long—and Root knew better than anyone the items she would need that she would never think of for herself. When Fossey chose the food she liked best—orange squash, cakes, and starches—Root was horrified. She wanted her to take seasonings and herbs, and tinned foods to supplement local vegetables.

Finally Fossey barreled out of Nairobi, on her way at last. Her Land Rover was packed to the gunnels and hugged the bumper of Alan Root's Land Rover just ahead. Her bottle of tranquilizers bounced on top of the dash before her very wide, very innocent hazel eyes. She was bound for the Kabara Meadow, seven hundred miles away.

The last time Walter Baumgartel had seen Dian Fossey was the last time he had ever expected to see her. Three years earlier, on her way out with John Alexander, she had told Baumgartel she had every intention of coming back. She wanted to write a children's book about gorillas. But while everyone always wanted to come back, few did. Baumgartel was surprised and delighted at the return of this dark, towering Kentucky woman—until he learned what she was doing there. And then he simply could not believe it.

"This is madness," he said to Alan Root. "I cannot understand Dr. Leakey sending this woman to the Congo at a time when most of the whites have fled. Are you really so ignorant in Nairobi of what is going on in the Congo?"

Root and Leakey were somewhat less ignorant than Fossey, but they had no way of obtaining truly accurate information. In East Africa, the state-controlled press was hardly reliable. Negative reporting was not helpful to newly independent nations trying to get started. As for the world press, the Congo was hardly a priority. With

1. Mary White Henry (*right*) shared an office with Dian Fossey at the Kosair Crippled Children's Hospital in Louisville, Kentucky. She introduced Dian to her family, whose home was nicknamed "The Henry Hotel" for its hospitality to strangers.

2. Mary's mother, Gaynee Henry (*right*), became Fossey's closest companion in Louisville—and helped steer her toward the Catholic church.

3. "That's my boy," said Dian Fossey when she was first shown a photo of Alexie Forrester, the man she almost married.

4. Louis Leakey—the most eminent prehistorian of his generation—believed that women were best suited, emotionally and constitutionally, to study the great apes. He gave Dian her start in Africa after she convinced him of her determination.

5. Joan and Alan Root were the first people to show Dian Fossey a real mountain gorilla. From that day in Kabara Meadow, they were her friends.

6. Dian Fossey arrived in Africa filled with drive and energy. She was completely unprepared for the demands of the job, but she didn't give up.

7–8. Fossey's cabin at the Karisoke Research Station was luxurious compared to her tent in Kabara Meadow. Still, Karisoke was a lonely place—wet and dark. Old Africa hands spoke of "going bushy" after too much time on the mountain.

9. Sent by the *National Geographic* to photograph Fossey's work, Robert Campbell changed her life. Some friends said she never got over her love for the reserved, methodical photographer.

10. For some time after her arrival in Africa, Fossey mimicked the conventional research methods of her predecessor, George Schaller, observing the gorillas from a distance.

11–12. On the day before Robert Campbell left Karisoke for good, Dian made her first prolonged physical contact with Digit, the silverback who became her favorite. Campbell snapped photo after photo.

13. Fossey's close contact with the gorillas was remarkable but left her open to charges of anthropomorphism, which occurs when scientists unwittingly project human characteristics onto their animal subjects.

14. Ironically, Digit—and the rest of Fossey's gorillas—became tourist attractions for Rwanda, despite the fact that the government made little effort to help protect them.

Come to meet him in Rwanda

Office Rwandais du Tourisme et des Parcs Nationaux, B. P. 905, Kigali

15. Sanweckwe, who tracked gorillas for Walter Baumgartel in his early days at Traveller's Rest, also worked for Fossey during her years in Rwanda.

16. Wayne McGuire, one of the students who learned to adjust to Fossey's moods, was eventually tried (in absentia) by the Rwandan government for her murder. Few believe he could actually have been her killer.

17. Like all Fossey's students, Kelly Stewart had her ups and downs with Dian. The worst moments came when Fossey realized that Stewart had fallen in love with fellow researcher Sandy Harcourt.

18. Sandy Harcourt, who argued with Fossey constantly over her research methods, would later found the Mountain Gorilla Project.

19. An Explorer's Club reception in New York in 1982 marked a rare meeting between Louis Leakey's "ape ladies"— from left, Birute Galdikas, Jane Goodall, and Fossey.

20. Fossey with her guards and a young poacher captured by the Digit Fund Patrol in the Parc National Des Volcans, Rwanda. On the table are the poacher's spear, bow and arrows, and a skinned bushbuck.

21. Late in her career, Fossey posed with her guards and a huge collection of poachers' snares collected by the staff.

22. Fossey inscribes a marker in the gorilla graveyard where she buried the murdered Digit.

23. Four days after her murder, Fossey's funeral was held at Karisoke. She was buried in the gorilla graveyard.

24. Dian Fossey's grave is marked, at her request, with the word "Nyirmachabelli." It means "the woman who lives alone on the mountain."

more than two hundred dialects and one hundred twenty political parties, it was a difficult place to cover. In time, the world would learn about the trouble in the Congo—and the estimated half-million casualties. But in 1967, if you weren't caught up in it, you couldn't be expected to know what was going on.

But Baumgartel knew what he saw. Belgians fleeing the Congo had set up camp on his lawn, providing him with information Root and Leakey lacked. The Belgians told of being chased out by the Simbas, a rebel horde moving against the central government in the name of the assassinated Congolese premier Patrice Lumumba. The Simbas were especially active in the northeast in the vicinity of Stanleyville, the largest city west of the Virungas. They hated all whites and they professed allegiance to the Chinese Communists.

Led by witch doctors, the Simbas believed themselves impervious to bullets. They stoked their courage on hashish, and dressed themselves in monkey skins and whatever else might be at hand—lamp shades, women's panties, chicken feathers. Some were dedicated ideologues, but as a mob force they were savage and grotesquely cruel. In one sector of the eastern Congo they murdered between 2,000 and 4,000 Africans. Many of these died by being forced to drink gasoline, then their stomachs were cut open and set on fire. One specially prized victim, a moderate politician named Sylvere Bondekwe, saw his liver cut out and eaten while he was still alive. Eating his body was the most direct way to acquire his power. In their extended siege of Stanleyville years earlier, the Simbas had held 1,100 Belgians and Americans hostage. "We shall cut out the hearts of the Americans and Belgians and wear them as fetishes," the Simbas had announced. "We shall dress ourselves in the skins of the Americans and Belgians."

Such horrors as these had driven the Belgians from the eastern Congo into Kisoro. They were grateful indeed for the "oasis," as Alan Root had described Walter Baumgartel's Traveller's Rest in more pleasant times, though some of the charm was missing now. Ugandan soldiers were pressing Baumgartel to redecorate with photographs of the new Ugandan president, Milton Obote, and the inn's clientele had come to consist mainly of black marketeers and gold smugglers, sitting in the dark corners of the bar negotiating over their gin. Things had turned ugly there, and Baumgartel feared greatly for the safety of Dian Fossey, living alone on a mountaintop in the eastern Congo.

Baumgartel's fears would prove well founded, but Fossey and Root didn't slow down to think. After Fossey promised Baumgartel that she would come down at least once a month for a hot bath and a long talk, she and Root drove down the deteriorating road that led into the Congo. They stopped only briefly, at the Indian shops in Kisoro, to establish credit for the replenishment of her supplies.

It is almost inconceivable that Fossey could have made it to Kabara on her own. Beyond the Uganda border, the roads alone would have defeated her. The mud ruts were deep, some impassable, and night driving was considered suicidal. Prudent drivers carried along all the fuel there was room for and traveled at the top negotiable speed to take advantage of daylight.

Not far into the journey, climbing an escarpment and scared witless by the drop at road's edge of several thousand feet, Fossey complained to Root that something was wrong with the steering of her Land Rover. He told her it was her imagination. And so she drove grimly on, trying to keep up with him, until her right front wheel fell off. He fixed it. At the border crossing, they encountered their second delay. Fossey had no registration papers, and Root had no visa. For four hours, Root spoke quietly to the Africans and listened respectfully to their responses. Often he cracked jokes drawing their laughter, and when finally he handed around some of his gorilla photographs, the guards let them through.

In all, he got them past two customs posts and four police barricades. At Ruindi he convinced the Africans in charge that Fossey's planned study was the best thing to happen to Albert National Park; they agreed to help her out and to keep Kabara off-limits to tourists.

At Rumangabo, he found Sanweckwe, the wonderful tracker who had worked with George Schaller and who had led Root himself out of the poachers' lair in the Bushitsi escarpment three years earlier. To staff her camp, Root arranged for a cookboy, a woodsman, Sanweckwe and their alternates, working on a two-week cycle. At Kibumba, he hired forty-two porters to take her gear up, and once there, he set up her camp, dug her a latrine, and put in a drainage system.

Perhaps she could have managed all this on her own. Certainly she would have tried. But since she didn't have to, who can say? Alan Root had told Leakey he was interested in coming back to film her study (assuming the National Geographic came through with the grant), and so it was to his advantage to get her set up on the mountain and her study under way. But Fossey also suspected that, beyond self-interest, Alan had accompanied her because both he and Joan thought it was so unlikely she would be able to get there otherwise.

She had never seen a man like Root before. Except for his maniacal humor, which could explode without warning, he was quiet and reserved, almost shy. There was no posturing in Alan Root. He was certainly not imperious or impressed with himself; he was gentle and soft-spoken. But he was never in doubt about *anything*. He just did what he intended to do, and did it better than anyone else. No matter how dangerous a situation might be, he got through it. He was a real man. Fossey was deeply impressed by Alan Root. He was the standard by which other men would be measured.

At nightfall on January 15, the day Root headed back down the mountain, Fossey was so depressed and lonely that she could do nothing at all. Leakey had given her a shortwave radio so that she might at least hear English over the BBC, but she couldn't bring herself to turn it on. Root had put up her tent, seven by nine feet—this would be her home. She would sleep and work inside. The three Africans were staying in what was left of the burned-out cabin, and had a fire going in the middle of a room. Since there was no chimney, smoke filled the structure. Fossey avoided the place—and the Africans. The language they spoke was incomprehensible; her Swahili glossary was no use at all. But even if she had been able to understand them, what was there to say?

In the wilderness night, there was nothing to do but go to bed, and her tent on the edge of the Kabara Meadow was a very remote place to be. All the BBC had to tell her was how far away she was, a reminder she didn't need. She lay in the darkness, amid African sounds she had so longed to hear again—the soft buzzing and the sharp clicks, the ringing bells, the sudden airless silence lasting too long and then shattered by animal screams. But she hadn't expected what it would be like to hear such sounds in utter solitude.

Her first night at Kabara Meadow was the night before her thirty-fifth birthday, and when she awoke the next morning, believing as she did that the turning points in her destiny were clearly marked, the single event that occurred was neatly appropriate to the occasion. Even before she left the meadow she came upon a gorilla. It was a male, and alone, resting on a heavy tree trunk extending over the edge of the small pond at the far side of the meadow. "Learning later that gorillas avoid water and cling to cover—she would never again see such a sight—she came to regard the event as even more singular than it had seemed at the time.) Thus was her serendipitous introduction to the object of her intended study. All doubts vanished. She had told Leakey she would stay there for two years at least, and she would if it killed her.

Catching sight of Fossey transfixed and watching him, the gorilla slipped from the tree and vanished into the forest.

12

THE PRIVATE LIFE OF THE MOUNTAIN GORILLA

Through advancements in molecular phylogeny and DNA comparisons, we have learned just how closely humans resemble the three species of great ape—the orangutan, the chimpanzee, and the gorilla. Biologically, we are cousins, although the orangutan, having evolved earlier than the rest of us, is more like a cousin once removed. Molecular phylogeny reveals the chimpanzee and gorilla actually to be closer to man than they are to the orangutan, though they look a lot more like orangutans than like humans. Are we to believe they are really *that* much like us?

The story is told of a Harvard psychologist who sought to prove it possible to teach an ape to play squash. He led the ape to a rear corner of the squash court, and there, with exaggerated motions, lifted a squash racket and ball in front of the animal's eyes. For the next half-hour, looking encouragingly toward his pupil from time to time, he ran around the court chasing and slamming the ball against the walls. Then he placed the racket on the floor, put the ball on top of it, looked penetratingly at the ape, and left the court. After an interval of several minutes, the psychologist bent down to peer through the keyhole. On the other side of the door, he saw a soft brown eye looking back at him.

The degree of intelligence of the mountain gorilla is unknown. But the quality of its awareness is estimated to be higher than most in the animal kingdom. The behavioral psychologist Francine Patterson claimed that the zoo-bred lowland gorilla she worked with in sign language had a vocabulary of more than six hundred words, the equivalent of a six-year-old child's. Other researchers have made similar claims. When Alan Root first filmed the gorillas of the Virungas, he remarked on their curiosity upon encountering the rare human visitor. Peered at, the gorillas peered back. In 1960, they indulged Schaller's intrusion into their lives for 466 hours. His pioneering work provided Fossey with her only real scientific instruction.

Schaller observed that unless the sky was overcast (in which case they slept in), the gorillas rose gradually and without enthusiasm to meet the new day at around 6:00 A.M. It took a while for them to get going, but when their attention was focused, it turned to food—their first concern of the day, their last at night. Of the more than one hundred food plants available to mountain gorillas, they were interested in only twenty-nine. Some of these—stinging nettles, for example—were of little appeal to other creatures. But the gorillas' jaws were powerful enough to handle them; they could crunch bamboo as though it were celery. They didn't drink; the moisture in the plants provided them with all the water they needed. They tended to avoid water, in fact; the distribution of the entire species across the African continent has been restricted by the course of rivers.

Organizing themselves into groups, the mountain gorillas formed communities of varying sizes, as few as two, as many as thirty, the average being eleven members. At the center of the group was the silverback, a sexually mature male whose coat had turned gray across his massive back. About twice as large as the adult female, he weighed close to four hundred pounds. Most of this bulk was taut muscle, but his exact strength would be a matter of conjecture. No one had devised a way to measure it. The gorilla group was a patriarchy and the silverback accrued all rights and responsibilities. Other adult males present in his group were there by his sufferance.

By 8:00 at the latest, when the group was alert and ready to go, the silverback rose up and faced in the direction he intended to take. The procession then followed behind him for what would become the principal activity of the day—cross-county feeding. Browsing leisurely from one plant to the next, the group covered about five hundred feet an hour. Mountain gorillas did not share their food, Schaller wrote, nor did they devise tools to secure it. They didn't have to. Though they were confined to a strip of land a fraction of the size of New York City, that environment provided the gorillas all the food they could eat.

Around 10:00 or so, the group stopped for a midday break. Distributing themselves within a circumference of two hundred feet, they spent two to four hours in a bucolic interlude of snacking, sunbathing, and dozing. All activity took place in the vicinity of the silverback, who was always the center of interest. The females rested against his broad frame; the juveniles and infants romped over him, sliding down his rump and pulling on his hair. A benign despot, he abided the disruptions. All the elders indulged the young, who chased and wrestled one another, playing at diversions strikingly similar to Follow the Leader and King of the Mountain. They pushed to test their limits. Although the females might restrain them by hauling them in, the young were never physically punished. Should they be threatened in any real way, the silverback would lead the group defense, fighting to the death if need be. (In 1948, sixty adult gorillas were killed before local authorities could capture eleven infants for delivery to zoos. None survived in captivity.)

The gorillas made their intentions known to one another through postures and gestures, facial expressions, and sounds. Schaller recorded some twenty-one vocalizations, from low moans of contentment and barks of annoyance to roars of displeasure and shattering screams of fear and rage. Open quarreling rarely broke out, but when it did, it was usually among the females. The silverback would ignore the disturbance. More serious conflicts were often resolved through body language. To signal submission, the gaze was averted and the head shaken rapidly, and, if all else failed, the penitent would fall flat on his stomach, head down, arms folded under, with only his back exposed. Most of the time, however, life within the group ran smoothly enough—a warning glance or a bark from the silverback was all it took to maintain the peace.

The gorilla had little interest in other animals but did nothing much to discourage their presence. The gorilla's physical power was so obvious that more than ordinary caution was taken by other animals. The water buffalo—one of the most fierce and least predictable of African animals—granted the mountain gorilla instant right of way. The gorilla had no enemies but man; no creature dared to provoke its charge. While the silverback sometimes bluffed a charge as a form of intimidation, deliberate harassment of the group or any of its members could provoke the real thing. The several phases of the silverback's charge were ritualized and frightening enough in themselves to freeze the heart of a transgressor. First, there was a hooting noise. Then the silverback rose to full height and beat his chest, a *pock-pock* sound that could be heard at great distance. Barks of annoyance were followed by an explosive roar, and then a shrill scream. The great jaws opened to reveal daggerlike canines, and the gorilla hurled himself forward in a sideways fashion, the momentum alone sufficient to flatten the target. At the end of the charge, he pounded the ground with one or both hands.

Around 2:00, the silverback would get his group going again, and they resumed feeding in earnest, moving a bit faster than during the morning. The land they foraged was dominated by the sixty-foot-high Hagenia trees, spaced widely apart and suggesting, quite eerily, given the remoteness of the setting, a landscaped park. At 11,500 feet the Hagenia trees gave way to open slopes dominated by lobelias. The group would move to these heights on occasion and sometimes even higher—to the 13,000-foot line, where the temperature dropped to freezing. But unless there was reason for haste, they took their time, covering more ground in the afternoon than the morning, and coming to a stop around 5:00. For an hour or so they milled about, until the silverback began to break some branches for his night nest. This was all that was needed for the others to follow suit. Some built their nests in trees; some on the ground. The branches were pulled together and crushed down into a bed, which would be used twice. The group then retired for the night.

Such was the information Schaller had collected in Kabara, covering a range of twenty-five miles along the saddle between Mikeno and Karisimbi. Some two hundred gorillas lived there then, in ten groups. In September 1960, because of political turbulence in Kivu province down below, Schaller brought his study to a premature end and returned to the University of Wisconsin, where he spent the next two years writing his doctoral thesis on gorillas. The year after that, at the Stanford Center for Intellectual Studies, he wrote *The Year of the Gorilla,* a more informal account of his experience for the general reader.

Looking back over Schaller's extraordinary career today, one gets the sense he never squandered a second's time nor a moment's opportunity. He was as much a pioneer in his own territory as Louis Leakey was in his, the first field zoologist to observe systematically under wilderness conditions not only the mountain gorilla, but the tiger of India, the lion of Africa, the wild sheep and snow leopard of the Himalayas, the jaguar of Brazil, and the giant panda of China. Of each of these studies he has written an account, often with such eloquence that he has come to be regarded, along with Archie Fairly Carr on turtles and Howard Ensign Evans on insects, as one of a very few zoologists who can reveal the wonders of his subject with true literary grace.

There is no question that Schaller came to Africa with significant advantages over Fossey. He was twenty-six and tough as a nail. As an undergraduate, he had studied birds and caribou in Alaska, and by the time he arrived at Kabara he had degrees in both zoology and anthropology. His emotional life was as well anchored as his education: a year or two before coming to Kabara he had married an anthropologist who shared his interests. George and Kay Schaller had lived in the same cabin Fossey's African assistants now occupied.

In his first six months, working in collaboration with John Emlen, his teacher from Wisconsin who had accompanied him, Schaller surveyed 15,000 square miles of the countryside about the Virungas in an effort to count the gorillas. At that time, the species was believed to consist of two subspecies: the eastern mountain gorilla and the western lowland gorilla (of which very little was known). Schaller and Emlen came up with a population figure of between 5,000 and 15,000 for both, although to their surprise they found only a few hundred to exist in the mountains—400 or so. All the rest were in the tropical rain forests below, and because of the density of the vegetation, virtually invisible.

After the census was completed, Emlen went home and Schaller chose Kabara as the site of the next phase of his study. The gorillas were easier to see there. Reuben (who was also Baumgartel's guide) taught Schaller how to track them, which was not quite so formidable a task as it might seem. So heavy are the animals that they crush down the vegetation they move through, and they leave behind food remnants, distinctive feces, night nests, and a powerful smell. Soon Schaller was tracking the gorillas on his own.

Schaller preferred being with the animals by himself. With patience and persistence, having managed to work his way to within

150 feet of a group, he would stand quietly and unobtrusively and make his notes. Once the gorillas became used to his presence, they began to approach *him*, some coming as close as fifteen feet. He made no move to touch them; he believed interaction could cause problems. Occasionally, he traveled with a group and slept nearby. As a result of his intrepidness, he gained information no one before him had gathered. A generation after his departure, his report would remain the basic reference in the field.

But Schaller had left some questions open. Most of his research was devoted to range behavior; only three pages of his monograph discussed social behavior.

Other than the research of Osborn and Donisthorpe, the only significant data available to him as comparative measure had come from zoos, and it was now recognized that animals lived and behaved differently in captivity than they did in the wild. Consequently, Schaller knew very little about the population dynamics of the mountain gorilla, of their birth and death rates. He saw only two copulations. He believed most gorillas died from disease, as he saw few natural reasons for death otherwise. He believed also that infant mortality in the first year was high—he estimated 23 percent, roughly equivalent to that known to exist among human infants in the region. He observed lone males from time to time, but never lone females. He never learned why gorillas transferred from one group to another, and he discovered little about the social dynamics within the groups. He found the animals to be as gentle as Donisthorpe had believed, and there was at least one obvious reason for this. There was no competition for food or territory, conditions which very often accounted for aggression in other species.

There was no precedent for some of Schaller's observations, namely his descriptions of the gorilla sensibility. He perceived the animals to have an immense innate dignity. No matter how excited or flustered they might become, they went to great lengths to preserve it. He was bemused by this characteristic, which he attributed to introversion, and was moved by a certain quality in their eyes. "The eyes have a language of their own," he wrote, "being subtle and of emotion that in no other visible way affect the expressions of the animal. I could see hesitation and uneasiness, curiosity and boldness and annoyance."

For a scientist as capable of George Schaller, and one so obviously ambitious, this was a risky tack to take in describing an animal subject. What peer review groups look for in such research projects is data that can be objectively analyzed: feeding habits, social organization, group behavior, and the like. But in the case of this particular animal Schaller was insisting on adding something more, a *subjective* interpretation the intent of which was unmistakable. Schaller was suggesting that these animals behaved in certain ways very much like people. As a talented young scientist with a future otherwise virtually assured, Schaller was clearly inviting the devastating charge of anthropomorphism—of crossing the line that separates man from beast.

Anthropomorphism, the attribution of human characteristics to animals, is regarded, particularly in the behavioral sciences, as an antiscientific attitude which results in the loss of differentiation between the object observed and the person observing it. Human reason becomes undermined by human feeling. Primate researchers are particularly prone to the problem. (In her biography of Louis Leakey, Sonia Cole tells of a female researcher going topless among a community of chimpanzees until an adult male came around. Then she put on her shirt.)

Schaller was well aware of such dangers. But he believed it impossible to observe any animals, particularly gorillas, without interpreting their behavior in human terms. "If a person thinks he understands a creature," Schaller maintained, "he must be able to predict its behavior in any given situation, and with gorillas I was able to do this only if I followed the bare outline of my own feelings and mental processes." By the end of his study, Schaller felt he had come to regard gorillas as he might a human child before it was able to talk.

By the time he left Kabara, he was more than a little concerned about the survival of these extraordinary animals, which were clearly dwindling in number. Although he was sensitive to the poverty of the peoples of Central Africa, he came to regard the enemies of the mountain gorilla as his own enemies. In this respect, he risked crossing a different sort of line. When Sanweckwe shot a cow as a deterrent to the Watutsi roaming through the park, Schaller did nothing to restrain him. On one occasion he himself cracked a heavy walking stick over a cow's neck. With a guard, he charged a Watutsi hut in the park, sending two men and a boy fleeing naked into the woods. He told a band of eleven Watutsi that if they didn't leave the park the next day he would shoot all their cattle.

He had come to take the welfare of these near-human animals quite personally.

13

KEEPING OUT OF TROUBLE

The first time Dian Fossey was charged by a gorilla, she shut her eyes, held on to a tree, and lost control of her bladder. The second time, she was following an animal path through a blackberry thicket when a silverback and a female came roaring and screaming down the path at her. For a few moments she held her ground as Louis Leakey had told her to do. When they continued to hurtle toward her, she yelled at them. They kept coming. At the very last second she dove into the blackberry bushes, the two massive apes whistling past her like a diesel train.

There were other adventures, too. One night, she heard a low rumbling sound and her tent began to move. She wondered if one of the volcanos was about to erupt. The tent began to sway back and forth, pitching and snapping like a heavy sail in a windstorm. An elephant had gotten caught in the guy ropes and couldn't free itself. Frustrated and increasingly annoyed, the elephant began to defecate.

She could see herself, if not pounded to pulp, entrapped in tent canvas and elephant shit. She whispered as loud as she dared for Sanweckwe, but there was no response. Then she whistled. The tent was billowing and swaying and beginning to go. She yelled at the elephant. Then she started banging on a pan, and finally it moved away. Another time, crawling beneath a long log, she reached out for what she thought was a small tree trunk. It turned out to be the leg of a water buffalo. She yelled at the buffalo and it ran away. She wrote Fred Coy's family in Louisville that in addition to her encounters with gorillas, elephant, and buffalo, she had been charged by a forest hog, two wild dogs, and an eagle that mistook her fur collar for prey.

But in the face of what had seemed at first to be inescapable annihilation, she was learning to cope. She was, after all, quite a formidable creature herself. In response to a silverback that would not stop bluff-charging her, she made a fright face, the kind of horrible grimace she had sometimes used to straighten out the kids at Kosair. The startled silverback sat down at once and began to eat, nervously, with one eye on her. Then he got up and walked away.

After a shaky start, she had quickly come to love her new home in this sylvan meadow on the saddle land of Mount Mikeno. Every day brought something new and unexpected. She was in the best physical shape she had ever been in, and she was surrounded by the animals she loved, including her own domestic stock. Sanweckwe had given her a chicken and a rooster, and she had named them Lucy and Dezi. When fed oatmeal in the morning, Lucy would lay an egg. There were also two Egyptian geese in the pond she had named Smith-Corona and Olivetti, and two ravens which patrolled the meadow. She knew that two ravens had kept an eye on the Schallers during their stay and she wondered if it could be the same pair.

When the sun shone, the Kabara Meadow was every bit as beautiful as described by Carl Akeley, but the sun didn't shine much. And when the fog and the rain came, which was most of the time, Akeley's Kabara was transformed from the most beautiful place on earth to the last outpost at the very end of the earth. At times hailstones large as golf balls pummeled the meadow. In the heaviest of the rains, in March and April, it was so bad even the gorillas moved out.

By the end of March, Sanweckwe was sure the gorillas had gone down the mountain. To verify this, Fossey set out with him for the Bushitsi Valley, the one place Alan Root had warned her not to go. They moved down through the bush in a steady downpour and inevitably—as had happened to Root and Sanweckwe before—they came upon poachers. This time, most of the poachers ran off, but Sanweckwe managed to capture one at gunpoint. He kept the man in front of them, hoping the presence of his captive would discourage the others from harming them. But once they entered the rain forest, the man slipped away into the dense jungle. Fossey was certain there were hidden eyes, watching them from behind.

Having circled the base of the mountain, they decided to go on to Rumangabo fifteen miles away, and they hiked for it in the pouring rain, through jungle, across fields and farms, arriving somewhere—Fossey had no idea where—six hours later. She was frightened and exhausted; she was certain she couldn't walk another foot. And so Sanweckwe arranged for her to sleep in an African hut. But as she lay down on a straw pallet—with goats in the room, and a fire burning in the middle of the floor—everyone in the village crowded in to have a look at her. She decided she wasn't all that tired, and so they walked on through the black night, all the way to park headquarters.

Well, she hadn't expected things to be easy. But on balance, she couldn't be happier. Leakey was very pleased with her progress—she had sent him monthly field reports as well as long, chatty letters—and she was thrilled with the splendid way he had come through for her. He had all the money he would need for her now and for some time to come—$3,000 from the New York Zoological Society, $1,000 from the African Wildlife Leadership Foundation, $1,500 from a wealthy conservationist named Royal Little—and best news of all, the jackpot sponsorship of the National Geographic: $11,368! Fossey had now become an investment of the National Geographic Society. This meant among many other things (lectures, personal appearances, and the instant credibility this august institution accorded her) that Alan Root would film her study, and she herself would write of her research and adventures for the *National Geographic* magazine—quite a step up from the Sunday supplement of the Louisville *Courier-Journal*! (They also wanted her to sign a release exempting them from liability in the event anything happened to her. She thought that was reasonable.)

Only a year before, she'd been deep in her plans to become Mrs. Alexie Forrester. Now, thanks to Louis Leakey, Dian Fossey, at thirty-five years of age, was going to turn out to be somebody after all.

Dian Fossey thought a lot about George Schaller. He had left enormous footsteps to fill. What was there left for her to do? She envied Jane Goodall, who had no predecessor to compare herself to.

Schaller had set standards that nobody had any right to expect Fossey to understand. At U.C. Davis the best she could get in her science courses were C's. Schaller was a trained observer, a qualified scientist. He was regarded by his colleagues as a brilliant researcher who had published a ground-breaking study. But Fossey, perhaps because she felt competitive with him, said she disagreed with his methods. (Later she would credit Schaller with inspiring her from the very first. It was his book, *The Year of the Gorilla*, she said, that motivated her to borrow $8,000 and go to Africa to see the gorillas for herself. But she had gone to Africa in 1963, and Schaller hadn't published his book until 1964.)

When the National Geographic first asked her for a study proposal, she had plotted a course that would enable her to produce something beyond Schaller's research. She chose to use Goodall's methods of habituating apes rather than Schaller's, which meant she would eventually try to interact with them rather than simply standing aside and observing them. This would allow her to compare the receptivity of gorillas and chimpanzees toward humans. Furthermore, she would study the consequences of human encroachment—farmers, poachers, cattle herders—on the movements of the mountain gorilla and undertake a census to see how many gorillas were left. After that, she might move 650 miles away to West Africa to study the lowland gorilla, about which almost nothing was known, by Schaller or anyone else.

But most of all, she emphasized, she was determined to stay up there two full years, twice as long as Schaller had stayed. In this way, if she was as diligent as she intended to be, she ought to see twice as much of the mountain gorilla as Schaller had.

No matter how much Fossey liked Kabara—she thanked God fervently for having let her come—she couldn't say that she never got lonely. She was frightened sometimes, downright *scared*, but less often than she was lonely. This was an increasing problem, until the time came when she was desperate. But it would take a while for things to get that bad.

Possibly, if there had been just one person she could have talked to occasionally . . .

At least the Africans could talk to each other. All she had to talk to was herself, sometimes a tiresome companion. She hated to bitch and complain, she felt it to be a failing in herself. Going down the mountain was not the solution. This meant choosing between Goma in the Congo or Kisoro in Uganda, and either choice meant a five-hour expedition, an ordeal she could afford neither physically nor financially. Besides, who was down there for her to see? Walter Baumgartel welcomed her like the father she didn't have, and she loved him for it. She had also made friends with a seventy-year-old Italian and his teenage Belgian wife who lived on a plantation in the middle of the Congo. They kept Arabian horses, hogs, a houseful of orphaned African children, twenty-four dogs and even more cats, a chimpanzee, and an infant gorilla. A day with them was weird,

146

intriguing, entertaining. But a menagerie was hardly what she needed. What she sorely missed was someone who had *some* connection with the world she had known before. Someone she could talk to.

But there was no one. She understood her three Africans no better than they understood her. The day Alan Root left, one of them had ventured a few words in Swahili to her. But with her nerves rubbed raw and the isolation suddenly choking her, she had run into her tent, terrified, and zipped herself in. After an hour of attempting to translate his words, she realized he had asked if she wanted hot water. The situation did not improve with time. She felt as if she were camped out on the moon, and she couldn't bring herself to trust the Africans. Except for Sanweckwe.

Even though they could not communicate, Sanweckwe had been her mainstay, a link to George Schaller and to Joan and Alan Root. Pleasant and understanding, anticipating her problems before she encountered them, puffing at his pipe with a half-smile, Sanweckwe had been indispensable, her silent tutor. The incredible man *thought* like a gorilla, and he could track even when he couldn't see his own feet in the fog. On the day the silverback charged her, Sanweckwe had been right there, with his rifle drawn. But even though the gorilla had come to within six feet (and she was peeing all over herself), he'd had the presence of mind not to shoot. Once when they were being charged by a herd of buffalo he had fired his rifle into the air, which was enough to scatter them. Wheezing and panting as she struggled to climb hand over hand up through the wet bush, she knew that he alone among the Africans would patiently wait until she was able to catch up. From Sanweckwe she had learned how to handle herself out there.

And no matter how furious she would later become with him, there was one special thing that had sealed him in her heart forever. In her second week at Kabara she had found a gorilla skeleton, which she knew Leakey would want. In her tent that night, cleaning up the skeleton, she heard a liturgical chant coming from outside—the same chant she had sung at Mass. *In Latin!* Sanweckwe was a Catholic, too, and the following Sunday, high up on the mountain, they had made a stab at saying Mass together.

Fossey knew very well that Sanweckwe was all that stood between her and exposure to disaster. Entrusting her life to him, she should have been able to trust him in other ways. And she did, until she finally realized, sadly, that he was just as bad as the rest.

Those Africans! The language problem was the least of it. Living with them hadn't been her idea. If there was a culture gap between herself and them, that was their problem. To her, people were all alike. She didn't care who they were or where they came from. The Africans had certain responsibilities like anybody else, and they were expected to live up to them. If she could do it, so could they. These people worked for her, after all, not the other way around. Toward the Africans, she was exactly as she had been with the crippled children at Kosair—compassionate when they hurt, but pretty demanding otherwise. Tough but fair. She was just as tough on herself, and she expected fair treatment in return from the Africans. She had, after all, gone out of her way to be nice to these people, especially to Sanweckwe, who had done so much for her. She had raised his salary to 3,000 francs and given him rubber boots and a uniform of pants and shirt. To the other guard, who did nothing but sit around on his butt, she gave extra chores.

There were certain things about the Africans that she simply could not understand. On February 10, coming in from eight hours in the bush, tired, famished, and soaking wet, she arrived at the meadow in driving rain to find a horde of them swarming over the grass, literally covered in blood. Poachers had killed a buffalo and its calf, and one of her guards had discovered the carcasses. He had sent word down the mountain to Kibumba, and everybody had come up to take his share. For three days and nights, they ate, sang, danced, burped, and quarreled over the carcasses. They even argued over the eyes. It was like a Stone Age orgy. They had offered her what they considered to be the delicacies—the intestinal sac and the brains—and she thought she might vomit.

But that wasn't what had really got to her. The point was, killing buffalos was wrong, and feasting off the remains of an illegal kill was just as bad. This was a national park, for God's sake, not an abattoir. Even Sanweckwe was indifferent to her indignation. He acted as though there was not the slightest thing wrong about any of this— once the buffalos were dead, what difference did it make if the meat was taken by people who were hungry?

This grisly scene was the opening of a war that Fossey would wage for the rest of her life. Poachers were outlaws. They had been no less to George Schaller, they were no less to her. Anyone who harassed these animals—whether deliberately or inadvertently—was an outlaw, and this included farmers who tried to grow crops on park land that was meant to provide fodder for the wildlife and the Watutsi who brought in their cattle, taking over the buffalo grazing fields. Their spoils were as illegal as they were.

She had done nothing to stop the villagers of Kibumba from cutting up the buffalo, but she didn't have to speak his language to let Sanweckwe know how she felt about such things.

As far as Leakey was concerned, Fossey was no problem. She didn't bother him or draw his attention away from his other projects. Whatever his initial misgivings, he could say now that she had turned out to be the perfect choice. In the Congo she proved a conscientious correspondent, and her reports pleased him inordinately. In her first two weeks, she wrote, she had accrued 23 hours, 17 minutes of observation from nine contacts with two gorilla groups. By February 24, she had recorded (but not seen) two new births. Soon thereafter, she sent to Nairobi a blood sample for laboratory analysis and the odiferous remains in formaldehyde of an infant gorilla. These materials arrived while Leakey himself was in the States foraging for

149

funding—a more productive expedition that year than before. (Thanks to a National Geographic television special seen in prime time by 26 million, Leakey had become a "draw." He had also attracted the interest and enthusiasm of a California millionaire, a young fellow from Pasadena named Alan O'Brien, who decided Leakey shouldn't have to work so hard on his solicitations. O'Brien had seen to it that Leakey's lecture fees were increased to $500 minimum.)

Arriving back in Nairobi, Leakey felt somewhat remiss about Fossey. With one thing or another, he had been too far removed from her work, and her offhand references to some of her problems gave him concern. He worried about the elephant incident she described, and he was openly distressed about her trip to Bushitsi, where she had run into the poachers. He wrote back saying she should stay clear of such problems whenever possible. And he advised her to fix up that burned-out cabin and live there, instead of in a tent. He said he would make it a point to get in touch with Anicet Mburanumwe, the park director, about the poacher problem.

He also wanted her to know that he considered the work she was doing absolutely first-rate. He beamed his pride around town, and made it a point to write her sponsors in the States of her impressive progress. She had by now, after only a couple of months, compiled two hundred typed pages of field notes, covering more than a hundred hours of contact with the gorillas. She was fast catching up with Schaller!

Alan Root, who had told Fossey he would be coming back to film her study, fully intended to do so as soon as he could clear his schedule, and that seemed to be always in the indeterminable future. The Roots were with Schaller, filming his lion study in the Serengeti, and could not make other plans until they had all the footage they needed.

Somewhat tougher to impress than Louis Leakey, who was more

than twice his age, Alan Root had come to respect Fossey, too—perhaps because he had known so much better than Leakey just how abjectly unfit she was when she started. In answer to one of her letters about her progress on the mountain, Root had written back cheery words of encouragement, but striking one admonitory note as well, which he labeled "Lecture time!":

> May 14, 1967
>
> People . . . are going around saying "She's done fantastically well, she has got 120 hours of observation." I assume Leakey is trumpeting this around and I wish he wouldn't, for the number of hours spent observing is an indication only of tenacity and is not necessarily correlated with success. Leakey gleefully points out that this is so much more than the number of hours George Schaller spent, but critics will gleefully point out that it is possible for some people to observe a phenomena for 1000 hours without discovering anything, whilst someone else may find the key in just an hour or two.

But in that letter, Alan hadn't said any more than he had earlier about when he would come back.

Fossey soon became absolutely convinced that the Africans were all taking advantage of her (a surefire way of making an enemy of Dian Fossey). They begged things from her, and she was sure they stole. If she didn't sleep with her mouth shut, she was certain they would take the gold from her teeth. She fired the cookboy for stealing, and if she had been able to find someone else she would have fired his replacement, too. The Africans didn't like it at Kabara, so she couldn't depend on them. On two occasions the guards (including Sanweckwe) failed to come up at all for five days. She didn't like the idea of being there with no one around but the cookboy. When she fixed up the cabin and started taking her meals inside, they would sit in the other room and watch her while she ate. So she had put up a bamboo door in between. Then she started having problems with Sanweckwe. He tried to take over her observation time, moving in on the gorillas too closely, growing impatient when she wanted to stay longer. She was losing control of him, as she had lost control of the others.

In her letters home she had begun to refer to the Africans as "wogs." When Gaynee Henry innocently wrote back to ask what the term meant, Fossey said it was like calling a black a "nigger," and she supposed she shouldn't do it. But she didn't stop. Writing a friend in California several weeks later, she said what she really needed up on the mountain was a "wog-whacking mzungu" (*mzungu* is the Swahili word for European).

Her problems weren't just with her African servants. Every time she went down the mountain, she found other reasons for complaint. The Africans at park headquarters, where she left her Land Rover while she was on the mountain, drove it around, once putting three hundred miles on it in a month. At the customs post, the military were always drunk on pombe, the ubiquitous banana beer. Once they searched her purse (anticipating this, she had removed her money and pistol). Another time, when she had a flat tire at the post, her spare turned out to be flat, too. It was pouring rain and the guards just laughed at her. Were it not for a French priest who helped her, she would have had nowhere to turn. There were other problems, too. Her visa was up in June and registration fees for her car were due. She worried less about that than anything else, however, because she could count on the guards being too drunk to notice. All in all, despite her problems with her staff, she felt safer on the mountain than down below. She thought this was a hell of a comment on her situation.

What she needed was someone like Alan Root, who could speak her language, straighten out her staff, and tell her what to do. What she needed was a man up there to help her. She decided to write the Roots and level with them. She knew very well she couldn't expect them to drop everything and come baby-sit her in Kabara, but Alan had said he was coming back, and apart from her own problems, the time was right for photography. She had established contact with three groups now, and the animals in Group 3 (which included a young blackback she had named Alexie) had become extremely receptive to her. Though she doubted anyone but Leakey would believe her, she thought it possible she might eventually be able to mix with them—if the wogs didn't jinx it. When Anicet Mburanumwe sent patrols up from below, ostensibly to protect the animals, they came in mobs of thirty, wearing steel helmets and armed with everything from hand grenades to machine guns. All night long they yelled and laughed and drank pombe. And, of course, they frightened the gorillas away.

In a letter begun on June 18 but not mailed until June 28, Fossey tried to entice the Roots with the wonderful things she was seeing in Group 3. She also told them frankly of her fears. Sanweckwe had become a real bastard. Once the rains ended, a drought had drawn all sorts of animals—elephants, buffalos, antelopes, warthogs, even a bongo—to the pool at the edge of the meadow. Sanweckwe brazenly took the position that this was a good time to thin the herds. They were entitled to shoot what they needed to eat. On two occasions he loaded his rifle and aimed at a buffalo. When she yelled and scared the buffalos away, he had turned sullen and gone down the mountain early, leaving her once again with only the cookboy for protection. Was it possible they could come up in July, she asked the Roots. If not, could they send someone else? She really didn't want to bother Leakey about all this. Could they come? Please come, she wrote, *please*!

Between June 18, when she started the letter, and the 28th, her dark gray mood had turned black. She described the Africans as "thugs," and, in an odd inversion of her fear and distrust, as "apes." She was now convinced that they had come to view her as fair game. Having been up on the mountain alone for six months, she must have seemed to them as though she hadn't a friend in the world. A defenseless woman. They could therefore bully her with impunity.

She had no intention of getting off the mountain just now. Independence Day would be celebrated in just two days, on June 30, and this meant more drunkenness and trouble in the towns below. She had resorted to the "silent treatment." No matter that she couldn't speak their language. Now she no longer tried. She didn't speak to the Africans at all.

On the 28th, having added a desperate postscript in her letter to the Roots, she decided she had no choice but to write Leakey about the extreme urgency of her circumstances. She didn't like doing this—she began her letter with some deference—but the plain fact was, she needed help. She enumerated her problems and said she was writing the Roots, too, hoping they might come. But if they could not, could he please send someone else? And as soon as possible? Would he let her know about this immediately? She was sorry to have to ask, but he should consider her request to be *urgent*.

By the time her letter got to Leakey, it was too late. Because of some new outbreak of violence—he had no idea of what the problem might be—the border between the Congo and Uganda was suddenly closed to all movement. A state of national emergency had been declared inside the Congo, and the government announced that any aircraft violating its air space would be shot down. Although he agreed with her entirely and promised to do everything he could, Leakey unfortunately had no idea whether his letter of July 6 would even reach her.

14

TROUBLE

Of course, if the shoe had been on the other foot, it would be just as presumptuous for someone from the Congo to come into Kosair with no experience and try supervising Fossey's working methods with the children there. Someone like Sanweckwe, say. Especially if by some freakish shift of history Sanweckwe had become her boss. Coming as he did from a country which hardly knew of hospitals, what would he know about occupational therapy? Or how he should behave toward the locals in Louisville, Kentucky? Would he have the right to feel resentful, even betrayed? To clam up altogether and refuse to talk to Fossey and her associates? Looked at in this light, "her" Africans had been quite forbearing.

But it is a measure of how extreme the differences are between our separate ways that such a comparison seems so inappropriate—one Fossey herself would hardly have entertained. She had come to Africa to study gorillas, not to harass the natives. Why should they harass her? In July 1967, however, she was about to find that the shoe was indeed on the other foot. How she might feel about the Congolese was considerably less relevant to her immediate welfare than how they felt about her. High up on the mountain, without the slightest inkling of what was going on, and in direct consequence of a particularly virulent form of racism, Dian Fossey had suddenly become an enemy of the state.

"The less intelligent the white man is," André Gide wrote after his tour of the Congo forty years ago, "the more stupid he thinks the black." Fossey was intelligent about many things, but about Africans she was dangerously uninformed. Boning up almost exclusively on Schaller, she had neglected to look very closely into the country in which she would work.

In the late nineteenth century, the Congolese people were victims of one of the most brutal genocidal massacres in modern history. It was ordered by the Belgian king Leopold, who at the time literally owned the country. The Belgians killed an estimated five million blacks inside of five years. A favored form of torture was the cutting off of hands—a punishment the Belgians devised for Africans who didn't work fast enough collecting rubber for them. In 1960, when the Belgians had suddenly pulled out, the country's administrative infrastructure disappeared with them, leaving political chaos in its wake. Unlike the Kenyans, who took over the institutions left in place by the British after independence, the Congolese were left without any of the political systems needed to govern themselves. The Kenyans still respected white people and deferred to them; the Congolese were less sanguine.

Although she had by now a pretty good notion of the geography of the eastern Congo, Fossey didn't have the faintest idea of its politics. For all she could see, the Congo was made up of incompetent officials, lazy park guards, and drunken soldiers. If it had any history at all—in the formal sense of the word, some intelligible record of the past—she was unaware of it. This was unfortunate, as she was about to become a victim of it.

At four in the afternoon on July 9, coming back into the meadow with Sanweckwe, Fossey was met by a group of thirty park guards and porters. They handed her a note written two days earlier by Anicet Mburanumwe. There was trouble down below, it said, and her life would be ruined if she remained on the mountain. Anicet didn't say what the trouble was. He had sent the porters to break up camp for her and bring her to Rumangabo. She tried her shortwave radio to see if she could pick up some word of what was going on. She heard nothing. She cried and she protested—pointlessly, she realized—and finally consented to the dismantlement of her camp. Later, in Rumangabo, she was told only that she was being detained. She had brought down everything she had come with, including her chicken and her rooster, and she was made comfortable in a large Belgian farmhouse, in a room looking out on the Virungas. Nothing much was expected of her. Anicet was as solicitous as always, but he seemed to know little more about what was happening than she did. She decided to bide her time reviewing her field notes and studying French. For the next eight days, nothing out of the ordinary happened. She was simply detained, and even though she didn't know it, it would prove highly significant that those who saw fit to detain her believed themselves to be complying with orders issued by none other than Joseph Désiré Mobutu. In the Congo, this small man with a big head who wore horn-rimmed glasses and a hat made from leopard skin was the supreme authority.

A former sergeant under the Belgians (whose officers were all white), Mobutu had emerged from the seven-year civil war as president, holding office largely through his control of the army (such as it was) and the patronage of the United States, which admired and financed his resistance to communism. If by 1967 Mobutu was not as

157

powerful as he soon would become, he was at least a point man in the effort to put down political opposition as it arose. This was similar to the role he had played when Western interests defeated the rebellion of the savage Simbas who had held 1,100 Europeans and Americans hostage in Stanleyville three years earlier.

A careful man, Mobutu had come to know the limitations of his strength. In a crisis, Congolese soldiers tended to drop their guns, take off their shoes, and run. To bolster their fighting efficiency, Mobutu had enlisted a small group of fierce white soldiers of fortune, mostly European and South African war veterans. They were paid well and encouraged to fight as they chose. These white mercenaries or "mercs," were as savage and bloodthirsty as the Simbas. Moreover, because they used modern military equipment and techniques, including bullets that did not turn to water, they tended to terrify all Africans, who called them the Terrible Ones or the White Giants. The White Giants killed easily and without mercy, and the balance of casualties was always heavily in their favor—twenty Africans to one of theirs. As racist as Nazis, they believed in white supremacy; but Mobutu had kept them on as a special force within his unreliable army because, in an emergency, they could make the difference. And so they could, until they turned against him.

The trouble had occurred in the eastern part of the Congo, in the country side near Lake Kivu. At the southern end of the lake, looking out on a view which has been described as a combination of Lake Lucerne and the Bay of St. Tropez, is the lovely little resort called Bukavu. The town, once a favored vacation destination for the Belgians, became, because of its strategic importance, an outpost for the Congolese army. At the northern end of the lake, 120 miles away and a hard day's drive even in good weather, rose Mount Mikeno with its Kabara Meadow.

By the time Fossey got down the mountain, Bukavu had been under siege for four days. While there were no other Americans at her end of the lake, there were a hundred or so in and around

Bukavu—missionaries, U.N. workers, plantation managers. There was also a tiny American consulate, where the ranking officer was a young Harvard man. On the Fourth of July, Frank Crigler and his wife had held a large barbecue at the consulate for the community at large, especially the Americans. There were balloons, confetti, hamburgers, Cokes, and folk songs on the grass, led by the consul playing guitar.

The next morning, July 5, Bukavu had exploded. The scene of the consul's barbecue became a battleground. Gunfire was exchanged across the lawn. Who was shooting at whom, and why, was at first something of a mystery. With fifty of his guests huddled inside the consulate praying for their lives, all the consul could see was a gunfight going on outside. Eventually it would become clear that the invaders were white mercenaries and their targets were Congolese soldiers. The White Giants were attacking their own comrades in arms—Mobutu's army!

Within hours, the Congolese soldiers had fled the city, and by the next day the mercs had departed as well, leaving Bukavu's city center a silent and eerie vacuum. Taking a paper American flag from the table decorations, the consul attached it to the front of his car and led a convoy of twenty vehicles carrying his family and guests across the border into Rwanda.

It is at this juncture of events that Mobutu came to figure directly in the affairs of Dian Fossey. On July 5, Mobutu authorized Congolese Radio to broadcast a warning to the nation that foreigners were trying to take over the country. The foreigners were anyone white. They should be killed.

Frank Crigler—the young consul on duty in Bubavu in 1967—is an experienced foreign officer in Africa, serving today as ambassador to Somalia. In 1974, when he and his wife, Bettie, came to be Fossey's closest friends, Crigler was the ambassador to Rwanda.

But the first he had heard of Dian Fossey was in 1967, a week or so after all the shooting, when a cable arrived from the State Department's African desk in Washington, checking on her status. Surprisingly, the initial source of concern was her errant father, George Fossey, with whom she had begun to correspond. Reading of the uprising in Bukavu, Fossey had checked its location on a map and concluded it was close enough to Dian's camp to cause alarm. He called Senator George Murphy of California, who called the head of field research at the National Geographic, a man named Ed Snider. Snider had called State. Eleven whites had been killed in and around Bukavu, and several more back in the west, but Crigler knew of no incidents occurring in the vicinity of Rumangabo, where, he learned, Dian Fossey had been taken.

Crigler had his hands full in Bukavu, where, it was becoming apparent, the mercs had tried to overthrow Mobutu. They weren't paid enough. They had become fed up with Africans. They had decided they would simply annex the eastern part of the country—the wealthiest part—and turn it into an orderly civilized place like Rhodesia, for White Giants like themselves.

Although they were surrounded and heavily outnumbered by the Congolese army, the mercs had decided to hold Bukavu until it suited them to launch an all-out attack. The Congolese could do nothing. "What you had was an agonizing situation for the Congolese army," Crigler says. "Here they were, trying to organize themselves without their white commanders—to fight the very men who had led them! They were not only frightened, they were humiliated. And they were boiling mad. The mercs had briefly hit Goma and Rumangabo before pulling back to Bukavu. So it was at this very time that Dian found herself in the hands of an enraged, angry military force." They would have been particularly enraged at anyone who happened to be white.

How much of this eventually got through to Fossey—sitting in the Belgian farmhouse at Rumangabo, fretting because she was away from her gorillas—is uncertain. She apparently behaved at first as though her detention was nothing more than the sort of harassment one had to endure in this benighted part of the world. But Louis Leakey knew more than he wanted to know. On July 5, the day Mobutu declared a state of emergency and closed the borders, two civilian planes from East Africa were shot down by the Congolese. On July 8, Leakey thought maybe he ought to raise some quick money to get Fossey out—Kabara Meadow could serve as a helicopter landing site. On July 10, he received a letter from George Fossey, anxiously inquiring about the welfare of his daughter. By now, Leakey was beside himself with concern.

And then, quite astonishingly, well into the second week of the uprising, Leakey received a letter from Fossey—mailed out of Kisoro! In the same manner as she recounted her field observations, she matter-of-factly related to Leakey how she had been brought down the mountain—she was certain the porters stole half the items she had packed! Once at Rumangabo, she had been treated very considerately by Anicet Mburanumwe. As for all the soldiers around, they were as you might expect—drunk on pombe. She believed she would be released from detention within the next several days, and once she was, it was her intention to drive into Kisoro to pick up her mail. While she was there she would post this letter. (Since he had the letter in hand, apparently she had done so without incident.) And then, she said, she intended to resume her research at Kabara.

Leakey reacted swiftly. He dispatched a small plane to Kisoro to bring her out. By the time the pilot landed, she had come and gone. Leakey had no idea what was going on. The American Embassy cabled that the trouble was in the towns, not the countryside, and although it was expected to go on for some months, Fossey should be safe enough on the mountain. Then another cable arrived: an American mountain climber named Tom Staley had seen Fossey up in Kabara. Though she looked like she needed a holiday, Staley reported that she seemed well enough. For a brief moment Leakey allowed himself to believe it possible she had weathered the worst of it. But Crigler's cable was based on an assumption, and Staley, it turned out, had seen Fossey back in February, five months earlier.

•   •   •

161

Fossey was under detention in the Congo for sixteen days. She arrived at Rumangabo on July 10 and she departed on the 26th. While there, she wrote a letter to the Prices and four to Louis Leakey. While she was effectively isolated from help outside the Congo, she was able at least to get some word out.

Of her ordeal during this time it is possible to fashion something of a rough approximation. But any construction must allow for the diversionary tactics of the principal witness—Fossey herself. To be sure, she had to tell people something. Everyone, from her friends in Louisville to the State Department to Louis Leakey to the National Geographic, wanted to know what happened. But, as she had done during earlier hurtful times, Fossey closed up. She told nothing but the bare details of her movements. Yet as interest in her career grew, and as she herself came to see those sixteen days as critical to her legend, she told more, though sparsely and sometimes with contradictions. The truth remains elusive. She wrote her old friends Patty and Bud Hjelms on November 4, four months after the event, that she would never be able to recount exactly what happened to her to anyone.

There are three sources which bear on this episode: her letters, her book, *Gorillas in the Mist*, and the accounts of those with whom she discussed this time some years later.

Three of her letters to Leakey covering events through July 21 are the most detailed and straightforward. According to those letters, she was allowed to go into Kisoro to pick up money she needed to register her Land Rover. At the border post of Bunagana, she was menaced by drunken soldiers. They ordered her to surrender her Land Rover. She put the keys in her pocket and dared them to touch her. (She made it a point to say that in spite of their threats she was not touched physically or harmed in any way.) She persuaded the soldiers that it was to everyone's advantage if she went into Uganda after the money, as she would be bringing it back into the Congo. They took her passport, assigned a guard to accompany her to assure her return, and let her pass through. At Traveller's Rest, Walter Baumgartel tried to dissuade her from going back, but she was determined to resume her study. He helped her get the money she needed, and called the Uganda military to assure her safe return across the border. Back in Rumangabo, without further incident, she sent her equipment ahead to Kibumba for her return to Kabara and was about to leave herself when word came that she was being detained by military order. She became angry and upset. She told Leakey bluntly she was very disappointed in his failure to send someone to help her out.

Her account in *Gorillas in the Mist* leaves out most of this and is only helpful in recounting what happened next by adding a single piece of information that provides for her continued confinement: from a military cable, she read she had been "earmarked" for a general expected to arrive soon from Bukavu.

"And then I was taken into a cage," she told the writer Sara Ann Friedman fifteen years later. "I stayed in that cage two days and two nights. It was an open cage so all the people— It was not very pleasant. Let's put it that way." Friedman did not press her further. At Cornell University, during her tenure as a visiting professor, she told her secretary, Stacey Coil, that she was confined in a cage at Rumangabo; and while working with the editor of her book, Anita McClellan, who assisted her closely in the writing of it, she talked about it some more. "She was in the cage for two days," McClellan says, "and during this time she was spat and urinated upon." McClellan believes Fossey suffered all the emotional trauma of rape but may have managed to escape a physical sexual assault by defying her tormentors with the force of her rage. "She screamed at them, 'You don't have the balls to rape me!' "

But Fossey told the wildlife cameraman Warren Garst that she was repeatedly raped. In 1974, she told Birute Galdikas (who went to Borneo to study the orangutan for Leakey) that she was put in a cage with several other people. They were white men, and all of them were killed. She was kept alive because they had other uses for her. "She told me she had been held in a cage and raped," Galdikas says. "Also, Louis Leakey told me twice that Dian had been raped—once during a conversation when he said, 'She's been through so much.' Whether Dian was raped or not I do not know, but I do know that both Dian and Louis Leakey believed she had been raped by Africans." She told Father Raymond, Betty Schwartzel, and Kelly Stewart, a researcher who came to the Karisoke Research Center in 1973, that she was raped; she told Alan Root she was kept as a pet and raped. And in 1983, in a night-long walk with a trusted friend in Santa Fe, she put away a quart of scotch and spoke to Katherine Rust about it, not so much in sentences but in broken phrases. "It was like a flood," Rust says, "like a dam opening. I remember her saying, 'And they raped and raped and raped. . . .' The way she said this, it was as though she were going through it all again. Then she didn't say anything more, and I didn't ask more."

Whatever it was that did happen to her, she carried away from Rumangabo her own private horror. She had been the last white to get out of the eastern Congo alive after July 4, she wrote her Cambridge tutor, Robert Hinde, in 1975. She told Hinde, without elaborating further, that within fifty kilometers of Rumangabo eighteen white people had been eaten alive.

The day after her escape from the Congo, Fossey wrote to Leakey, but this letter, dated July 27, speaks of no physical duress of any kind. What is noticeable is a shift in the pitch of her voice. In contrast to the other letters, which range from annoyance to outrage, this one is emotionless. She learned (she writes) that she was being held for a general from Bukavu as well as a major in Goma and a major in Rumangabo, and on the strength of this, decided she had better get out. She used the same ruse as before—another bill to be paid on her car—to get across the border at Bunagana. To avoid the suspicion she was trying to get away, she packed only a few things: her field notes, a pistol in a Kleenex box, her typewriter and camera. She brought along her cookboy, Phocas, and her chicken and rooster. At the Bunagana gate, the guards said they didn't have a key and couldn't let her through. She waited five hours. A Belgian priest arrived with a sick person he was taking into Uganda. She gave the priest a note for Baumgartel, telling him she was trying to get out. After the guards had opened the gate for the priest, she bribed them to let her through. They agreed to let her go so long as, once again, she was accompanied by a guard to guarantee her return. The guard got in the back of her Land Rover with Phocas.

With good reason Fossey would hold Baumgartel in high esteem for the rest of her life. Baumgartel's version of what happened next is roughly confirmed in her book. Arriving at Traveller's Rest, she leaped from the Land Rover, ran through the lobby to a room in the back of the inn, and hid under a bed. Baumgartel took charge. To the Congolese guard, who demanded she be returned to his custody, he said, "Miss Fossey is not your prisoner. She is going to stay here. If she wants to return, I shall tie her to that tree out there!" The guard said he would be shot if he came back without her. "Better to shoot you than her," Baumgartel said with a flourish, bringing together, like the fittings of a fine cabinet, the last pieces that finally joined these two lives. Heading back to the border in the company of the Uganda military, the guard said if Fossey ever tried to enter the Congo again she would be shot on sight.

In a long postscript to her letter of July 27 to Leakey, Fossey said she needed visas and his assistance in getting her back to Nairobi. But these were logistical details. What was uppermost in her mind was getting back on the mountain—if not in the Congo (perhaps she would be able to enter through another border gate?), at least on the Rwanda side, where she had heard there were gorillas. On the day after her flight out of the Congo, this was her only concern. She needed no rest, no vacation.

There was only one thing on her mind.

"She knew very well that the second anybody suspected what she had been through, she would have been sent straight home," says Anita McClellan. "She wasn't about to let that happen. What had become more important to her than anything else on earth were those gorillas."

15

ALEXIE'S ADVICE

After her escape from Rumangabo, Fossey wasted no time. The first thing she did was cable Leakey she was out and awaiting his instructions: what did he want her to do now?

The U.S. Embassy in Rwanda—in Kigali, the capital, a red-dirt village a five-hour drive away—had sent word that she should come there immediately for interrogation. She would go the next day. And then? Baumgartel had asked her. After that? Certainly she did not need him to remind her that the Congo was now out of the question!

If she had to give up the Virungas, Fossey said, she would go somewhere else—to the west perhaps, to study the lowland gorilla, or possibly to Borneo to observe the orangutans, the third of the great ape species Leakey wanted to see studied. But she was willing to bet there were gorillas on the Rwanda side of the Virungas. The border between Rwanda and the Congo ran right down the spine of the volcano chain. The gorillas couldn't be expected to know one side of it from the other. She was certain they were there, just down the saddle from Kabara to the southeast, toward Mount Visoke and the towering Karisimbi. If there were gorillas in Rwanda, and Leakey agreed to her plan, she would go there and start over again. Under the circumstances, Fossey seemed remarkably composed.

Very well, Baumgartel said. If she was so determined, the person she should see when she got to Rwanda was his friend Alyette de Munck, a Belgian woman who had grown up out there. De Munck was a self-taught naturalist, expert in the wilderness of Central Africa. She had lived among the Pygmies of the Ituri Forest, filmed erupting volcanos in the Virungas, and collected poisonous snakes for the Corydon Museum in Nairobi. If there were gorillas in Rwanda, she would know it.

Baumgartel agreed to look after Fossey's rooster and chicken while she was gone, and the next day, with Phocas, the cookboy, she drove to Kigali. When she told the embassy people there about what had happened to her and raised the possibility of resuming her work in Rwanda, the response was not what she expected. Of all people, they asked, couldn't she understand there was a war going on only a few miles away? The mercenaries were still holding Bukavu, plundering what was left of the place and terrorizing Congolese soldiers, who in turn were looking for white people to terrorize. The refugees Frank Crigler had brought out only a few weeks earlier were still in Kigali, and they had no idea when they might go back, if ever. With the slightest provocation, all of it could spill over into Rwanda. The American Embassy bluntly informed Fossey that her research project was not wanted in Rwanda.

Fossey asked if anyone at the embassy could direct her to a Mme. Alyette de Munck. No one could, but someone did suggest an American woman living in Rwanda who might be of help. This was Rosamond Carr, a former fashion illustrator from New Jersey who lived alone on her farm outside of Gisenyi, near Lake Kivu. Mrs. Carr had come to Africa in 1949 and now ran a nursery, selling flowers to nearby resort hotels on this, the friendlier shore of Lake Kivu.

The two women met for the first time over lunch in Kigali. "She was terribly, *terribly* nervous," the willow-slim and very formal Rosamond Carr recalls. "She was really a surprise, this tall, very pretty girl. Really, you can't believe how pretty she was! Absolutely lovely. She was wearing the most elegant pale lilac-colored linen dress with an old pair of dirty tennis sneakers! It was the most peculiar costume. But it was all she had. The Congolese had taken *everything.*"

When Fossey learned Carr's farm was located near Karisimbi (a slope of the soaring 14,500-foot mountain began at the rear of Carr's flower garden), her ears perked up. "She asked if she could make my house her camp, and when I wondered why she should want to do this, she said it was so that she could look for gorillas up on this side of Karisimbi. But that was hopeless, I said. There were no gorillas on this side of Karisimbi. And she said flatly, 'I don't believe you.' Which"—Carr does not hesitate to speak her mind to anyone—"I didn't appreciate." Furthermore, she was not immediately disposed to direct this stranger to her friend Alyette de Munck, who had only recently suffered a terrible tragedy.

But as she thought more about it, Carr realized that each of these remarkable women had something to offer the other. She decided to tell Fossey about her friend.

Alyette and Adrien de Munck had had a wonderful life together in the old Belgian Congo. He was a mining engineer, a bit older than Alyette, and wonderfully indulgent of her tendency to wander the African wilderness. They had raised two boys there, their son Yves and a nephew named Philippe. When the trouble broke out in 1960, they had sent the boys to school in Belgium. In 1965, things had become so bad that the de Muncks themselves had to get out; they gave up their farm and moved to Rwanda, to a plantation Rosamond Carr had found for them only two kilometers away. In May 1967 the de Muncks had gone to Europe, and on June 6, about two months before Fossey's arrival in Rwanda, Adrien de Munck had died suddenly, from a burst aorta.

"The boys had graduated from college, and their graduation present from Adrien was to be an African safari. They had bought an old military-type jeep, and they were bringing it down on the boat, the first time they'd been back since they'd left for school. When they arrived in Nairobi, the Belgian ambassador brought them word from Alyette that Adrien had died. But Alyette said she was certain he would have wanted them to go on with their safari. She said she would meet the boys in the Nairobi airport, on August 6, and ride with them back to Rwanda. Alyette was the most adventurous woman I've ever known," Carr says.

Carr decided that the challenge posed by this intense young woman before her now was exactly what was needed by her grief-stricken friend. The sort of expedition Fossey wanted to make up Karisimbi, looking for gorillas no one knew were there, was the sort of therapeutic activity that might offer Alyette de Munck diversion from her deep sorrow.

In Nairobi, Louis Leakey was as proud as he was relieved. Once he was certain Fossey was safely out, he had begun to spread the word about her uncommon dedication, presence of mind, and incredible courage. The response from those who counted was exactly what he had sought. Leighton Wilkie, confessing he found her escapades "blood-chilling," sent another $3,000 to get her outfitted all over again. "What new breed of human being is this?" asked Fairfield Osborn of the New York Zoological Society. "These young women go out alone to far places, obviously relishing the risks involved . . . Do you think," he asked suspiciously, "they are trying to prove they are better than men!"

But the once and future career of Dian Fossey rested mainly with the response of the National Geographic Society, to whose executive secretary, Melville Payne, Leakey had written a progress report that strained his capacity for understatement:

> She has had a pretty thin time, but she is completely undaunted, and when I spoke to her on a special radio telephone yesterday, she tried to avoid coming down here [to Nairobi], as "it would waste precious time and money," and she was anxious to make an attempt to proceed forthwith up the mountain from the Rwanda side, and make contact with her gorillas again.
>
> I told her firmly that although this might seem feasible, she must come down for adequate discussions and further planning and I will write you after a couple of days of discussion with her.
>
> She has already achieved a vast amount of most important results, running to over 300 pages of typescript notes, and has achieved in fact more than Schaller did in his whole 18 months. She is most upset at having to get out of the Congo, but clearly it is now impossible for her to work there for several months.
>
> In the meantime, there seems to me to be two alternatives: (1) she should do what she would like to do—try and get back to the gorillas on the Rwanda side, or (2) have a pause and spend some six months at Cambridge at the Animal Behaviour Research Centre, gaining knowledge of existing literature and gaining in background discussions and talks with others working in the animal behaviour field.

Melville Payne, who had seen a lot, was as impressed as everybody else. Fossey's escape read like fiction, he wrote back, and he couldn't imagine anyone, man or woman, with less courage and determination getting out of such a mess safely. Since it had been obvious to the National Geographic from the first that she lacked scientific background, perhaps now would be a good time for her to go to Cambridge. Most emphatically, however, she shouldn't be allowed to go anywhere that was beyond what he called, somewhat euphemistically, "civilized control."

While Leakey believed that the ultimate decision about her future course was hers, he intended to make sure that Fossey addressed the question with care and objectivity. If anything, she tended to be even more impulsive than he! When she arrived in Nairobi on August 1 (he had chartered a plan to fly her in from Kigali), he cleared his calendar and spent five days conferring with her.

It would take Fossey a while to forget Leakey's failure to send someone up to Kabara to help her, but she still considered him her mentor. He was, after all, the one who arranged her funding. After listening very carefully to him, she drew up a list of her possible alternatives:

1. LOWLAND GORILLA
(−)	(+)
A. Someone else's study	A. Good comparative study
B. Terrain?	B. Work continuation
C. Delay of visas, shots, etc.	
D. Distance	
E. Language	

2. CAMBRIDGE
A. Lack of adequate material	A. Has to be done sometime
B. I certainly don't want to leave	
C. Length of time required?	

3. RWANDA
A. Government red tape	A. Proximity to Kabara
B. No camping equipment	B. Able to return to Kabara when things get settled
C. What if *no* gorilla?	
D. Cattle, poaching, park organization	

But at the bottom of this list she wrote: "Find out when plane [of] Mrs. de Munck is arriving on the 6th."

•　　•　　•

By August 5, Fossey had got Leakey to agree they should bank everything on the response of Alyette de Munck—assuming Fossey could find her the next day at the airport. Since she knew de Munck would be seeing the boys for the first time since her husband's death, she realized that her timing for proposing such a venture was unfortunate at best. Nevertheless, on August 6 she arrived at the airport early, prepared to stay all day if she had to. As passengers filed through the small wood-frame terminal, she stopped any single woman who conformed even remotely to the description she had of de Munck: short and wiry, about five foot three, short brown hair, vibrant with energy. At forty-five, she would be getting the raisinlike wrinkles European women could expect from living out in the African sun.

After only an hour Fossey found Alyette de Munck. She was surrounded by the three young men Rosamond Carr had told her about, her son Yves, her nephew Philippe Bribosia, and their friend Xavier de Failly. When Fossey explained her reason for being there, the de Munck group enthusiastically offered their help. They all met again the next day with Louis Leakey, and they agreed to go forward with the expedition out of de Munck's plantation, two kilometers down the road from Carr's house, once they had regrouped in Rwanda. De Munck would drive with the boys in their open jeep and Fossey would fly back on August 15. They would start from the slopes of Karisimbi behind Carr's house. If gorillas lived in Rwanda, de Munck would help Fossey find them, and the boys would do some filming.

Shortly after the de Muncks had departed, a cable addressed to both Leakey and Fossey arrived from the U.S. Embassy in Kigali:

ALL THE PEOPLE WHO WERE EVACUATED FROM THE CONGO HAVE BEEN ORDERED BY THE RWANDA GOVERNMENT TO LEAVE RWANDA *IMMEDIATELY* UNDER PAIN OF EXTRADITION TO THE CONGO AS THEY WILL BE REGARDED AS POTENTIAL MERCENARIES AND ACCOMPLICES. AMERI-

173

CAN EMBASSY TAKE THIS ORDER *VERY* SERIOUSLY AND THINK THE ORDER HAS BEEN MADE BY REQUEST OF THE CONGO GOVERNMENT. IT WILL THEREFORE BE IMPOSSIBLE FOR DIAN FOSSEY TO THINK OF RETURNING.

Having read this cable, on August 15 Fossey flew out of Nairobi for Rwanda as planned.

Even in an old jeep, the drive from Nairobi to Kampala, Uganda, just under halfway to Rwanda, is not an uncomfortable one. The British put in a good macadam road, which has since been well maintained. But at Kampala in 1967, the macadam merged into a dirt track, and in Africa any dirt track promises a hard day's ride.

When the boys stopped in Kampala to make some repairs, Alyette de Munck ran into some friends, who immediately insisted she drive the rest of the way with them in their car. It was certain to be more comfortable than the jeep. The boys could follow behind. Expecting them to arrive at her plantation a day or so after her, she waved good-bye to the three young men and drove away.

Once the repairs had been made, the boys followed the road from Kampala to Kabala, arriving late in the afternoon in Kisoro, only a few hours away from their new home this side of Gisenyi, Rwanda. They decided to spend the night at Traveller's Rest, where they were made to feel most welcome by Alyette's good friend Walter Baumgartel. After dinner they spent the evening in the bar. The next morning, at the crossroads just outside Baumgartel's place, they took the wrong turn. Instead of heading south into Rwanda, they drove west along the road leading through the Bunagana gate into the Congo. And this was the last Baumgartel, or anyone else, would see of them.

The account of what happened next comes mainly from Fossey, who revealed what she knew (said she knew) to a very few people— cryptically at first, and in fragments, and then, as she learned more, with a degree of hysteria that she never thereafter allowed herself in any of her correspondence with anyone. For others even indirectly involved with these events, the details were too distressing to speak of. Rosamond Carr could bring herself to mention them in only the sparest and most elliptical of allusions, and Walter Baumgartel, in a tight-lipped reference to the young men's fate in his memoirs, gave it as the principal reason why he packed up, sold his beloved Travellers' Rest, and left Africa forever. ("They had spent the last night of their lives under my roof. I had been the last person to shake hands with them. Suddenly, I felt that I had had my fill of Africa.")

How accurate Fossey's account in its more grotesque details may be is open to question, for reasons stated earlier: the absence of creditable records, reliable witnesses, and so on. Two historians of modern Zaire, including the civil disturbances in Kivu province of the 1960s, Thomas Turner and David Newbury, are unable to dispute or confirm her account. (In matters having to do with the eastern Congo in the 1960s, Newbury says, his own inclination is to err on the side of sensationalism.) But the relevance of these events to Fossey's own story has less to do with their historical accuracy than the effect they had on her in the years to come. She believed them to be true, and the effect on her was so powerful as to cause her to react irrationally, the intensity of her feelings for her new friend Alyette de Munck without precedent in her own emotional life except possibly that which she had felt for her battered young patient at Korsair, Norma Kelley.

Fossey was next seen on August 15 by Frank Crigler when she flew into the Kigali airport. It was his first meeting with her. "Inside this tiny waiting room there was this extraordinary-looking, very tall, obviously American woman," he says. "She was trying to organize an enormous quantity of luggage, and frantically giving instructions to everybody in sight. She was dressed all in white!" On behalf of the U.S. government, Crigler tried to discourage her from staying. It was feared that the mercenaries were about to move north through Goma and directly into the area where she proposed to camp.

Fossey ignored him and continued on. Dismayed but undaunted, the American Embassy did what it could to keep up with Fossey. Another cable went out shortly thereafter:

FOR WHAT IT MAY BE WORTH, CRIGLER MET MISS FOSSEY IN LATE AUGUST ON HER RETURN FROM LEAVE. WAS HEADED THEN FOR GISENYI WITH LARGE BATCH BRAND NEW EQUIPMENT WHICH SHE WAS STRUGGLING TO GET THROUGH GOR [GOVERNMENT OF RWANDA] CUSTOMS WITHOUT PAYING DUTIES. HER BEHAVIOR AT THIS MO-MENT OF PERSONAL "CRISIS" LEFT CONSUL WITH IMPRES-SION SHE WAS RESOURCEFUL, INDEPENDENT BUT HIGHLY EMOTIONAL AND ERRATIC YOUNG WOMAN. SPOKE NO FRENCH AND MADE NO ATTEMPT TO USE ANY SWAHILI SHE MAY HAVE KNOWN, AND ATTITUDE SUGGESTED SHE HELD AFRICANS IN LOW REGARD. CONFESSED TO BEING FRIGHT-ENED AT PROSPECT OF RETURNING TO WILDERNESS AT TIME OF CIVIL UNREST AND MILITARY HARASSMENT NEARBY AND DESCRIBED DR. LEAKEY IN MOST UNFLATTER-ING TERMS FOR "CALLOUSLY" HAVING ORDERED HER BACK.

According to Fossey, when she arrived at the de Munck plantation the next day, Alyette ran toward her screaming that she was the only one who had known the dead boys. Dian must move into her house and be as her daughter. Alyette was just then leaving for Kigali to meet with the Belgian ambassador about the circumstances of the boys' murder. When she departed, friends of hers came to the plantation and pleaded with Fossey to stay. All Alyette had talked of, they said, was how she and the boys would help Fossey find the gorillas. She had planned to fix up the small house on the upper plantation for Fossey to work out of. It was imperative that she stay there and help Alyette somehow survive this latest tragedy.

Fossey abandoned her plans for the mountain. How could anyone think of gorillas, or anything else, at a time like that?

What had happened to the boys was made all the more horrible by her awareness that it could have happened to her. In the bar at Traveller's Rest, the night before their death, she learned, the boys had struck up an acquaintance with a Watutsi, who offered to show them the way into Rwanda. Before their departure, the Watutsi sent word to the guards at Bunagana that he was directing three mercenaries into the Congo. When the boys arrived at the gate in their military jeep, they asked if they had come to the Rwanda border. They were told that they had, and the gate was opened. They were seized as mercenaries and executed.

But there was far more, Fossey later wrote Leakey, which she discovered when she returned several days later to Traveller's Rest. To help out Baumgartel, she had gone out front to paint a sign, and while she was working there, a French priest from the Congo passed by. Weeping, he told her the full story of the boys' fate, a version which she said was later corroborated by an investigation held by "an honest judge" in Kinshasa. The boys were seized at 9:00 A.M. and tortured until 4:00 the next morning. Their remains were eaten over the next three days, she told Leakey. But she wrote Father Raymond that they were castrated and burned alive. (It was the beginning of Fossey's loss of her newfound Catholicism. Later on, she asked Father Raymond how God could have let such a thing happen. "He gave His own son to be crucified, didn't He?" Father Raymond replied. Fossey said that wasn't good enough for her. "Then may He have mercy on your soul," Father Raymond said.)

In the same letter, dated August 24, 1967, Fossey wrote Leakey that Alyette de Munck must never know of these unspeakable events, for the knowledge would kill her. She told him she held four men directly responsible, whose names she knew, the same four men at the Bunagana gate who, but for Walter Baumgartel, might have subjected her to the identical fate. Since justice was impossible in the Congo, she declared, revenge was the only answer. And it must begin at the Bunagana gate. She told Leakey that she was writing important friends in the U.S. and raising money to help carry it out.

This was not an idle threat; a State Department cable (released under the Freedom of Information Act) confirmed it. She was described to be in a highly emotional condition, and according to State, she had written to a friend asking help in avenging the murder of three Belgians. She vowed "that she herself would kill the [men] responsible unless someone else did it by October 31st." This cable was sent to the consulates and embassies in Rwanda, Kenya, Uganda, and the Congo. It was signed by Dean Rusk, the Secretary of State.

It was at about this time, in the last week of September, that Alexie Forrester at Notre Dame received a letter from Fossey, asking for his help.

Sister Gerald tells this part of the story:

"One day Alexie came to me and said, 'Here's a letter from Dian. She wants me to go right out to Rwanda. She evidently has been attacked. I've contacted her parents. I've contacted the State Department.'

" 'Where are you going to get the money, Alexie?' I said.

"Well, he was in touch with her parents, he said, and they were going to give it to him.

" 'How is it the parents are giving you the money?' I said. 'Doesn't the mother have enough interest in her own daughter to go with you? Why is she letting you go alone? Why is her stepfather letting you go alone?'

"What I read burned into my brain. Dian said: 'I couldn't tell you what these Africans have done to me. You've got to come out and avenge this. You may have to do it yourself, or get some mercenaries.' I finished reading the letter and handed it back to him without comment.

" 'Aunt Maura,' Alexie said, 'aren't you going to help me?'

" 'No, Alexie,' I said. 'You've made your decision, and I'm not moving in between you and your decision. You're a mature man. You've told me what you're going to do. I've nothing to say.'

" 'But you're the only one I have in this country,' he said, 'the only one I have to come to for help. You're letting me down. You're refusing to talk to me.'

"So I said, 'She's asking you to commit murder. I didn't think it was necessary for me to comment on that, what with the moral education you're getting at Notre Dame. This of course is outside of reality. One of two things has happened, as I see it. Either none of this ever took place, and she has just gone over the edge from the life she's leading alone up there—she's no longer mentally sound—or it *did* happen, and the result of it is that she's mentally disturbed. This is not normal. She is in need of help. So when you get out there to help her—and I'm glad you're going to help her, Alexie—I would ask you not to tie yourself up in marriage out there. Bring her back here. I'll help you in every way possible. I'll find a place for her to stay at St. Mary's. Do everything to help her, and then have a decent marriage at Notre Dame. She needs to get some psychological evaluation because that letter is not the letter of a sane woman.'

" 'I'm going to marry her, Aunt Maura,' Alexie said."

Forrester called Richard and Kitty Price, and he says, Richard Price insisted on paying the $3,000 it would take to get him to Rwanda. Before his departure, he called the State Department in Washington and Louis Leakey in Nairobi. Both parties, he says now, agreed with his expressed intention to bring Fossey home.

On October 9, after a day of tracking gorillas, Fossey returned to her new camp on the saddle between Visoke and Karisimbi and found Forrester sitting in front of her tent waiting for her. He had got there in a most circuitous fashion. He had bribed his way across the Rwandan border with two hundred cigarettes and a bottle of wine, and en route was detained by soldiers, who held him for four hours before allowing him to go on.

The events of the second week of October 1967 are a long way removed from the life of Alexie Forrester today. Like anyone else after twenty years have passed, he is more sure of his conclusions about the events of those times than he is of the facts leading to them. ("I'd rather you look at what we've said, and put down what I intended to mean rather than the words themselves. Words themselves are pretty lethal," he says.)

After he had talked with Fossey, Forrester changed his view of what had happened to her. He knew Africa a lot better than she did, and he had no intention of avenging anything. He was skeptical of all the events leading to her arrival on the Rwanda side of the Virunga Mountains. He accepted the fact that she had been detained against her will, and while he had no doubt she had been terrified, scared out of her mind and humiliated, he did not believe she had been physically abused. "First of all, if that happened, she would never have got out of there alive. If *any* African raped a European in that part of the world, you might as well forget that European's existence. And if it was a military incident, she would never have come out of there alive. Never. And especially, as she implied, if a senior officer was involved. He simply would never have let her come back. No way in hell." Nor did Forrester believe her story of her escape. "You don't get out of those kinds of camps—I've been there, and I know what it's like. If the military people are in control, there's no *way*. Just no way in blazes. You're totally at their mercy."

He simply ignored her requests for vengeance against the murderers of the de Muncks. "She was extremely lonely up there and very frightened. Despite her bravado, things tended to get out of proportion. She had in fact overstepped her environment by a great deal. Most Americans have not much sensitivity for living outside the U.S. Certainly she didn't have any—she felt Africa was just another Sunset Strip, and she could go around insisting on her rights. It doesn't work that way.

"In the end," says Forrester, "she was white. She was a woman. She was on a mountain. And she was terribly vulnerable."

•   •   •

They were together five days. During that time they had long talks, and Fossey took Forrester out to see the gorillas. His memories do not suggest the poignance of a lovers' reunion. "I told her to get off the mountain and we would get married right away. Or she could stay there. But that would be the end of any marriage plans." This time Forrester had no intention of equivocating. He had brought along a ring. "I said, you either come down this mountain with me, or you stay here and I keep walking."

Whatever response she may have expected from Forrester, it was most assuredly not his proposal to escort her down the mountain and back to the United States. Except for her demand that he avenge the atrocities at the Bunagana gate, Forrester had been out of her picture for a long time. Almost a year earlier she had indicated in her application to the National Geographic that she planned to devote at least two years to her study of the mountain gorilla, meaning she intended to stay in Africa well past her projected marriage date to Forrester.

By the time Forrester arrived on the mountain, Fossey had discovered the gorillas she was seeking and was highly elated at her success. She told him she had made some three hundred sightings. "She watches them by day," reported American ambassador Leo Cyr, and "types her notes in a wet tent and clothes by night."

Nothing had stood in her way thus far; nothing would now. Although it was her fury that prompted her to seek his help, her own references to Forrester's visit suggest she was less than grateful for his solicitude. Only two days after his departure, she complained to Louis Leakey that she had just lost five days' work because of the arrival of a visitor from America who was "both unannounced and unwelcome." Several weeks later she wrote the Hjelms in California that Forrester had told fantastic lies to everyone who mattered to her. He had told the Prices and George Fossey she was in mortal danger; told the CIA she should be evacuated by force if necessary; told Leakey she was returning to America as his wife and that her study was therefore terminated; and worst of all, he had gone to Alyette de Munck and told her all the details of the boys' death. And now she was faced wtih the problem of restoring Alyette's faith in her, because Alyette could not understand why Dian would keep these details secret, knowing how hard Alyette had been trying to find out what had happened.

And so Forrester had kept on walking. But before he left—and since Fossey had asked, he says—he gave her some advice.

"I told her that if she stayed, I fully expected she would have her throat cut by the end of the year. It was absolutely ludicrous to live on a mountain out there, harassing a bunch of poachers and expecting to stay alive."

Forrester pauses.

"It took a lot longer than I thought it would take, but in fact it actually happened. You can't project *when* in Africa, you can just project *what*. And I was right.

"I told her this in so many words. When she refused to come down, I said she had one option. And she asked me what this was. I said to her, 'The only option you've got to stay alive is to make yourself into some sort of spiritual witch. You've got to do this with such effectiveness and create such a sense of terror about you, people will give you a wide berth.'

"This was not capricious advice, not in any sense of the word. All over Africa, there have been European women who lived on farms by themselves while their husbands went to war—my mother was one of them. The only way they survived was to become known as some sort of banshee. All Africans, you know, live in a spook land. They believe almost everything is invested with spiritual meaning. Every single perception of reality is some form of sacred existence.

"I suggested she should make herself into someone no one would want to go *near*—that she should get wailing systems, smoke bombs, false faces, that sort of thing. And I told her to leave these things lying about everywhere, and to make sure everybody knew they were there.

"At the same time," Forrester says, "I told her she should beat the bejesus out of anybody she felt like beating the bejesus out of."

She should strike them?

"That's right. And then they would get to feeling there was a woman up there who was behaving totally unwomanly. I told her this in 1967. I didn't think she would do it, although if anybody would, she would."

16

BEFORE CAMPBELL

At the time Dian Fossey arrived in that country, Rwanda was every nation's poor cousin. There was little living space left; it was the most densely populated country in Africa. It was also the most impoverished, one of the most underprivileged nations in the world. But, like some poor cousins, Rwanda was no less proud than any other nation in the world community.

Because Rwanda lay outside the old slave-trade routes and at the far edge of Belgium's colonial interests, its indigenous culture was influenced very little by the West. The first white man through here was a German soldier, in 1894. The nation's history is venerable, however. It was first settled by the Twa Pygmies, developed by the Hutus (90 percent of the current population), and, five hundred years ago, invaded and ruled over thereafter by the very tall Watutsi, or Tutsis as they are more commonly known. Until recently, the principal medium for Rwandan history and culture was oral—stories, legends, and proverbs handed down from one generation to the next in Kinyarwanda, one of the world's all-time most difficult languages, in which a single word can stand for a sentence.

In Rwandan society, the family is the binding force. Most of the people live in kin-group clusters, cheek by jowl with the next. Rwandans are generous, honest, introverted, and oblique. They consider it impolite to look another in the eye—indeed, such presumption announces to the offended that the offender is probably a member of a more powerful class. Unlike the Congo, where the Belgians had committed endless atrocities against the blacks, in Rwanda white people are respected and liked, mainly because the West supported the Hutus in their revolt against the oppression of the Tutsis. (This was yet another genocidal African war of the 1960s. In 1963, the year Fossey first came to Africa, the Hutu majority cut down the tall, aristocratic Watutsi by the tens of thousands, sometimes cutting them off—literally—at the knees. But Rwanda became quiet thereafter, especially for Europeans. Dian's murder was the first white fatality from criminal violence in over thirty years.) A most surprising fact about this poor and tiny country—so bucolic and inviting it has come to be known as Africa's Little Switzerland—is that it has somehow managed to avoid being swallowed whole by the Congo, its giant neighbor to the west.

For Fossey, her new country of residence offered several considerable contrasts with her former one, the most obvious and unavoidable being their extreme difference in size. The Congo (soon to become Zaire) was one of the largest countries in Africa; Rwanda was one of the smallest. If the Congo is equivalent in land size to the eastern half of the United States, then Rwanda is the size of Maryland. And while Rwanda is every bit as arable as Maryland, it has become so densely populated it is a demographer's nightmare, a paradigm of Malthusian imbalance, so bloated today it seems only seconds from the inevitable crash. When Fossey first got there, there was not enough food to go around. By the time of her death the situation was much worse.

In Rwanda, as in much of black Africa, modern hygiene has slowed

185

the death rate, while the birth rate has remained high. In 1967, the population of Rwanda was 3.2 million; in 1985, it was 6.9 million. To make matters worse, Rwandans live by a patriarchal tradition which guarantees ever-diminishing returns. Whatever land is held by the father is divided equally at his death among his sons. As fathers have increased and multiplied, small farms have shrunk to minuscule gardens.

For these pressing reasons there is very little natural vegetation left in Rwanda; all possible land has been turned to cultivation. The wilderness remaining totals only 3 percent of the land. Nearly all of this is to be found on the volcanos—in the Parc National des Volcans, the Rwanda side of the Virunga chain, which is, as well, the nation's watershed. To be sure, one side of the chain is just as dense as the other. The trouble is, for the mountain gorilla as well as any other form of wildlife, when you come down the mountain on Rwanda's side all you find are people. Moreover, while it is true that nearly any plant will grow in the fertile soil and there is in consequence food to be had, there is very little meat. The people suffer from protein deficiency. Traditionally they have looked on their side of the Virungas as a last desperate resource for small animals like bushbuck and duiker and for the few open places left to graze their herds. In 1960, George Schaller reported thousands of people roaming the Virungas with tens of thousands of their stock. When Fossey arrived, they were still there, but the park had shrunk and was about to shrink some more.

"Since its creation as a national park over 50 years ago," writes Bill Weber in his master's thesis on gorilla conservation, "the size of the original Albert reserve has been steadily shrinking. This has been most serious on the Rwandan side of the [volcano] chain. In 1958, responding to local population pressure, Belgian colonial authorities allowed the clearing of 7,000 hectares (25 percent) of forest from what is now the Parc National des Volcans. In 1969, the independent Rwandan government, acting on advice from a Common Market development agency, authorized the clearing of an additional 10,000 hectares for agricultural use."

Watching her beloved gorillas about to be crowded out of existence, Fossey took the long view: the Parc National des Volcans was all that was left of the 20-million-year-old Miocene forest in which these magnificent animals had evolved. It measured just twenty-five miles long and four to twelve miles wide. When the Parc National des Volcans was gone, the mountain gorilla would be gone, too.

To the people of Rwanda, however, the Parc National des Volcans was important mainly as a source of food and water.

It is certainly true that Alyette de Munck got Fossey established in Rwanda. She helped her find Karisoke, the camp on the southwest slope of Visoke which would become her home, and helped her put it in place. In June 1968, when she found Fossey living there in a rotted tent and trying to stay alive on a diet of potatoes, she was so appalled that she immediately set about building her friend a cabin. That way, she could at least stay dry.

At first the two women were together often. It was only in the wilderness now, Alyette told Dian, that she could find any joy, any peace. The excitement of the discovery of gorillas in Karisoke—more gorillas than they could count—helped cheer her, at least momentarily.

With the presence of the gorillas confirmed, Dian was off and running. Alyette checked into the camp from time to time, bringing up essential equipment and offering Dian a place to stay when she came down from the mountain to replenish her supplies. She was more than invaluable to Dian. She was for a time her soulmate, and Dian did everything she could think of to help assuage the misery that had befallen Alyette. But there was too much ever to be forgotten, and the time came when Alyette left to travel throughout East Africa, as she does still.

But for the first few years, the two women clung together, each looking after over the needs of the other. Rosamond Carr served up a hot meal from time to time, and worried constantly about them both.

Karisoke was now Fossey's home, and this she accepted without qualification. The first half of her life was so remote it seemed to belong to someone else. Although Gaynee Henry kept up her Blue Cross payments and had her films processed for her, Fossey hadn't made contact with anyone in the States for months. Her Kentucky friends were extremely anxious about her, and so was George Fossey. By December, Father Raymond had written Leakey asking for some word, and from San Francisco, even more desperately, so had George Fossey:

> My wife, Kathryn, had a stroke in Sept. along with a clot on her brain she is paralized & has been steadily confined in the hopital. Consequently my hours are completely tied up between her & our business. I have not had any word from Dian since August 22 and naturally Kathryn & myself are frantic with worry. . . . Would you inform me if I have been writing to the right address, Dian Fossey c/o Mrs. De Munck, Gisenyi, Ruanda, East Africa.

Leakey had answered George Fossey briefly to reassure him, and then received a letter from Dian that left him bemused. She asked him please to stop writing to George Fossey, who was not her parent. She apologized for involving him in a family matter, but said he should know that George Fossey, who was her natural father, had nothing to do with bringing her up. Her real parents were Mr. and Mrs. R. C. Price, who would be very unhappy to learn that George Fossey was in the picture at all. They were already so displeased with her for not having come home with Forrester that they had stopped writing to her. She had not heard from her mother since September, and this had hurt her very much. Anyway, would he please write the Prices assuring them of her safety and of the respectability of her study in the interest of restoring their confidence? And please remember not to mention the name of George Fossey?

Leakey immediately sat down and wrote the Prices. "The reports I get from her," he told them, "show that she will achieve an outstanding place in the scientific world by the time she has finished. What she is doing is comparable to what has been done by Jane Goodall with the chimpanzees . . . and I assure you that Dian will have equal fame and success." And he let it go at that.

But such blandishments were an understatement. Fossey had become more than just a badge of his perspicacity; she was his Galatea. Against the most formidable of obstacles, she had surpassed the best he had expected of her. For twelve years he had waited for the right person to come along. With her industry and courage the young woman he had chosen to fulfill his vision had by now exceeded George Schaller's 466 hours of field observation by an impressive margin. In a single year, despite a disaster that would have sent a lesser person home for good, Fossey had accrued 485 hours. Already in Rwanda she had located and identified four new groups. Her commitment was dogged and unquenchable. On his swing through the United States he had received an excited cablegram from her: I'VE FINALLY BEEN ACCEPTED BY A GORILLA. Lecturing at UCLA, he had pulled the crumpled cable from his pocket and read it to his entranced audience, among whom sat Birute Galdikas. (Like Fossey before her, Galdikas would approach Leakey immediately thereafter, and thus became the third member of his visionary scheme. Under Leakey's sponsorship—with her appendix *and* her tonsils removed—Galdikas would go to Borneo to devote her life to the study of the orangutan, the oldest in evolutionary age of the great apes.)

By 1968, Dian Fossey's name was known to the most important people in her field. She was under exclusive contract to the National Geographic, and was receiving tentative inquiries about coming to take her Ph.D. at Cambridge, the most advanced learning center in the West for the study of wild-animal behavior. This was a must if she was to be regarded as a true scientist. Reading of her ordeal in the Congo, an American publisher had invited her to write a book for a popular audience (not the right time for *that,* Leakey had told her), and an invitation, all expenses paid, had come for her to speak at an international symposium on the great apes at the Yerkes Primate Center in Atlanta in June.

But Leakey couldn't honestly say he was ever free of worry for Fossey's safety. In one of her first letters from Rwanda she said her cookboy, Phocas—the one she had brought out of the Congo—had turned bad and threatened her with the same fate that had overtaken the de Munck boys. Another time, when she sacked a staffer for smoking marijuana, he came back to the camp to accost her and she had fired a bullet over his head. One of her guides said the Congolese had put out a reward for her capture, and that the mountain was crawling with soldiers looking for her. Leakey was alarmed and immediately cabled her: HAVE WRITTEN FIVE TIMES. YOU MUST TAKE NO UN-NECESSARY RISKS. IF THINK NECESSARY ABANDON PROJECT.

But there was no point in alarming the people back home. So Leakey had reassured the Prices on this count as best he could. He said Dian was not in any grave danger, "although naturally her living conditions are those of camp life."

Dian Fossey really did hate to complain, and didn't, most of the time; and not only because there was no one around the camp to complain to. After sixteen months, she knew very well what to expect up there. But she believed she had every right to more institutional support than she was getting. Leakey had said there was plenty of money for her now; he told her to expect a check from National Geographic in February. By March it hadn't come and she wrote him in England about it. He said it would be mailed in April.

And now it was the first of May, and still no check. The tires of her Land Rover were gone. The axle was broken. She had to borrow money from de Munck to pay her staff and buy them food; and to do this, she herself was reduced to living on potatoes. At least they were soft, for now her teeth were bothering her. To assuage the pain, she took codeine to sleep, and during the day an African concoction called dawa, which she said looked like a mixture of *merde* and vacuum-cleaner fillings. She was lancing her jaw now, on a weekly schedule. When her gold inlays fell out, she collected them in a little bag so that—if she ever got to a dentist again—she might be able to save some money. Since February there had been five days of sunlight. But what could you expect when you set up camp in a rain forest— your feet turned to mold.

After sixteen months in these mountains she could use a break, and for a while, back in January, she thought she was about to get one. The Yerkes people had said they would pay her way home if she came to speak at their conference. Dutifully she had informed them she would have to obtain Leakey's permission first, and she had written him on January 22. But though they exchanged several letters there- after, he made no reference to it one way or another. Finally, she cabled him: *Could she go or not?* Besides, she had to get her teeth looked after. By the time she received the permission she sought, four months had passed, and by then it was too late—the invitation had been rescinded.

There was no one in Africa, or anywhere else, whose approval she sought more avidly than Louis Leakey's. But this was certainly not the first time he had shaken her confidence. She really didn't know what to expect from him anymore. Since December he had been spending a lot of time in the States; a group of wealthy Californians were setting up a foundation in his name to fund even *more* of his projects, ostensibly to keep him from killing himself on the lecture circuit. But while he was gadflying about with these people he had still been overseeing digs all over the world and continuing his personal ap- pearances. And now he was in a hospital bed in London, recovering from a hip operation.

Leakey was her lifeline. She knew how proud of her he was, how assiduously he had worked to finance her study and further her interests, and she was grateful for his sponsorship. She was still awed by the sweeping vision of this great man. But she knew, too, that there was only so much he could give of himself when he was in a hospital bed on the other side of the world. What was she to do? She couldn't understand what was going on at the National Geographic. How did they expect her to survive up there? In one of his letters, Leakey had sent word that they had assigned Alan Root to film her study, which was wonderful. But Root had been supposed to come back to Kabara in the Congo, and he had never gotten there. Now that he was officially assigned to Karisoke, *when* would he come? Some of the things that had happened to her she wouldn't expect anyone to believe without seeing it for themselves. Recently the silverback from Group 8 had come so close she had to blow cigarette smoke in his face to keep him at three feet. Who would ever believe it? But if Root were here, he could get it all on film.

She had immediately written the Roots, both delighted and relieved they were once again riding to the rescue. She told them of the wonderful things she was seeing, and how thrilled she was that they would be the photographers to make the record of her study. All she had to show for her months in the Congo was a bunch of notes. She certainly didn't want that to happen again. When might she expect them?

They would be there in a couple of months or so, Alan Root wrote back. But in the meantime, he delivered another little lecture. The least of her worries, wrote Alan Root the filmmaker, ought to be whether her observations were recorded on film:

> My understanding is that you are doing a study of gorilla behavior, therefore the fact that your time with the Kabara groups is now just a pile of notes should not be considered too terrible. Ninety-nine percent of all scientific studies end up as a pile of notes . . . as long as your notes are of interest, then nothing is lost from the scientific point of view. I get the feeling that you are so disillusioned that you want photos to *prove* what is in your notes. . . . Dian, please believe me, this isn't necessary. No one of any standing will doubt your word or your work. This is the very backbone of research, that what a man puts down on paper he stands by and it is accepted. I intend to make

pictures that will show the world what we have always known—that you have the guts it takes to succeed with these animals—but whatever you do, don't feel you must have this coverage as *proof.* O.K. Analysis over, you can get up off the couch now and Dr. Root will send the bill.

That argument left Fossey unmoved. She still wanted a photographic record—and wanted no one but Root to do the filming. And he could tell her how to handle the poachers and the cattle people. He was the *mzungu* she needed now. The outlaws had become open and fearless in their trespassing—far worse than in the Congo—and she had no idea what to do about them. They seemed to regard the Virungas as a community resource. They were brazen—they openly crossed her meadow and one of them had blithely skipped across the guy ropes of her tent. To prohibit illegal entry, the Rwandan government had assigned twelve guards and one conservator. Pathetic. *Hopeless!* Only the weather was a reliable deterrent; the rain kept the intruders out. Once the sun broke through, the gorillas fled, and so now she found herself praying for rain.

There was no one to advise her what to do about this. When she had gone into Kigali to ask for help from the government, she was received with total indifference. The gorillas were good for nothing; they served no purpose for the people of Rwanda, most of whom had never seen them and were scarcely aware they were there. In three years, after the presidential elections, something might be done to strengthen the guard force. But not now.

In his letters from abroad, the best Leakey had been able to offer was moral support. Somewhat distractedly, he reminded her not to take too many chances. What concerned him most at the moment was getting her into Cambridge so that she could take her Ph.D. As quickly as possible, Leakey wanted her to establish contact with Jane Goodall's professor, a man named Robert Hinde.

Fossey was less enthusiastic about the next phase in her career than Leakey. She had more immediate things to think about than Hinde, who was largely responsible for making Cambridge the most important center for the study of primates at that time.

But Fossey held great interest for Hinde. There were only three species of great ape. Through association with Goodall, Cambridge could claim expertise in the study of the chimpanzee. If Leakey's latest "discovery" proved equally successful, Cambridge could have a lock on two out of the three. Hinde had told Leakey he would like to visit Karisoke to see how Fossey's study was coming along.

Leakey had moved quickly. Hinde wanted to come out that summer if possible, he wrote Fossey, imparting this news with an air of urgency. This confirmed Fossey's opinion that Leakey didn't have a very good idea of what was going on in Rwanda. So far as she was concerned, higher education was the lowest of her priorities. If something wasn't done soon to protect the few gorillas remaining on this earth, there would be none left to study. What *she* needed, and with plenty of urgency, was (1) some money to live on, and (2) Alan Root.

This was almost exactly where Fossey had been a year earlier—calling for help and waiting for Alan Root. The main difference was, last year her teeth didn't hurt.

By coincidence, Root and Hinde arrived in Karisoke at the same time, toward the end of July. Both were British by birth. Both were tall, lean, and intense. But they came from radically different traditions.

Hinde was the prototypical Cambridge don, a protégé of the great ethologists W. H. Thorpe and Niko Tinbergen, and now head of graduate studies in animal behavior at Madingley, a subcenter of Cambridge University. During the war, as a pilot for the RAF, he trained in southern Rhodesia. Because of his austere appearance, rigorous standards, precise reasoning, and forceful challenge to their own thinking, Hinde was regarded by his students as an intimidating figure.

"So much so," recalls the primatologist Richard Wrangham, "the story was told when I was there that the graduate students got together and elected a representative to inform Hinde they preferred to have seminars among themselves because so many of them were frightened to speak up in his class. Robert listened to this proposal, and as he was a very wise and sensitive man, he said he thought it was a good idea and that they all should meet to talk about it. At the meeting Robert said, 'I have heard that some of you are rather intimidated by me. Anybody who feels this way I should like to ask to stand and say what the problem is.' There was a dead silence, and everything went on as before."

Hinde came to the study of apes as an ornithologist; the work done at that time with birds was the most advanced in behavior ecology. He then turned to monkeys, to research mother-infant relations. On Louis Leakey's recommendation, Hinde had accepted Jane Goodall as a Ph.D. candidate even though she lacked a bachelor's degree. Later, he sent Ph.D. candidates to Goodall's camp in Gombe for a firsthand look at her work. When Leakey called upon him to take on Fossey, Hinde had the foresight to see the opportunity for a generation of students still to come.

In a very short time, Hinde would become Fossey's academic supervisor at Madingley and—as age, crippling disabilities, and his unremitting, vaulting ambition wore Louis Leakey down—Leakey's successor as her scientific mentor.

Alan Root, Fossey's first guide to survival, was so far removed from the academic life that he made Robert Hinde look as though he had just emerged from a cloister. Root was a born naturalist. At four, he had collected butterflies and flowers; at ten, snakes; at seventeen, he left school; and at eighteen he, along with Michael Grzimek, Berhard Grzimek's son, shot the footage for *Serengeti Shall Not Die,* a pioneering film study of East African ecology. In a comparatively new field which was becoming increasingly complex as scientific knowledge accumulated, Root had taught himself. Much of what he knew came from firsthand experience, and he applied that knowledge directly in the films he wrote and produced with his wife Joan. Not only did the Roots' films meet scientific standards for accuracy, they often went beyond what was known in the field and were regarded as original data in themselves. Whatever interested Root (and nearly everything in the natural world did) became a likely subject for his films—the social life of the termite, the migrating route of the wildebeest, the evolution of the rain forest. Save for the voice-over narration, no humans intruded. The casts consisted of animals, plants, rocks, fire, and weather, all playing before the Roots' camera as though they'd been chosen only for their talent (for example, an extended sequence of a snake gulping down a small frog only to be gulped down itself by a very large frog).

In East Africa today, Alan Root is as close as one can find to the colorful adventurers of the colonial past. Most of his limbs have been mangled or pierced by one creature or another, nearly always for his persistence in coming too close. His vehicles for swift and comprehensive vantages include a hot air balloon, a Mercedes field wagon, and two small airplanes, which are so banged up that at any given time only one is serviceable. In the ever-dwindling community of white Africans, Root is the modern equivalent in raw dash of Phillip Percival, the great white hunter of the 1930s, several significant differences being that Root loves animals and does not kill them, carries a camera instead of a gun, and takes more chances.

Arriving at Karisoke, where their beleaguered hostess had almost forgotten what it was like to be surrounded by attractive, convivial men of her own race, Robert Hinde and Alan Root were made to feel exceedingly welcome. Both were roughly her age—and both were taller.

In every way but one, life had considerably improved for Fossey by the time they got there. Her check had arrived on May 7, and it was enough to pay her debts, fix up her Land Rover, and keep her in rations for the next several months. Intrusions into the park had slowed abruptly after she killed a cow. (Closing her eyes so she wouldn't have to see the carnage, she shot her pistol into a herd. She knew she got one. She sent word to the herdsmen that she would do the same thing every month until they stopped coming in.) And she was living now under a dry roof, thanks to Alyette de Munck. Alyette had organized a work force of ten Africans and put up a proper cabin for Dian; they had it up in a week's time. It had a lava-rock fireplace, bookshelves, cabinets, a work desk ten feet long, three windows looking out across the meadow toward the volcanos that surrounded her, walls covered with matting and framed with bamboo . . . Fossey at last had a home.

But her teeth were still killing her. A distraught Leakey had assured her he would find the money to buy her a plane ticket home. But now, she informed him, that would have to wait. It was imperative that she stay with Root, and besides that, she didn't dare leave without a European to run the camp in her absence. If she did, she was certain it wouldn't be there when she got back.

There were other developments, too. Just a few weeks earlier, thirty Congolese park guards, all armed, had appeared at the edge of the meadow, led by Jacques Veschuren. This was the same man who had fled the Congo with Schaller in 1960 and who had changed Fossey's life by directing her to the Virungas for the first sight of gorillas. As an indication things in the Congo were somewhat less volatile than they had been, Veschuren had been restored to his office as scientific director at Albert National Park under the Mobutu government. He had come to ask Fossey to resume her studies at Kabara—which of course was out of the question.

He also brought distressing news: the Congo side of the Virungas had become as overrun by poachers and cattle people as the Rwandan park. There was nothing left of her old hut, nothing but bones and dried blood. Kabara Meadow was filled with cattle; and all the gorillas were gone. As he spoke of these dreadful developments, Veschuren broke into tears. Walking part of the way back with him, Fossey counted four hundred head of cattle and sixty-four huts.

197

Fossey informed Leakey that the same thing could happen in Rwanda. She would not leave Karisoke until she had a *mzungu* to look after it.

Except for Fossey's tooth problems, the Hinde/Root visit was a smashing success. She cooked for them, a most convincing proof of her pleasure, and she took them out to see her most responsive gorilla group. Leakey had warned Hinde not to expect too much. Fossey would have to decide if it was safe—an aroused silverback could kill them both. But when she got them there and the group tolerated their presence, it was like showing Hinde and Root—well, she didn't know exactly *how* to describe it. It was, she said, like giving birth to a seventeen-month-old baby.

Hinde was overcome by the sight of the gorillas. Like any other first-time observer, he couldn't have imagined such an experience. When he could tear his eyes away, he took pictures for himself (one of them hangs in his office today), and when they got back to camp, he took some time to introduce Fossey to techniques of statistical analysis of behavior. Hinde could see that she actually was not much advanced beyond Schaller's research of eight years earlier, but he had the good sense to keep it to himself. He urged her to come to Cambridge. He was certain her long-range study would prove of major scientific value, but it was critical that she approach her subject properly.

It was the self-taught naturalist Alan Root who gave Fossey the harder time about her science—or lack of it. He was disturbed by her objective of moving ever closer to the gorillas, and he quarreled with her interpretation of the need for habituation. The point was not to touch the animals, or to be touched by them, but to *observe* them. To do this properly, Root said, the observer should strive to become neutral—to fade into the foliage. Once the gorillas had accepted her presence, she should become as unobtrusive as an antelope. The point was to observe *natural* behavior, not to affect it by her presence.

Schaller had stayed at the edge of a group, standing or sitting quietly, just watching.

Joan Root (who had stayed home to sort out their various projects) heard later from Alan about Fossey's strong-minded reaction. "She had her own ideas by then," Joan says. "She had been there more than a year, doing it her own way, without any experience at all. She tended to approach the problem of habituation as though she were another gorilla. We both thought she had more guts than anybody we'd ever known, but it was almost as though she had to do it that way because she needed the gorillas to like her. Alan is very forceful, but she was very forceful, too. He thought he had got nowhere with her."

Hinde, of course, had had no experience whatsoever, so he stayed out of it. But what he could see—and would remember most about that first visit—was something that had nothing at all to do with the emerging theories of gorilla primatology. What Hinde was struck by was Alan Root's sensitive evaluation of Fossey's considerable strengths and one unmistakable weakness. Hinde had the distinct impression that Root knew Fossey better than anyone.

"We were following a gorilla group up one of the volcanos," Hinde says, "and there were long deep gullies running up the slopes, some of them quite steep. The group crossed to the side away from us, leaving us the choice of going back down and coming up again or climbing a quite steep cliff on the other side. Alan said, 'You go first, Robert, then Dian, then me. Then if anything happens, we'll be all right.' I hadn't the faintest idea what he meant. When I got to the top of the cliff, just above her, Dian froze. Alan was pushing her from below, and I was on top of the cliff, pulling her. I got her by her blue jeans and her fly popped open, but somehow we managed to get her on top of the cliff. She was frozen for a few minutes, and then she was all right. Afterwards, Alan told me she had a phobia about heights."

She had told Root no more about it than she had to; he had seen it in her in Kabara. When gorillas traveled over a log bridging a ravine, she would, instead of following them, go down one side and climb up the other, her progress so impeded she would sometimes lose her quarry.

Where her acrophobia came from, at least in part, was an experience she had at a ranch in Bolinas, California. In 1951 Fossey spent a weekend with a friend named Sally DuBray, a classmate at college, and they decided to go riding at the Bolinas ranch, whose western-most boundary was the Pacific Ocean. DuBray recalls that painful sequence of events Fossey had thereafter shut out of her mind.

When they got to the ranch, it was drizzling, too wet for riding; and so they decided to drive around instead. On a narrow dirt road, which followed the contour of a hill and emerged at the top of a cliff overlooking the sea, they stopped to admire the view. As they sat there, with DuBray behind the wheel and Fossey in the passenger seat on the side toward the sea, the muddy road began to give way, the car sliding slowly toward the edge. In a fraction of a second, they realized the only way out of the car was through the driver's door; but the instant DuBray was out, Fossey's weight could be enough to tip the car over. Fossey froze. DuBray grabbed her wrist, leaped out, and yanked Fossey after her. The car disappeared over the edge.

"I think," Hinde says, "it was a great testament to Dian's courage that she was up on that mountain all the time, and all that time she had that awful fear of heights."

After Hinde left, Root stayed a few days longer. But the rain hampered his filming, and so did Fossey, whose jaw was so swollen she wouldn't let him take pictures of her until it went down. But they talked on, and they agreed on two things: that she must get her teeth fixed (she was now willing to have all of them pulled if that would enhance the future of her mission); and that the worst thing possible would be to leave the camp untended. Already close, in their few days alone together, they became closer; and before they parted, they slept together. Later, when Fossey desperately needed someone she could confide in about an emotional misery so crushing she could not handle it alone, she turned to Root. "I think it was because of this closeness she had with Alan when I wasn't along," says Joan Root. "At such a time, I think a woman can get closer to a man friend than a woman friend if they have already established that closeness."

In any event, Fossey took deep satisfaction in the fact that Root admired her, not only for what she was able to do, but for what she was willing to do. She planned now to go to the States in September, and Root assured her that before she left Karisoke he would find someone in Nairobi to run her camp while she was gone. He and Joan would return there later—when, he couldn't say—to resume their filming.

A week after his departure, Fossey received letters from both Alan and Joan. Alan's began with an apology. He hadn't been able to find anyone yet to relieve her, though he had got off a message to a photographer in Richard Leakey's camp near the northern frontier, a man named Bob Campbell. The reason he hadn't been able to do more was that "three days after getting back from Rwanda I was bitten in the right hand by a puff adder. For the first 24 hours it was touch and go whether I kicked the bucket or not."

Joan's letter was more informative:

I was going to write you but then . . . I forgot everything. For the first week he was very ill, and for the second week he has been recovering gradually, but his arm is still swollen and the hand is in a dreadful state, and it will be a long time before he can use it. . . . We had flown up to Joy Adamson's camp in the Meru for the day, and we found a huge puff adder lying in wait near a path near her camp. Alan caught it and Joy photographed him milking it. Then while she changed the film, he let it go, and then when he went to catch it again it bit his hand. As Alan had already milked it, we hoped that there was no poison left, but there obviously was because he was in a pretty bad way by the time we had flown him to Nairobi and we reached the hospital 2½ hours later. . . . With the help and influence of Dr. Leakey, we arranged for a specialist to fly up from South Africa.

Two weeks later word came from the Roots that Bob Campbell was available to come to Karisoke and would arrive on September 20. A methodical and punctual man, Campbell arrived as scheduled. Fossey reserved judgment. Campbell was very British in manner, quiet and reserved, with a clipped accent. He spoke Swahili fluently. And he was tall. He seemed comfortable among the Africans, and when she took him out the next day he showed no hesitation in moving in close to the gorillas, even though this was his first contact. *Too* close, she told him sharply, when they were back in camp. Otherwise, there was nothing very remarkable about him, certainly nothing that would indicate he would one day become the most important man in her life.

Before dark a porter came up from below with the mail, which included a cable. She read it in Campbell's presence and without a word retired to her cabin. It had come from Louis Leakey:

DEEPLY REGRET TO ADVISE FOLLOWING CABLE RECEIVED 18TH QUOTE FATHER SUICIDE FUNERAL TOMORROW GRIEVING LOVE KAY UNQUOTE

17

CAMPBELL

R. I. M. Campbell was an officer and a gentleman, and had seen action as a major in the King's African Rifles during the Mau Mau uprising. He knew more about what Fossey was trying to do than she did, but he was too polite to say so. He had been tracking and filming wild animals for fourteen years. A modest man with a touch of vanity, Campbell was nearing forty, and wore a beret to hide his bald patch.

Campbell believed things ought to be done right. It is fair enough to say he was fastidious. Cleanliness discouraged infection. If you were dependent upon equipment you should be certain that it functioned properly. In the bush there were too many things to cope with you couldn't count on. From his pressure lamp to his Land Rover, Campbell saw to it that his things worked. As Jonathan Scott, one of his young associates put it, "Campbell was like his Land Rover, tuned to perfection, ready to go." While he might not be an inspired filmmaker like Root, he was a welcome addition to any wildlife expedition. Before turning to photography, he had been a Jaguar dealer; he knew all about vehicle machinery. When a wheel fell off in the desert, Campbell knew how to put it back on.

He had been in the desert, at Koobi Fora on the northern frontier of Kenya, working with Richard Leakey, when Alan Root and Louis Leakey had sent word up asking if he would come out and spell Fossey. (By now, Richard had resigned from his partnership with Alan Root in the safari business to dig fossils full time.) Campbell and his wife, Heather, were old friends of the Roots, and of the entire Leakey family. The sculptor who cut the statue of Leakey which stands today in front of the National Museum in Nairobi worked from a Bob Campbell photograph. Heather Campbell, a veterinary surgeon, looked after the Leakeys' animals. From the time the younger Leakey began to pull away from his father's knee, Campbell had accompanied him on his digs. As Richard had succeeded—to the point now that the National Geographic was funding him, too—so had Campbell, whose pictures would appear in *National Geographic* magazine and whose films Richard would use in his lectures. In a sense, it was all in the family.

Before Campbell had time to settle in, Fossey was taking pains to show him the proper way to track the gorillas. He was listening and watching attentively, even though he knew what she was going to say before she said it. She quickly caught on to that fact. Few words passed between them.

When she introduced him to her staff, he took no particular notice of her open reference to them as "wogs." He accepted the epithet as less derogatory than she may have intended. In Kenya, the term was short for "Gollywog," the colonialist term for a long-haired race of people in the northeast. (Not too prudent to use it since independence.) But Campbell didn't worry much about Fossey's Africans. He had been in Africa since he was ten months old, the child of a British soldier-settler. He knew how to talk to the Africans and how to work with them. He was certainly not intimidated by them. Nor did he feel that they should be intimidated by him. Each, so far as Campbell was concerned, knew exactly what to expect of the other.

On his second day at Karisoke, after Fossey got the cable telling of her father's suicide and was obviously distressed, Campbell had done the only thing an outsider could decently do. He made himself scarce. He busied himself about the camp, seeing to his tent and equipment, making sure everything was in order for his stay. At that time, he was not especially impressed by Fossey, he would later recall. After Jane Goodall's early success with the chimpanzee, a lot of young women had come out to Africa trying to emulate her, hoping for some research project with one wild animal or another. In those days, the field was wide open, and many of these women were attracted by Louis Leakey. This one was older, hardworking, imposing because of her stature. The most remarkable thing about her, he reckoned, was simply the fact that she was there.

Nearly two years after Fossey left Louisville for Africa, she returned to the States to take care of her teeth and renew old friendships. She considered her return a triumphant one—and so did everyone else. She had succeeded in changing her life. At the Henry Hotel, where she spent most of her time, she was received joyously. Everyone was vastly relieved she had survived the terrors of darkest Africa.

In California she visited briefly with the Prices and got her teeth fixed. Much to Kitty Price's relief, Dian made no mention of her father's suicide (she seems to have discussed it with almost no one; whatever her feelings were about George Fossey's death, she kept them to herself), although she did take back to Africa some family jewelry he had left her. In Washington, she delivered a research report which was well received by various officials at the National Geographic. While she was there, a press conference was held to announce her accomplishments to the nation and the magazine asked her to do an article about her experiences. In London, on her way back, she stopped off to see Robert Hinde.

Hinde was full of enthusiasm for the work of his prospective student. She had begun to send him copies of her field reports to Leakey, and he was eager to get her trained in formal research analysis. When could she enroll at Cambridge? She needed solid academic grounding to guarantee her work got the proper attention. Fossey tried to explain how complicated her circumstances had become. Just to get away for a few weeks had been a major undertaking. She needed help on a permanent basis. She certainly could not come to Cambridge until there was someone available to run her camp. A census of the animals had become imperative.

Fossey estimated that the population of three groups Schaller had identified and counted had dropped off by half in the eight years since Schaller left. If this was true for the whole of the population, the mountain gorilla had become even more seriously imperiled, adding to the threat of genetic drift, in which there are too few animals to support a viable population (the phenomenon argues against the zoo as a satisfactory haven for endangered species). She wanted to see a research station established on each of the six mountains of the gorilla habitat, but for the moment she would settle for one able-bodied census worker.

Not only was Hinde most understanding, he said he would do what he could to help find her an assistant. He knew he couldn't press Cambridge for the funding, since the university had no money for such purposes. Fossey said the National Geographic might be willing; they were now her sole benefactor and insisted strongly on exclusivity. The talk drifted. She was now a week behind schedule and anxious to get back where she belonged.

Returning to Karisoke, she told Campbell, after a thorough look around, that she was very pleased with his management of her camp. Although coming from Fossey this was high praise, Campbell received it with some diffidence. He had only done what was expected of him.

(He had got some 4,000 feet of footage, too, which he was sending on to the National Geographic.) Campbell was a professional who, under any circumstances, would not have done less. When they parted, neither of them dreamed they would see each other again—although Campbell itched for another shot at the gorillas, which had fascinated him.

They stayed in touch. The typewriter was indispensable to Fossey, and she corresponded with anyone she thought had the slightest understanding of what she was doing. She wrote to Campbell about the fifteen poachers and their dogs who had chased a water buffalo right into the center of Group 5. She had been so mad she put on one of her Halloween masks, and with a water gun in one hand, her camera in the other, and a tear gas canister in her pocket, she chased after them, scattering them in all directions. Then poachers kidnapped her boxer dog, Cindy—a Polish count had given it to her a few months before—and she had taken eight Tutsi cattle as hostage, spreading the word through her men that she would kill one cow a day until her dog was returned. She got it back by nightfall. On Christmas Day, she had observed a copulation in Group 5. (In a letter to Hinde, she said that if anything came of it she was going to name the infant Jesus.)

Otherwise, things were going as she believed they should. She knew that everyone who cared about what she was doing was working earnestly in her behalf, and without compensation. (So was she; Leakey had promised her a salary but she had never got one, nor would she ever.) Even with his bad hand, Alan Root was planning to return. Hinde was looking for an assistant/census worker for her, and so was Leakey, who had written he would scour the U.S. for her. And the National Geographic (though late again with her check) had the financial resources to assure things being done right. And they were, she thought, solidly behind her.

Many years afterward, an astute observer of Dian Fossey saw what

207

she believed to be a key to her later pathological behavior. Whatever befell her, she seemed incapable of learning from experience—of changing her behavior in consequence of the reversals she suffered. But this was a misreading based on the observer's inadequate knowledge of Fossey's early years in Africa. Closer to the mark was Rosamond Carr, who believed there was always a reason behind what Fossey did. And in the winter of 1969, Fossey suffered enough reversals to provide her plenty of reasons to change. Everything and everybody suddenly came down on her at once. And from these unhappy experiences she *did* change: she began to distrust those who were the most eager to help her.

Undoubtedly the mail delivery in that remote part of the world was at least partially to blame. Even cables came through the postal service, such as it was. Fossey once ran a check within a single month of the letters going out and expected in at Karisoke. She counted twenty-four of them lost and gone forever. Trying to climb out of the doghouse, Leakey claimed he had a letter returned to him in March 1969 that he had sent her in the Congo in July 1967!

Counting mail delivery as the wild card, then, this was the hand Fossey was dealt in the first week of February 1969: She was still awaiting definite word from Alan Root. If his hand didn't recover sufficiently, someone else had to be found. For reasons unclear to her, Leakey didn't want to use Bob Campbell, and so she considered Campbell out of the question whether he was interested in coming back or not. If Root proved unavailable, Leakey said he would find someone else. Fine, she wrote back; she would leave the decision to him. She also wrote the National Geographic inquiring about the availability of funding for the graduate work everyone seemed so eager for her to have at Cambridge. Hinde had located a possible candidate for a census worker, a well-qualified man named Wilson.

In the second week of February, a letter came from Campbell, pulsing with enthusiasm. He had just received a cable from the National Geographic asking if he would be interested in accepting an assignment to photograph her work in place of Alan Root. Was she aware he had been asked to do this? He hoped so, for he was eager to take it on. He would be with her a year at least, giving the project 98 percent of his time. In the same day's mail there was a cable from Leakey's secretary in Nairobi. A man named Shackford was ready to work for Fossey as census assistant. When would it be convenient for him to come to Karisoke?

Campbell to photograph? Had Root been told that Campbell was replacing him? Shackford to census? Who was Shackford? What happened to Wilson? Who was making these decisions, and why wasn't she consulted? Then word came from Rwandan park officials that two infant gorillas had been captured with government approval to supply a zoo in Cologne. The payment was a Land Rover and a nominal sum of money; the government must be in a very bad way. The gorillas seemed ill, and the park conservator wondered if she might lend a hand.

By now Fossey knew that the adults in a gorilla group would fight to the death to defend an infant. For each of the infant gorillas, she suspected that many adults had been killed. (She later determined a total of eighteen lost to take them.) What was the Rwandan government doing, capturing its own precious gorillas? It was a direct violation of the international park treaty. What was the Cologne Zoo doing, ordering their capture? This was an outrage, a crime against the principles of international conservation! Of course she would look after them—and she would pay the conservator not to interfere with her care of them. By the time she retrieved them, both were half dead. Through Leakey's office came advice from Heather Campbell, the veterinarian, whose only sources relating to gorillas were zoo books. Fossey must become their surrogate mother, she said. And this Fossey did, tending them night and day as though they were her own babies, feeding them, cuddling them, sleeping with them in her cabin, covered with their diarrhea.

Meanwhile, the letters kept coming. She was steaming at Leakey.

209

She accused him of "mother knows best" manipulation of her interests, showing no concern at all with what she might think of his choices. She blasted Leakey to Hinde and to Campbell. She complained to the Roots about all parties involved. She was being barraged by various demands for data. She was expected to provide computerized reports of behavior, tape recordings of vocalizations, photographs of unusual events—and meanwhile, the dwindling gorilla population went uncounted. On top of all this, the survival of two infants had become her sole responsibility. She was expected to do all this work but felt she had the least to say.

In the third week of February, a letter came from Campbell—the longest he'd ever written to anyone other than his wife, he says. He had been in touch with a trusted contact at the National Geographic. Trying to untangle it all, he managed instead to pour a little more fuel on the fire. His N.G. contact had confided that Leakey wanted to replace Root with a young man of dubious qualifications whose father was prepared to finance some of Leakey's projects. This created some confusion among the N.G. people, who hadn't expected an all-new candidate. As it happened, Richard Leakey was there at the time, and his advice was asked. Why not use his friend Campbell, Richard had said. He already knew the territory. "Richard and his father then had a bit of a row, which ended by Dr. Leakey reluctantly giving in," Campbell wrote. As to the man Shackford, Campbell had seen the fellow in Nairobi. He had said that he expected his payment for assisting Fossey to come out of her grant. "Don't blow up," Campbell said, correctly anticipating her reaction. "I'm sure all this can be sorted out." Finally, Campbell concluded helpfully, "It would appear that the N.G. has very little knowledge about your research. Leakey seems to be running the show without reference to you, and the N.G. meekly do as he suggests without considering what it is they want, let alone what you want."

And then came word from Leonard Carmichael at the National Geographic regarding her request for expenses at Cambridge. Where could she have got the impression National Geographic funds were available for such purposes? Out of the question.

That did it. Fossey wrote Hinde that Cambridge was out. She ignored Leakey. And she turned her full attention to the survival of the infant gorillas.

As Campbell had optimistically predicted, it would all get sorted out. Eventually a letter would arrive from Leakey in Washington suggesting to Fossey (not telling her) that Campbell might make a suitable replacement for Root, who had to go to England for further treatment on his hand. Was Campbell acceptable to her? If she didn't want him, she certainly didn't have to take him. He had thought the man Shackford, who was already in Nairobi, would make a good census worker. He reminded her that she had said the choice was up to him. But of course he wanted her to be satisfied.

Leakey's letter was dated February 5, the same day Campbell had received his cable from the National Geographic. Leakey had been the victim of slow mail (although it was true he made no mention of the potential backer's son as his candidate for photographer, or of his row with Richard over Campbell). Anyway, by now the man Wilson had withdrawn his candidacy, and as for the Cambridge business, this in the end would get straightened out, too. Hinde would dig up the money from the Wenner-Grenn Foundation in Germany, and Fossey would go to Cambridge for the winter term, beginning in January 1970.

But her greater grievance was not to be relieved. It was both her responsibility and her intention to return the two infant gorillas to their native habitat. She had weaned them from soft bananas and liquids to their own foodstuffs, and somehow, miraculously, they had responded to her treatment. In the midst of the chaos over her immediate future, she managed to launch a mail campaign against the Cologne Zoo, enlisting Leakey, Hinde, and Melville Payne of the National Geographic to assert their influence in the conservation

211

community to keep the animals where they belonged, in the Virungas. Cologne received letters of protest from Harold Coolidge of the New York Zoological Society, R. F. S. Fitter of London's Fauna and Flora Preservation Society, Bernhard Grzimek of the Frankfurt Zoological Society, and Peter Scott of the World Wildlife Fund—all of which achieved nothing. Cologne would not be swayed; and Rwanda ordered Fossey to ship the animals out the minute they were ready to travel. (They survived nine years in the Cologne Zoo, dying within a month of each other in 1978.)

After the experience with the infant gorillas, Fossey never had much confidence in conservation agencies, which practiced what she came to dismiss scornfully as "theoretical conservation." The sale of these two animals to a zoo encouraged illicit traffic in endangered species. It was illegal and immoral, and there was evidently nothing anyone could do to stop it. Fossey became convinced she would have to work outside the boundaries of conventional wildlife conservation. She had to practice "active conservation," which to her meant waging a war against forces outside Rwanda as well as inside. She would do whatever she deemed necessary to keep any and all enemies of the diminishing mountain gorilla out of the Parc National des Volcans.

Leakey, as always, commiserated with her, and she by now had forgiven his transgressions. He wrote to assure her that he was still on the case. In San Diego he had found a young man (better than Shackford) to assist her with the census. He was a graduate student in animal behavior at San Diego State, big, rugged, and mature, a former construction worker. His faculty advisers spoke highly of him, and he seemed eager to help her out. His name was Michael Burkhart. She needn't worry about where the money would come from. Leakey had arranged for the National Geographic to fund him. Burkhart ought to be there early in July. But if for any reason he didn't work out, she shouldn't hesitate to sack him.

In early April 1969, Campbell had arrived to begin his photographic coverage of her study. He had set up his tent thirty yards from her cabin, on the other side of the creek, under a Hagenia tree. He hadn't been there very long before Fossey decided she couldn't stand him.

The trouble with Campbell (she wrote to the Roots) was that he was on her back all the time, looking for conversation, getting on her nerves. He expected to be fed three meals a day, and he was in the cabin every five minutes "to warm up in front of the fire." He refused to go off to photograph the gorillas without her, because, he said, the National Geographic wanted her in his pictures. Even when the sun was out and the gorillas of Group 5 were no more than twenty minutes away, he was still in her cabin, sitting on his duff. It was about to drive her crazy.

Bob Campbell wears glasses now. Otherwise, he looks much as he does in the pictures from his days with Fossey. He appears very much the professional, with a manner that seems less that of a wildlife specialist than an academic or cleric. His voice is soft; he is deferentially correct and even in informal conversation works at being precise. His restrained nature shows in his face. Little about his past is inaccessible. He has carefully filed away logs, diaries, film footage. He is as finicky and methodical as Fossey described him.

Heather Campbell is a cordial woman with searching eyes, as soft-spoken as her husband, comfortable in his company even as he speaks of his affair with another woman. But perhaps this is because so many years have passed since that time.

Except for the two extended occasions when Fossey left the mountain to attend Cambridge, and her short leaves in Nairobi, Campbell was with her constantly from April 1969 through March 1972. From the time of her arrival in Louisville in 1955 until the day of her death in 1985, this was the closest anyone would *ever* get to Dian Fossey.

Since leaving Karisoke so many years ago, Campbell has had nothing to say about Fossey other than to express his admiration for her.

In an October 1987 letter, he said he would not be speaking his piece now except for the appearance of various accounts of her life (including the film *Gorillas in the Mist,* which he considers to be more fiction than fact). "In light of [these] revelations I am not so reluctant to hold on to what is essentially private information that, as far as I am concerned—and I'm sure Dian would have felt the same—was never intended for public consumption. On the other hand, I wish to correct false information already given and misconceptions that stem from it."

When Campbell arrived at Karisoke, not long before Fossey was forced to surrender the infant gorillas, she was in a highly emotional state, bitter and angry over the failure of overseas organizations to help her get the animals back into the wild. She was abusive toward the Africans and curt in her manner toward Campbell, alternating between violent outbursts of temper and fits of crying. Campbell was terribly embarrassed by this, for all of them. But he helped her with the animals however he could. When the time came to crate the gorillas up and ship them out, he supervised their trip down the mountain—to spare her the ordeal. It was a horrible defeat for her, an awful moment. "I ran out of the cabin," Fossey wrote in her book, "ran through the meadows of our countless walks, and ran deep into the forest until I could run no more."

Immediately afterward, she and Campbell went into the field. It was her first opportunity for research since the infants had arrived. She didn't like having him along, and he knew it. "This was the first she'd had of anyone hanging around her constantly. She couldn't even sit down in the bushes and have a pee if she wanted to." Even more disconcerting for her was her awareness that Campbell knew something about proper research procedures. "She knew that *I* knew she was far from making much progress. And here I have to say that Dian became very good at exaggerating things that happened. Very often there was little going on. When something did occur, she would write her report to make it as exciting as possible." But he expressed no criticism of her methods. He did his best to do as he was told.

But when he became aware that she was testing him, the tension between them quickened. Campbell was no amateur, and it was clear enough that he knew what he was doing. Nevertheless, he felt her attention always fixed on him. She evaluated him constantly, and by a most singular criterion. "She tested my patience—my ability to do nothing. She was very good at this. She could sit for hours in the cold and the rain, and sometimes up there, the temperature could drop to freezing. At first it was quite a shock to me. When it was obvious nothing was happening with the animals, she watched *me* to see if I altered my position to see if something *was* happening." By the middle of May, Campbell was ready to quit.

He stayed with it because he had committed himself to the job, but it was more demanding than he had ever expected. "The problem was to carry enough clothes to keep yourself reasonably warm, but then you had to throw them off when you were climbing. It was a mixture between heat and sweat and inactivity, and the cold inevitably creeping in. You just had to learn to ignore it." Eventually he got used to it, and came to appreciate the toll it took on Fossey, especially when they had to climb.

"She wasn't in good shape, her lungs were unequal to the task of getting the oxygen she needed for her muscles. Her face would get drawn and she would puff like the devil going up—her whole face would change. I avoided shooting her at those times. At ten thousand feet, even if you're fit, it's hard—I was reasonably tough and quite thin when I went up there, but I lost a lot of weight. I went out at 148 pounds and came back at 135 two months later, just pure sinew. If you have to carry things and then climb to eleven thousand, it is *really* hard. On a rock slope she would turn rigid and start cussing. But with me along she'd make herself do it anyway. She could make herself do anything."

The strain between them didn't go away. Fossey remained just as tough, abrasive, and distant as she was when he first came. But Campbell found his own view of her gradually tempered by the extraordinary circumstances. "For anyone who hadn't been there, you simply couldn't equate Dian's problems with Jane Goodall's at Gombe. The altitude, the weather, the walking conditions, the temperament of the gorillas, and many other things made this study a particularly hard one. She was constantly being bothered by people who came up without any invitation or warning, expecting her to take them out and show them the gorillas. They also expected to be put up and fed. These were mostly local people who had friends, or diplomatic people from Kigali." With the U.S. ambassadors, whose support she needed, and who came and went every two years or so, she had little choice. She cultivated them and went out of her way to make them comfortable. But each time she did, it cost her time and energy.

"What she cooked for herself was what she could get—most often tough meat from down below, which she would grind into hamburger because of her bad teeth. She never had any money and her finances weighed heavily on her mind all the time. She was extremely frugal—never wasted a penny. When she shopped for curtains for her cabin she got the best material at the cheapest cost. Nobody back in the West could ever understand what it was like to be without cash in Africa." Throughout her entire time in Rwanda, no one in authority at the National Geographic Society visited her camp to see the nature of her problems, and her funding was never advanced for more than a year at a time. "She was always in agony over this part of it," Campbell says. "Her installments didn't arrive when they were due." Campbell lent her what he could, but she was mortified at having to ask.

Campbell had been eating at her table, too; but by early June he had got the message. Back in Nairobi for a couple of weeks, he gathered everything he might need to be completely independent of her, most especially food supplies. When he returned, he began to prepare his own meals, staying away from her. He kept to himself in his tent, working on his equipment or listening to his shortwave radio. After he decided not to try to socialize with her, he noticed that things between them began to improve. She started to relax about his behavior in the presence of her gorillas. He hung back, even though he couldn't get his shots, to avoid disturbing the activity of the animals. He followed her lead. She realized now that he knew it was *her* study. He agreed not to publish a book until she had published first (it would take her twelve years), and soon a sort of truce prevailed between them. Moreover, help was now on the way. Leakey's new man, Burkhart, was coming to make the census, and that would lighten the load, even though he would be situated in another part of the park. She would have time to work on the *National Geographic* article, and Campbell's pictures were intended to illustrate it. So they had got on with it. His job was to make her look good.

This wasn't easy. "She did not pay much attention to her appearance," Campbell says, "and the stress of living and working at so high an altitude showed strongly in her face. She considered herself to be too large and tall, and she was exasperated by a body that gave her far too much trouble. Her expressed wish to be 'stacked like Dolly Parton' stemmed from the fact that she was very flat-chested, a condition she hated with a passion. Off the mountains, though, with rest, makeup, and feminine clothing, Dian could transform herself into a startlingly attractive woman. But in Rwanda she did not often make the change. I had great difficulty with her looks in the field—in many situations where there was no possibility of preparation, she looked terrible."

For this reason—and others—Bob Campbell had little sexual interest in Dian Fossey. And the feeling was mutual; he wasn't her type. Their relationship might have remained platonic throughout Campbell's long stay had it not been for a new problem—a problem only Bob Campbell could solve.

•   •   •

There are three versions of this story—Campbell's, Fossey's, and Burkhart's. But all of them agree on one point: Michael Burkhart didn't work out. Campbell says that poor Burkhart arrived at the wrong time. Fossey had had another siege of disasters. Her dog Cindy had been kidnapped again (later returned) and all her best transparencies from the Congo had been lost in the mail. To top it off, the night before Burkhart's arrival, her cabin had been broken into. All her money was taken and, much worse, all the jewelry left her by her father. This disaster occurred on the night of July 20, just as the spacecraft *Apollo 11* had set down on the surface of the moon. Campbell was listening to the coverage over his shortwave radio from the warmth of his bed.

"This chap had just stepped out of the capsule and was saying, 'One giant step,' or whatever, and Dian banged on my tent yelling, 'I've just been robbed!'"

Members of her African staff were suspected, and the next morning they had all gone down to report the theft to the police—and to meet Michael Burkhart, who was coming in at the airport. Burkhart, a bearded, burly man, never quite got his bearings. After several days of indoctrination by Fossey and Campbell, he was moved to the other side of the mountain, where he was expected to count the number of gorillas in the area.

"He was set up to work on his own," Campbell observes with some sympathy, "and I think that was fatal. He wasn't able to stick with his own company. He felt lonely, and he was said to be smoking marijuana and not doing his job. He couldn't give Dian any information that was really accurate. He didn't know how to assemble reports. He couldn't even describe where he'd been." Michael Burkhart rapidly became a problem.

In *Gorillas in the Mist,* Fossey refers to Burkhart, without naming him, as an example of her many problems with student assistants ("A steady stream of porters . . . brought me distressing reports of the young man's activities, many of which were not related to census work. I was left with no alternative but to send him back to America"). But in a series of letters to Leakey, she really let loose. She said she had worked her guts out setting this "idiot" up, and all he could say was, "Nobody ever tells me anything." She said he spent all his time sleeping, tinkering with his camera and radio, and "taking trips" with the ingredients of what he called his "girl scout kit." He was making no progress on the census. Once again, she accused Leakey of letting her down.

Her complaints about Burkhart continued in a later letter, in which she quoted segments from Burkhart's reports: "One elephant carries its young over its neck"; "nearly pissed on by a silverback"; "I split open an African's scalp"; and "dead man buried near drinking water."

Leakey cabled back that clearly Burkhart had to go.

Burkhart's account of his unhappy interlude with Fossey begins with a visit by Leakey to San Diego State University, where Burkhart was a graduate student working in anthropology, animal behavior, and ecology. Burkhart sought Leakey out just as Fossey had, convincing him that he would make a fine field worker. He was quiet, patient, six foot two, and plenty rugged. "I was pretty tough," he says. "Easygoing but tough. You could scratch a match on me."

Burkhart had his appendix out and his teeth fixed, and flew to Nairobi. He had some early misgivings about Leakey which remain vivid in his memory. "When I was trying to talk with him about my safari," Burkhart says, "he was trying to track down some potatoes for somebody up north. I said, 'How about you assigning this petty shit to the locals and let's you and me talk?'" When Burkhart left for Kigali, Leakey gave him some cheese to take along and a 100-foot steel tape for making surveys. "The man was daft," Burkhart says.

Nor was he prepared for what he found at Karisoke. "They take an innocent surfer boob from San Diego—you know, to *me* a wildlife adventure was skin-diving for *abalone,* okay?—and they put me in with Dian Fossey, this tough-talking, chain-smoking, mean son of a

219

bitch. She says, 'Somebody stole my jewelry. Get out of my way.' I was absolutely dumbstruck. Hey, bitch, I just came nine thousand miles, you know? And she all but pushed me aside and said, 'I'll give you some time later.' "

Burkhart does not recall the indoctrination phase spoken of by Campbell, but he remembers Campbell very well. "She called him 'Twinkletoes' to me," he says, "and she didn't respect him or like him." He says that Campbell spent all his time in his tent and that Fossey considered him to be homosexual. (In her letters to Leakey and Hinde, she also said she thought Burkhart was a homosexual.)

Another significant memory is the day Fossey took Burkhart to the other side of the mountain where he was to work. "Okay now," she said to him, "we're going to set up your own place, and here's how you study gorillas." Then the instructions began. "She took me out and spent the whole afternoon counting gorilla turds," he recalls. "Why the hell she did this didn't make any sense to me. The only thing that mattered was that she get a grasp of how many gorillas were up there. I told her she was going about it the wrong way. She should track them with poachers' dogs, or better still, with motor-cycles.

"I said, 'Dian, this is nuts, man. You call up Yamaha and Honda and you get them a deal that says you'll publicize their equipment, and they'll give them to you for free. And you can do five days' work in four hours! You don't have to walk a half a mile an hour up a vertical hillside. You sit on a motorcycle, and *putt-putt-putt,* you're there. They'll scare hell out of poachers. Nobody can get away from a motorcycle!' "

But as far as he was concerned, Burkhart says, he was on the mushroom patrol. He was out there, lost, for thirty days with his three African assistants. He had put in a garden, growing "killer black Congo marijuana" among other things, but he still wasn't getting enough to eat. His weight fell from 195 to 145. Meanwhile, he was sending Fossey reports, in which he urged her to use dogs, tracking collars, and motorcycles. But increasingly he became convinced that she was deranged. Finally he hiked over the volcano to her camp to have it out.

"Dian was drunk and belligerent. And then I looked down, and that bitch had a stack of aerial photographs. I held them up to her, and I said, 'Listen, you. I've been lost for thirty fucking days and you've got aerial photographs of my study area? What's goin' on?' She said she needed to use them every day for her study count.

"I said, 'Bullshit! You've been blowin' smoke up my ass.' And then she said, 'Leakey wants to see you.' "

That suited him fine, Burkhart replied. He wanted to tell Leakey how crazy and incompetent she was. Then he could come back and run the camp right.

At the museum in Nairobi, Leakey's secretary tried to head him off, but he saw Leakey sneaking out a back door and cornered him.

" 'Dr. Leakey,' I said, 'we have to have a talk. Dian is having a mental breakdown. She's ruining the gorilla study project. She has alienated the Africans, the park rangers, and a couple of Rwandan officials, and she is smartass and hostile with them. Look, we've got to build a hotel. We have to get people coming in here. We have to get publicity. I want to get Lindblad [operator of adventure tours] up here, have people come look at the gorillas. We have to appease the local people, get them food and medicine. They have this horrible internecine war up there where the Hutus kill the Tutsis, and then after twenty years the Tutsis get together and kill the Hutus. Just like Vietnam, or any other place where the country is terribly crowded. The only thing that works is death. That's population control. And this is one of the reasons why I study gorillas. I want to find out what went wrong in human origins.'

"Anyway, I pitched Leakey and all the time he was back-pedaling out the door."

What did he say to all this?

" 'Well, I have to go, and I'm really busy, and that's nice,' and 'er, ah, um-hum,' bullshit, bullshit, 'ah, er, I have to go.' And he closed the door in my face. And that was the last time I saw the bastard."

Burkhart left Kenya for Israel, where he spent some time in a kibbutz, trying to calm his rattled nerves.

Campbell's account differs sharply from Burkhart's. He says that Fossey wasn't drinking in those days, except on occasion, and that he never saw her drunk. "When Burkhart was called back to our camp by Dian, she let me tell him he was fired, because he would take it better coming from me. I think he might have had a shouting match with her if I hadn't been there. He was a strong man. If he had let himself lose his temper, it would have been a disaster for him as well. But he also knew what he had failed to do, and with me there, he just had to back down because he wasn't prepared to go at the two of us, particularly me, who knew what had been going on. So there was a witness to his lack of effort, and his failure to get on with what was expected of him."

Most likely it was around this time that "Campbell" became "Bob" in the letters Fossey wrote to Rosamond Carr. Campbell believes this is likely, for one night not long thereafter, he was in his tent, half asleep, when a commotion at the entrance caused him to think someone might be breaking in.

" 'It's me,' I heard her say. It was a bit embarrassing because it was in the dark of the tent.

" 'Dian, no,' I said. 'You don't do this.'

" 'I never had a man say that to me before,' she said.

" 'No, I'm sorry, I can't,' I said. 'I just can't do this.'

"Then she just went out again in a bit of a huff—angry. The embarrassment of it took a little while to wear off, but she spoke of it the next day. She said she wanted to come thank me for all the help I'd given.

"The incident was never again referred to between us. I was in the habit of going over to Dian occasionally, after I'd had my meal—to

222

discuss the next day's work, and so on. Sometimes I stopped to have a drink and enjoy the warmth of the cabin fire. I was by now, after some three months in the mountains, beginning to like Dian much better. We had some pleasant, wide-ranging talks, as I recall—until, on one occasion Dian again decided to make love to me, and I did not resist."

18

THE BEST YEARS OF THEIR LIVES

Despite Bob Campbell's later words, it is certainly true that late 1969 through the spring of 1972 were the best years for both him and Fossey, although for different reasons. Fossey had become accustomed to a cliff-hanger's existence. Tune in for another chapter in the perils of Dian, she would write the Roots. There had never been a time since she left Louisville when her life was serene, or even remotely untroubled. But apart from some reversals during this period, her time with Campbell was productive, and for a while, toward the end of their relationship, she was happy. From the time of Burkhart's departure, Fossey's dependence on Campbell helped soften the part of her that was obdurate and unyielding. It didn't happen right away. For a while, they maintained the distance they both seemed to need. She stayed in her cabin and he remained in his tent, later transferring to a cabin he built himself. Though she might go to bed with him—invite it, even—she did not drop her guard alto-

224

gether. Yet in a slow and cautious way she came to see him differently. Need sharpened her desire. By the time he rode to her rescue again, two years later, she was deeply in love with him and quite at a loss as to what she could do about it.

"Bob had come to her late in her life," says Anita McClellan. "She really didn't want marriage, but she hadn't thought that through. She wanted children and a family, but she didn't want to give up what she was doing. She had had no experience with a man who might share the part of her life that was nonsexual, which was her work, and at the same time be a lover to her in the most romantic way possible. She found this in Bob Campbell, and for her that was a miracle." Her years with him were definitely the best years of her life.

They were for Campbell, too, but not because of Fossey. "I regard the period as a highlight of my filming career," he says. "No other experience in all the time I have spent with wild animals even matches it." He says that his relationship with Fossey gave "a curious twist to events" and "enhanced the general upgrade nature of those years." But that was all. Campbell does not speak of being in love with Fossey. During this time, he acquired some 1,245 hours of gorilla observation, a good part of it on his own. Independently of Fossey, he earned the animals' trust, and like every researcher there before him, was captivated by their intelligent behavior. They were what kept him at Karisoke, along with his commitment to National Geographic to record Fossey's study in depth. As for his relationship with her, their working relationship developed into what he calls "a restrained affair."

"I did not indulge in a passionate romance," he says. "She and I retained our independence, kept to our separate establishments, cooked and ate on our own. For me it was not an affair of the heart. I grew to be very fond of Dian and protective of her, but I did not fall in love with her. Her attitude to me was governed in part by mine to her, and our relations were somewhat formal."

And so they would remain in his mind, and the minds of some

other observers throughout their two and a half years together. People coming into the camp to work for extended periods were unaware of anything between Fossey and the photographer. They were lovers, but their behavior was restrained and detached (except for once when, Rosamond Carr reports, she saw them together at a hotel, and even then they had taken separate rooms). During Fossey's long second stay at Cambridge, from the fall of 1970 through the winter of 1971, even their letters reflected their reserve. They corresponded more as dutiful business associates, signing these perfunctory reports with "Sincerely" or, at most, "As ever."

Even if the affair had been a consuming passion, there would have been little time to indulge it. Fossey had seven hundred pages of field notes (each page representing half an hour of work) to organize for her impending first term at Cambridge in January. Campbell, who would be looking after the camp while she was gone, was scheduled to return to Nairobi for two weeks in December; and there were daily observations, photography coverage, and field reports to maintain until then. Whatever they felt for each other, Dian Fossey and Bob Campbell both had work to do.

Early in November 1969, a poacher's dog came into the camp, sick and bedraggled. "Dian had just got up and was brushing her teeth outside her cabin," Campbell recalls, "when this animal came over wagging its tail. It walked past her into the cabin and then turned around and went straight for her, latched onto her shin and held on for all it was worth. I heard the yells and screams and rushed over to give assistance."

Campbell and the Africans clubbed the animal off her. Rabies was common in the Virungas, and they feared she might have contracted the disease. When she wrote Leakey about it, however, she told him not to worry—she had thirty-three days before the infection would set in. There was plenty of time before foam started messing up her papers. When Leakey cabled that he was air-mailing a fourteen-day series of rabies vaccine, she wrote back that she was no more rabid than usual. She had gone back to work.

In late November, Campbell accompanied her on a four-day trip back to Kabara. Her old camp was every bit as dispiriting as Veschuren had reported. The cabin was gone and poachers' traps were everywhere. Fossey swept away the debris that had gathered about the grave of Carl Akeley, and returned to Karisoke more pessimistic than ever about the future of the animals.

A few days later, sick with the flu, Campbell left for his scheduled two weeks at home in Nairobi. On December 16, Fossey came down with a fever. Maybe it was the flu, maybe not. She worried that she might have rabies after all, and when her temperature reached 105 degrees, she fired her pistol to summon her Africans. They carried her down the mountain on a stretcher to the Ruhengeri hospital, where she stayed one night before checking out and moving to Rosamond Carr's house. But she took the vaccine serum for the whole two-week course of treatment.

During her convalescence, Fossey learned of a new development that worried her more than rabies: the government of Rwanda was excising 10,000 acres from the Parc des Volcans. The land would be distributed among five thousand farming families. Already, elephants were being shot for the safety of the new residents; new roads were being put in. The entire area would be more accessible than ever to the cattle people and the poachers.

And then, after she had recovered and returned to Karisoke, something wonderful happened.

On her last day of field study, the day before she was to leave for Cambridge, Fossey, Campbell, and Alyette de Munck, who had come for the day, all moved to the edge of Group 8 and settled in to observe. (Fossey had by then habituated four gorilla groups—that is, got them used to human presence nearby.) Campbell and de Munck situated themselves in the bowl of a large Hagenia tree, and Fossey crawled past them into camera range. As she lay motionless, she was approached by a young blackback she had named Peanuts. She watched quietly as Peanuts squatted down quite close to her position. He seemed content for the moment, and somewhat indecisive about what to do next. To reassure him, she chewed the same leaves he was eating. She scratched her head. He scratched his head. Slowly she lay back and extended her hand toward him, palm up, resting her arm on the vegetation. She lay this way a few minutes more and then, tentatively, Peanuts reached out and touched her fingers—*touched her hand!*

Campbell started shooting. Fossey didn't move or seek eye contact with the gorilla. She could scarcely believe what had happened. When the animal touched her again, Campbell thought he looked faintly embarrassed. And then he rose to his full height, pounded his chest, and returned to the group. Dian Fossey had been touched by a wild mountain gorilla! What a going-away present, she later wrote Leakey. It was an apotheosis, something she had hoped for since she first arrived in Africa.

At Cambridge, Fossey knew more about gorillas than the people designated to teach her. She was finally gaining some respect for her work. She had been invited by one of the finest universities in the world to study for its highest degree; her first article (twenty pages, with a Campbell photo of her on the cover) had been published in the *National Geographic;* the distinguished Robert Hinde had himself met her at the airport and was personally guiding her into the maze of statistical methodologies. A whole new world was opening to her.

But she didn't much take to Cambridge. Her room smelled of cabbage. There was too much traffic, too many people, and they were always taking coffee breaks. It was cold and gray, and she had no car. She came close to losing her data, all seven hundred pages of it, when Hinde suggested she give it to a secretary to Xerox. The next day the secretary reported that her car, with Fossey's papers inside, had been stolen. Appeals were sent out over the radio and in the newspapers, and a search was made by refuse workers. The car was found abandoned three days later—with the notes intact. But their return did little to lighten her mood. She was already drained by the city.

She had wanted a room somewhere out of town. But none was available and she had wound up in Darwin College, the resident hall for graduates, some of whom were as old as she. But she had no interest in palling around with students, and she made few friends. All of this was predictable enough to anyone who had known Fossey in Louisville or the Virungas. But the truth was, none of it had much to do with her discontent in the winter of 1970. She had discovered that something not so wonderful had happened to her, something very inconvenient.

Though she had taken precautions to prevent it, Dian Fossey was pregnant.

Alan Goodall (no relation to Jane) entered Fossey's life at about this point. A man of modest stature, bespectacled, polite, intense, a graduate student at the University of Liverpool, Goodall was, like Fossey, a bit older than most of the other students. He had put in some time as a schoolteacher. Goodall was about the only good news that came Fossey's way during her first term at Cambridge. Or so she thought at the time.

Goodall had written to Robert Hinde asking assistance in finding him a research project for his doctorate in animal behavior. He had done some work surveying crop pests in North Wales, but was looking for something more challenging. His academic record was good. Hinde sent him along to Fossey, suggesting he might be the man she was looking for, the one all-purpose assistant to help her with observations, census-taking, and running the camp. Fossey was immensely impressed with Goodall. In a pro forma way, she sought Leakey's opinion of him.

As it happened, Louis Leakey was nearby, confined to a hospital bed in London. He agreed to look the man over. Since the sour experience with Burkhart was still an issue between him and Fossey, he was not about to withhold his approval of her choice. Fossey was pleased. Here, at last, was a man she could describe as "honest, forthright, intelligent, completely unself-centered." She even praised his humor, common sense, and maturity. Moreover (perhaps because of her own condition), she thought Goodall should be encouraged to bring along his wife, who was expecting. If Leakey couldn't find the money to make this possible, she would have to dig into her own meager savings. This meant, of course, that she wouldn't be able to come back to Cambridge in the fall.

Leakey, of course, fell for it. He vowed he would find the money somehow. Fossey and Goodall were encouraged enough to begin mapping out a schedule for his forthcoming stay at Karisoke. He would arrive in late July and his wife would join him some weeks later. In mid-August, Fossey would travel to the States for six weeks, and then return to Cambridge for the fall and winter terms, fulfilling her residence requirements. Afterward, she would return to camp to work on her thesis. In the spring of 1971, upon her return, Goodall would go back to England for his two terms, and then come back to work as her deputy for two whole years.

Fossey was very enthusiastic about this plan. Leakey was behind it; so was Hinde; and so was the National Geographic. Here at last was the perfect assistant, cut to order to Fossey's demanding standards.

Fossey was a busy woman during the winter of 1970. Besides occupying herself with the usual activities of any Cambridge first-termer, she had to decide how to handle her unexpected pregnancy. She decided there was nothing else to do but get an abortion.

At the time, she took only two people into her confidence, and only one of them is willing to discuss the matter today. Cynthia Alexander, then a secretary at Cambridge, was a married woman close to Fossey's own age. She was one of the few people at the university who actually became Fossey's friend. It was, however, Fossey's other confidant who arranged the abortion, locating a willing obstetrician and checking her into the nursing home where the procedure was performed. It was, not surprisingly, a traumatic ordeal. Verging on hysteria, Fossey accused the obstetrician of making sexual advances toward her. She was confined for three days. No one except her two friends knew it had happened.

"I have absolutely no doubt that Bob Campbell did *not* know about this," Cynthia Alexander says. "It was indeed a question I asked. Her response was, 'No, he must never know.' I think at that time her relationship with him was very close. She desperately did not want to lose it, and equally, I believe she knew that such an event running full term would interfere with her relationship with her animals on the mountain. But the fact that she was causing the termination of a pregnancy—of a little life—all to benefit herself in the long run bothered her very much. Once the event was over, I felt it was not for me to delve into her thoughts, and certainly she did not volunteer information."

When Fossey spoke of her abortion to Anita McClellan many years later, she chose an explanation that better suited the sardonic persona she had fashioned for herself by that time. "You can't be a cover girl for the *National Geographic* if you're pregnant," she told her friend.

"She did withhold it from me," Campbell says. "I had absolutely no idea. On March 18, 1970, I left Visoke early to go and meet her in Gisenyi. The driver had failed to turn up with my Land Rover. He hadn't been able to start it. I arrived in Gisenyi late, some hours after Dian had flown in from Kigali and had made her own way from the airstrip to town. She was very upset, thinking I had forgotten she was due. She spoke very little about her stay and work in Cambridge, and was clearly very pleased to be out of the English winter and back in Rwanda. We climbed to camp the following day. It was during discussions some considerable time later that she finally divulged what had happened. I was astonished—appalled would perhaps be a better word. She treated the matter calmly and as a thing of the past, and was relieved that she had not kept it to herself any longer. She had made up her own mind what to do, and as far as I know, she certainly never held any aspect of the situation against me."

Back at Karisoke, Fossey immediately turned her attention to the camp's pressing problems, which were manifold. Because of the shrinkage of the park borders and the lack of government intervention, the poachers and the cattle people had become even more aggressive. Her Halloween masks didn't work anymore. She considered her gun the only thing she could depend on.

Campbell did not actively dispute her in this regard. He knew only fragments of her experience in the Congo. (He knew nothing about the de Munck boys.) She once told him she could never respect an African because of what had happened across the border. But she never went into detail. Her tendency to resort to firearms didn't surprise him. Anyone acquainted with her now knew that the gun was an *idée fixe* of Dian Fossey's life in Africa.

She wrote Alan Goodall that it would be helpful if he could bring his own gun. If he could not, she would lend him hers, but he would have to provide his own ammunition—a hundred bullets ought to do him, figuring the expenditure of about ten a month. His wife would certainly need her own gun, for protection while she was alone. Fossey also mentioned that Hinde was planning to come out that summer. She said she wanted him to bring some ammunition. At about this same time, she asked Campbell to buy a rifle on his next trip to Nairobi. He protested, citing the problem of getting it through border posts. Wouldn't firecrackers do? he asked. No, she said. For crippling and killing cattle, fireworks were useless.

But Campbell knew the dangers. Just after Fossey's return from Cambridge, he himself had fired a Beretta over the heads of fleeing cattle people. A spent bullet accidentally hit one of them in the leg. Campbell was certain that the bullet did very little damage, but the incident worried him. Back in Nairobi in June, he received a letter from Fossey that increased his concern. She had done some shooting, too. Returning to camp in the rain, she found a water buffalo wedged into the fork of a Hagenia tree. Its rear legs were cut off but the animal was still alive. Forcing herself to ignore the courage of the buffalo's attempts to survive, she shot it, "falling to pieces" afterward. After she had taken her wrath out on her own men, who said the Watutsis had butchered the animal, she abandoned her field work to track the killers.

She saw three from a distance and "fired the clip at them," she wrote. Moments later, approaching an *ikibooga,* a temporary shelter, she spotted a child hiding behind a tree. "So I kidnapped him and said I'd hold him for a spear." She had just returned to camp "with the dirty little thing when, of all people, Mutarootkwa showed up, 'saluting' at a vast distance—the brat was his, and he had no spear, for you had already stolen it! Naturally I returned the brat. Also, it turns out that the man you shot was one of his brothers and now they won't come near the camp because of that—we'll see. . . ."

On June 21, she wrote to the International Union for the Conservation of Nature in Morges, Switzerland, urging its intervention in Rwanda's desperate park problems. Stringent methods were imperative, and she recommended her own solutions. To punish Watutsi cattle people who interfered with the gorillas or other wild game, she recommended the public slaughtering of cows for each illegal entry. She suggested that the number be increased with each repeated offense. For poachers, there was to be no leniency: "I definitely advocate giving the Conservator and qualified Park Guards full license to kill on sight any poachers fleeing when encountered within the *interior* of the Park . . . I would be willing to guarantee no more than 3 or 4 poachers would be killed, *if* the park were patrolled on a regular basis, before the interior would be rid of them."

There were precedents for Fossey's position. In the early 1970s, poachers were shot on sight by park authorities in some African countries (the policy has recently been reinstituted by Kenya's President Moi to stop the killing of the country's elephants). But Fossey was putting herself on the militant side of an international debate: In an overcrowded world of ever diminishing resources, who has the greater claim on life? Starving Africans or nearly extinct gorillas? And who are the judges to be? Those same civilized foreigners who have already destroyed all their own wildlife?

There were other questions. If poachers should be shot on sight, should foreign visitors be allowed to shoot them? Within the context of independent black Africa with its epochal history of racial disharmony, should African poachers be shot on sight by foreigners who were white?

Despite her vehemence on the poacher issue, there was nothing in Fossey's past to suggest a tendency toward violence. Rather, her inordinate (and perhaps compensatory) love for helpless things—for crippled children and abandoned pets—suggested the opposite impulse. But what she saw in Africa overwhelmed her. There were only a few hundred mountain gorillas left, only a few hundred of the rare, intelligent creatures she had risked everything to save. Their habitat was in a country ill-equipped and indisposed to protect them. They survived in a national park that, by international agreement, was committed to their preservation. But she saw what was happening. She couldn't ignore it. If nothing was done, the mountain gorilla would be gone by the end of the century.

The only person she trusted to save the gorilla was herself. So she turned to the gun and ignited a war every bit as dangerous as the one she had fled in the Congo.

19

HER WAR WITH
THE POACHERS

Alan Goodall arrived in Karisoke as thrilled and eager as a camper on the first day of summer. But Dian Fossey of the Virungas proved to be a different woman than he had met at Cambridge. There she had been soft-spoken, shy, and persuasive. Here she was tense, impatient, and sometimes explosively angry. Once when they were rounding up cattle to drive them off the mountain and he didn't know exactly how to go about it, she shocked him by yelling at him to get off his butt and make himself useful. But she did work to help train Goodall, and so did Campbell, who noted she was giving Goodall much more of her time than she had given Burkhart. Campbell believed that she still felt some residual guilt about Burkhart; that she considered Burkhart's failure partially her fault and was determined to see to it that Goodall succeeded. She even asked Campbell to suspend his own work while she was gone so that Goodall would have a free hand. (This was fine with

Campbell. He would go back to the northern frontier to work with Richard Leakey.)

Goodall was a conscientious student, anxious to succeed. He listened carefully. "Dian told me that by constantly checking the night nests and comparing the counts with visual sightings she had been able to find out the precise combination of each of her four study groups," he later wrote in his 1979 book *The Wandering Gorillas.* "In this way one could then monitor changes due to births, deaths, or emigrations and immigrations." This was a good deal more than she had told Burkhart. Goodall would be expected to keep accurate records of his field observations; report them to her; oversee the African staff; account for all expenditures; and look after her personal things, including her dog Cindy and her monkey Kima. She turned the whole camp over to him, including her ancient Land Rover, her new van, and, of course, her gun.

The night before she was supposed to leave, Goodall announced that he hated Karisoke. It was cold, dark, wet, lonely, and unfriendly, even with Fossey and Campbell still around. Everyone ate alone, and they expected him to do so, too. He couldn't believe it. Here, he wrote later in *The Wandering Gorillas,* "ten thousand feet up on a volcano, were living three people, each cooking his own meal and then eating it in the silence of his own cabin. After the pressure of my exams, I had been looking forward to some discussions about biological principles and research, particularly on gorillas. Yet here I was as isolated as one is in an examination hall, surrounded by others yet unable to talk with them. I began to think about my situation, and I seemed to be sucked into a downward spiral of depressions."

Goodall announced he was going home.

Fossey's reaction to this peremptory declaration was not what he expected. Her fierce demeanor softened and she became the warm, encouraging woman he had met at Cambridge. Gently and reassuringly, she drew out his problems and fears. His mother had died just before he left England. He desperately missed his wife, and he was eager to see his newborn daughter. He didn't want to wait through the weeks ahead before they arrived. What was he *doing* there? He was a schoolteacher!

Fossey talked at length with him about her own fears when she had first come to the Virungas, how frightened and lonely she had been. She said she understood how he felt about his family. She envied such closeness because it was something she had missed in her own life . . .

She seemed to understand him so well. Goodall agreed to stay.

In the summer of 1970, Fossey spent six exhilarating weeks in the United States. To her astonishment and delight (which she struggled modestly to conceal), she had become something of a celebrity. She wasn't known in every household, to be sure, but she was familiar to the 6 million or so readers of the *National Geographic,* which included all the people important to her now. And now that esteemed institution had assigned her to write a second magazine article. She would also be the subject of a lecture film to be shot by Campbell when she returned from Cambridge in the spring. This made her happy. It not only assured Campbell's continuing stay at Karisoke, but signified that she was fulfilling her promise, against very high odds, of becoming Jane Goodall's peer. The first of a succession of young women who saw her as a role model asked if they might come to work for her. The women, two researchers named Marshall Smith and Jackie Raine, said they would pay their own passage. Fossey said she would see what she could do.

Zipping from Washington to Louisville for a few days with Gaynee Henry, then on to Atherton and Los Angeles, then back to Louisville and back again to Washington, Fossey found her career accelerating at a rate she hadn't dared hope for. She was recognized now as the protégée of both Louis Leakey and Robert Hinde. And her credibility was certified by scholars like David Hamburg of Stanford, a leading psychiatrist in the academic community's growing interest in primatology. Hamburg declared Fossey's data to be unique in the world, equal in quality to "any previously obtained on sub-human primates."

In Pasadena, she was the guest of honor at a black-tie dinner of the Fellows of the Leakey Foundation. In her shy, husky, schoolgirl voice, she told what she had seen and done with gorillas, omitting the horror stories, screening Campbell's slides to prove it. She was a great hit, and all of it was joyous and rewarding. It was one of the high points of her life. Only one thing marred the celebration. On September 8, scarcely a month after her departure, at a time when she was nervously preparing for her talk to the very wealthy members of the Leakey Foundation, Alan Goodall shot two poachers.

At first, no one was unduly upset about it.

Goodall recounted the circumstances in an almost lighthearted fashion in letters to both Fossey and Campbell, who was in Nairobi. "I am now trying your technique with poachers & Watusi," he wrote to Campbell. "After firing over their heads & finding them still in the area I have now put a bullet from Dian's little pistol in two legs so far—both of poachers." Although Goodall would later contend that he had shot only one man, it is difficult to draw this conclusion from his letters. In a letter to Campbell, Fossey said she understood that two people were hit: "It seems you mentioned shooting Tutsis to him, so now he's been going wild—two (Batwa and Bahutu) in one week."

Stung by the implication that the shootings were somehow his fault, Campbell wrote back to Fossey saying that he had immediately written Goodall, warning him to be careful. "He knows darn well that the Tutsi I shot was hit by mistake, and that the whole affair could turn serious. Quite what's got into him I don't know, but he must feel he has a free hand to shoot around and we are partly to blame for letting him think that way."

Writing to Goodall, Fossey said she was proud of him but he should be careful. "Although these people are cowards," she wrote, he should remember "they are like animals when cornered with a pistol." What seems to have displeased her more was his sporadic correspondence; she had decided he was doing a poor job of keeping her abreast of what was going on in her camp. The longer she had to wait for what she considered to be essential information—his field observations, some word about her pets—the more irritated she became.

And then, somebody killed six gorillas. Goodall couldn't have been more conscientious about informing her; he said he was certain the news would break her heart. The animals had been killed in the small village of Cundura at the foot of Mount Karisimbi, well inside the old park border. He had done what he could to investigate the matter, going with the park conservator to the scene of the slaughter. The story there, he learned, was that a gorilla had bitten a child and the villagers had retaliated by killing all six of them—by stoning them to death. He was able to find no record at the hospital of an injured child being treated. Goodall was disturbed by the attitude of the locals. As he and his people cleaned the ants from the carcasses in preparation for moving them up to Karisoke, the conservator and his people stood aside amused. Through his trackers, Goodall tried to tell the villagers that what they had done was wrong.

The connection between the death of the six gorillas and the actions of the residents of Karisoke (including Fossey's own free-wheeling use of firearms, Campbell's wounding of the Tutsi, and Goodall's shooting of the poachers) apparently did not occur to any of them until, at Fossey's suggestion, Alyette de Munck went to Cundura to look into the matter. She reported to Fossey, who was now in Cambridge, that the gorillas were not stoned. The stones in Cundura were too heavy for anybody to lift. The gorillas had actually been chased out of the forest into a clearing by Bahutu and Batwa, then killed with bows and arrows. In a letter to Campbell, Fossey said de Munck had found out that the killings were in retaliation for Goodall's shooting one of the poachers in the back. The bullet, it appeared, had lodged in the poacher's stomach.

Her War with the Poachers

•   •   •

When Fossey received de Munck's version of the Goodall shootings, she reacted strongly but not quite so predictably as one might think. First of all, she didn't buy it. She was convinced that the gorillas were killed defending an infant taken by trappers. Leakey had written her of rumors that an infant had been brought through Nairobi, and that was it, she was certain. Second, she came to the conclusion she had had about as much of Alan Goodall as she could take. Her wrath was caused not by his shooting of the poachers but by offenses he was not yet aware of having committed. On Christmas Eve, he learned of these by cable:

AM FED UP WITH YOUR INABILITY TO COPE WITH SIMPLE ACTIONS. OBVIOUSLY NECESSARY TO ENUMERATE QUESTIONS VIA CABLE. PLEASE STATE CONDITIONS KIMA AND CINDY. PLEASE EXPLAIN HOW YOU HAVE SPENT MY NINETY DOLLARS FOR FIRST DAY ENVELOPE AND COMMEMORATIVE STAMPS. PLEASE EXPLAIN WHAT HAS HAPPENED TO MY FILM SHIPMENT FROM ENGLAND CONTAINING ORIGINAL SLIDES AND PRINTS. HAVE YOU ATTENDED TO THE CAR SERVICE IN KIGALI. PLEASE EXPLAIN HOW YOU MANAGED TO GO THROUGH FIFTEEN DOLLARS AND EIGHTEEN CENTS PER DAY FOR CAMP EXPENSES AND I LEFT YOU 2200 DOLLARS TO COVER 139 DAYS FROM AUGUST 15TH THROUGH DECEMBER 31ST. I CANNOT CONDONE YOUR USE OF CAMP MONEY FOR OTHER PURPOSES IN VIEW OF YOUR SALARY PLUS THE STOCK OF FOOD THAT WAS LEFT AT CAMP. I'VE GIVEN YOU EVERY CENT OF REMAINING NG FUND FOR 1970. I AM NOT A DISPENSER OF ADVANCE NG FUNDS SO IF YOU WISH MORE MONEY YOU MUST NOW WRITE TO THEM ALTHOUGH YOU HAVE PREVIOUSLY REFUSED THEIR HELP. I WOULD SUGGEST THAT YOU REEVALUATE YOUR GOALS IN UNDERTAKING THE STUDY OF GORILLA. PLEASE ANSWER VIA LETTER. DIAN.

From now on, she would refer to Alan Goodall as just another "boy"; the sooner she was rid of him the better. The repercussions of the Cundura affair appeared to be blowing over rather quickly; nothing had come of the investigations into Goodall's possible culpability. The names of the injured man or men were not known. But she was still angry at Goodall—and a good many others. She had again tried to arouse action from the international conservation community in protest to the slaughter of the animals, but with little success. Rwanda was a poor magnet for publicity.

Meanwhile, Fossey had her hands full trying to live up to what was expected of her at Cambridge—and what she expected of herself. Something called the Mann Whitney U test, which she considered statistical jabberwocky, was driving her crazy. She spent a whole day on a single mathematical equation. Alan Root had written her a teasing letter about her efforts to become a scientist, and she had written back grimly—it was no joke—that she had never been a scientist, wasn't one now, and had no interest in becoming one.

But that wasn't strictly true. With the same intensity that had once driven her to listen to opera because she thought she ought to know it, she set about arranging an ambitious program to develop Karisoke into a first-class research station. She told Smith and Raine, the two young women researchers, to come ahead (but, she warned, be sure to bring guns). They could do a census. She encouraged the Cambridge psychiatrist Nick Humphrey to make comparative studies of the Cundura skeletons. (Humphrey would find remarkable similarities between gorilla and human skulls.) She also invited Colin Groves, a taxonomist (who would demonstrate the existence of three gorilla subspecies rather than the two that Harold Coolidge had classified earlier). Other recruits included David Bygott, a scientist from Jane Goodall's camp at Gombe who would come up to make sketches of the gorillas, and two sparkling bright zoology undergraduates, Graeme Groom and Alexander "Sandy" Harcourt. They approached her after she had given a lecture one day and asked for the privilege of working through the summer for her—doing absolutely anything that needed doing. She signed them on.

To all outward appearances, in the winter of 1971 Dian Fossey was becoming a scientist who had positioned herself at the center of a movement. She was fulfilling exactly what people like Leakey, Hinde, and Stanford's David Hamburg expected of her. But one problem would not go away. Although she considered the Cundura affair to have been Alan Goodall's mistake, she had to admit the incident had caused a shadow to fall over Karisoke.

She had thought of the Cundura business as just another unpleasantness which she could quickly put behind her, as she had other misadventures. But it was a greater problem than she thought, and would continue to fester under the surface. Some of her most important supporters, including Robert Hinde and the National Geographic Society, would not quickly forget the incident, which would eventually become a major scandal in Rwanda, threatening the future of Karisoke and Fossey's work in Africa.

Much later Alan Goodall would write to her, "I cannot help feeling we have all been caught up in a whirlwind which has progressively wrecked all in its path."

Alan Goodall gets an acknowledgment in Dian Fossey's book, but no other mention. In 1979 he published *The Wandering Gorillas,* a good book about his experiences in Africa. When he went back to Rwanda to see Fossey shortly after its publication, she told him it was crap. She said that everything he said about her (he was quite gracious under the circumstances) was lies. *The Wandering Gorillas* never appeared in the United States, mainly, Goodall believes, because Fossey managed to have it suppressed. In his book, Goodall says he shot only one man, and merely nicked him in the calf of his right leg.

Today he describes the shooting differently. "We had become judge, jury and jailer about park management in Rwanda," he says. "I had accepted without question this was what we were supposed to do. Only afterwards did the enormity of it occur to me. I thought, 'My God! I could have killed him.' Who was I to do these things? I accept it now as an open question that those six gorillas were killed because of my action—as well as hers and everybody else's. It was as though Rwanda had become our own private empire, with no sense of responsibility on our part to those involved. I realize this now. I had the feeling after I left that the African people wanted to see all the gorillas killed so that all of us would leave."

But Fossey never did get the message. She went on believing for the rest of her life that the best way to deal with poachers was to kill off a few of them; then *they* would get the message. As she indicated in her recommendations to the International Union for the Conservation of Nature, such actions should be taken by duly authorized government personnel. Otherwise, she made no concession. In 1979, she wrote a letter to the American ambassador in Rwanda which made her sentiments all too clear: "It is now only a matter for the President to give the order—KILL—[because] the prisons are already over-crowded and this is the only way we are going to be able to protect the remaining gorillas."

On her way back to camp that spring of 1971, Dian stopped off in Nairobi briefly to see Louis Leakey. The old man's mortality was closing in on him. Six weeks earlier, stress having aggravated his heart condition, he had been ordered back into the hospital. Shortly after his release, he was attacked by a swarm of eight hundred bees and stung so severely that he was temporarily paralyzed on his right side. Had Fossey known that this would be the last time she would see Leakey alive, she might have stayed longer and talked with him more. And maybe not. They didn't visit very long together, and when it came time for her to leave, Leakey insisted on seeing her off at the airport. She implored him not to, but he came along anyway, and her last image of him was that of a crippled old man leaning for support against the railing of the second deck of the little Nairobi airport. His silver hair flying, he grinned and waved his aluminum cane, cheering her on.

Her feelings about Louis (or "Lewis" as she sometimes called him in letters or "Dr. Leakey" when she couldn't help herself) had become hopelessly mixed. She had tried hard to forget the many times he had let her down. Before her erstwhile associate Alan Goodall had gone to him for his interview, she had told Goodall to be patient with him. He was an old man trying to run things despite misinformation and his unreliable memory; he couldn't let go. He was peevish as a child and ruthless toward anyone trying to poach his territory, which was now vast and included his million-dollar foundation back in Pasadena. She didn't have to try very hard to remind herself of his faults. He always expected her to consult him, but he rarely consulted *her*. When she needed money (as she needed it now), he just wasn't there. Luckily, Richard Leakey had arrived on the scene and was helping run his father's affairs. But, as far as Fossey was concerned, this just meant that someone else was mismanaging her funds. She didn't have much use for Richard's administrative skills.

"I thought Dian treated Dr. Leakey abysmally," Birute Galdikas recalls. In 1970, for the first (and last) time, the three "Leakey ape ladies" had met together in the presence of their common mentor at the apartment of Vanne Goodall, Jane's mother, in London. It was a historic meeting but only the young Galdikas, on her way to study the orangutans of Borneo, saw that at the time. Here *she* was, she would later recall, with these two legendary women and the even greater legend, Louis Leakey himself. But in retrospect it had seemed less portentous than pathetic. Leakey was indecisive. "He was somewhat sick in another room, and he kept calling out for Dian to come to him. Dian wouldn't go. She hadn't seen Jane Goodall in a long time, and she said, 'There's just one person in the whole world I want to talk to, and that's Jane.' "

While Fossey might sometimes bad-mouth him in private, she paid homage to the feeble but still energetic Leakey in public. Like a dutiful daughter, she tended (when she thought of it) to fuss over the old man. She did write him of her continuing activities, but her letters dwindled in number; there was little more he could do for her and she didn't have time to waste on pure sentiment.

At the memorial service held in the halls of the National Geographic Society following Fossey's death, Jane Goodall concluded her eulogy with: "I don't think it's too much to say, if Dian hadn't been there, there might be no mountain gorillas in Rwanda today." And Dian Fossey wouldn't have been there if it hadn't been for Louis Leakey, and neither would Birute Galdikas have been in Borneo, nor Jane Goodall herself at the Gombe Stream Reserve in Tanzania.

Whatever admiration Fossey might have had for scientists like Louis Leakey, her idea of a suitable man was still based on white Africans like Alexie Forrester, Alan Root, and even Bob Campbell. (She did not count her former guide, John Alexander, in this company. She once ran into him at the Thorn Tree Bar in Nairobi in the late 1960s, and when he came over to suggest—rather charitably, he thought—that bygones be bygones, she cut him off and turned back to her companion, Alan Root.)

Fossey liked men who could do many things well. She used these self-reliant, powerful men as yardsticks to measure every other man who subsequently came into her camp. Most failed to meet the test. Many had the skills. Some were strong. But few managed to combine these qualities with gentleness. Gentle men stirred something deep in her. "It is true," Campbell says, speaking for himself, "that I was very gentle with her. I think she was surprised to find how gentle I was. For instance, as I've said, she was really flat-chested, and that was a total embarrassment to her. It didn't bother me, and she was grateful for that. Yes," he says, thinking about something he hadn't thought much about before, "I suppose I am like that anyway. She got the full benefit of it."

In the spring of 1971, they resumed their affair in a quiet way. The abortion had made her more tentative, and it seemed that after she returned from Cambridge, Campbell's wife and marriage weighed more heavily on her mind. Still, she began to cater to him in small ways. Because she knew he detested it, she quit smoking for a time, and she began to fix herself up for their photo shoots. She could also relax into a pleasant kind of mood that few people tended to associate with her in those days. Still, from Campbell's perspective, their relationship remained an affair of convenience. "If I had been a single man," Campbell says now, "I would not have married Dian Fossey. It was not that kind of relationship."

There were problems between them—and tacit understandings. "Once we were out together for nineteen days straight. That means we were in close association, within a few feet of each other for hours on end, every day. There was no more tension, resentment—only a common objective, with elusive animals to deal with. We seldom quarreled. There are only two instances I recall. Once, early on, she expressed some frustration—and lost her temper—saying some harsh things about Heather. That outburst led to a better understanding between us, but left Dian in no doubt that when my assignment came to an end I would be returning to my home in Kenya. There was absolutely no question about this, no possibility that I would divorce my wife and stay there. It was part of the delicacy of our relationship that that sort of thing was never discussed."

But Campbell also catered to her, in small ways and large. While she was in Cambridge, he went shopping in Nairobi for toys for her pet monkey, and kept up a steady correspondence with her about his own activities and what he heard from Rwanda. Throughout the period from 1969 through 1972, he became a regular on Richard Leakey's digs, and took most of his breaks from Karisoke at Koobi Fora at East Lake Rudolf (now Lake Turkana), chronicling the younger Leakey's successful expedition. (Theirs had become more than a collegial relationship; it was a mutual dependence evolving from many aventures together.) But Campbell maintained his loyalties to Karisoke, too. When a too optimistic report on the mountain gorillas of Rwanda appeared in the British nature magazine *Oryx,* he wrote a stiff rejoinder, using the occasion to point out the courage of the lone American woman who was single-handedly responsible for their survival.

And, in the case of the Cundura affair, he saved her entire project.

Before Fossey returned from Cambridge, Campbell had been called to Washington for a briefing on film technique at National Geographic headquarters. He discovered that a report of the Cundura incident had somehow made its way to Washington, where the smoke of rumor had quickly blazed into a raging fire. The news broke at a terrible time; Fossey's annual grant was up for renewal. National Geographic executives were horrified. What would people say if it became known that researchers connected with the magazine were shooting people? It might be best if Fossey sought another backer. (But, of course, there *was* no other backer than the National Geographic Society.) Campbell stood up for her. She was nowhere around when the shooting occurred, he argued; she had never shot anyone herself. Eventually, or so he was told, her grant was, however reluctantly, approved for another year. Because it was not in his nature to arouse alarm, he said little about the controversy to Fossey. He thought it appropriate for him to stay out of her affairs, and went about his own business.

When Fossey returned to Karisoke, there were many demands on her time—inexperienced census workers; her thesis; a second article for the *National Geographic;* and a paper on gorilla vocalizations. There were also many letters to write, including a long, tedious series to Robert Hinde in which she attempted to justify her firing of Alan Goodall. While she was doing all these things, Campbell turned his full attention to that which had made his years at Karisoke the best in *his* life. Working by himself more often than not, he spent more and more time with the gorillas.

Lumbering over the mountain with his heavy film equipment,

trying to negotiate the slippery bush, he managed to devise a more effective way of keeping the skittish gorillas in camera range. He had learned from Fossey not to push them, not to crowd them in any way, for it affected their behavior and gave misleading data. But by now Campbell had perceived that submission was the key to entry *inside* the group. If he stayed downhill from them and then inched his way forward, staying on his knees and below their eye level, and making reassuring sounds, they would tolerate his entry into the group. And once inside, there were *extraordinary* pictures to be made.

In this fashion Campbell got to know the gorillas on a very personal basis: one of the most engaging was a seven-year-old blackback in Group 4. Fossey had named him Digit because of his deformed finger, which probably had been injured in a snare. "He was always a gentle animal," Campbell says, and they developed a sort of camaraderie. "He was somewhat inhibited in play with the juveniles if they were close to adults, but could be very boisterous with them on their own. He obviously enjoyed messing about with me, and frequently chose to make a day nest only a few feet away."

From late 1971 through the first months of 1972, Campbell captured rare moments on film. He had begun to bank stunning footage of spectacular wild animals the world had never seen up close. Campbell had got his lens to within inches of their faces.

In camp, Campbell didn't like to talk; he later decided it had become painful to him because he had become so used to living by himself in the wilderness. Searching for a word, he could not always find it. He had become accustomed to silence, and so had Fossey; the two of them spent hours with the gorillas without exchanging a word. Campbell had never had a particularly social temperament. "Placid," he calls himself—unlike Fossey, whom he saw as fiery and irascible. In temperament they were direct opposites.

Though he kept his distance from the others, Campbell was amiable enough, and gave a hand when asked. He helped situate all the new census workers, including the two American girls (one of whom could never keep from hiding her head in the presence of the gorillas). He had helped Burkhart and Goodall, as later in the summer he would assist the two young Cambridge undergraduates Alexander Harcourt and Graeme Groom. (These two were impressive, even by Fossey's and Campbell's standards. From the first they were able to look out for themselves.) Otherwise he stayed off to himself, with an air of almost studied diligence, even when Fossey returned to camp.

She had arrived back from Cambridge on March 14, overlapping Goodall's stay by only one night. Later, she said she had been so furious with him that she managed to stay calm only by taking two Valiums. It had all been expressed before in her cable, but his unforgivable sin was his failure to give her the records (if there were any) of his field observations, a critical lapse of six months in the longitudinal study she had begun. She said hello and good-bye, and that was that. Campbell could see for himself what upset her, but said nothing.

And he remained quiet for the weeks thereafter until it finally became unmistakably clear that, despite his intervention, the National Geographic had decided not to continue Fossey's funding. There was no money to pay the staff, or provide for the new workers, or buy even the most meager of supplies. The National Geographic had abandoned her. The crisis had become life-threatening. Campbell decided it was time he stepped in. To his own supervisor at the National Geographic, Joanne Hess of the lecture division, he wrote:

> May 14, 1971
>
> The situation has now reached the point where something has got to give. Her checks have not arrived, and she is worried sick that some problems have arisen that have prevented their dispatch. I am going with Dian on this supply run to help with the small amounts of cash I have left, also to replenish my own stocks of food. By the end of next week, if Dian's funds have still failed to arrive, I fear some drastic action will have to be taken. The girls' census camp will have to be

closed down, and the majority of the base staff will be sent home. . . . Not a very happy state of affairs.

Three weeks later, although he himself had received a check for his expenses, she had received none. He wrote again:

> June 5, 1971
>
> I know Dian sent off a cable giving the details as to where and how she would like her checks, and Ed [Snider, head of the research division] should have received this around the 20th May. I can't help feeling there is more to the delays than a letter lost in the post. Dian was desperate for funds as far back as mid-April, when her personal money ran out. She borrowed cash and ran up credit accounts on the promise of early repayment, and now is embarrassed. I'm sure a small advance could have been sent to her long ago had there been no difficulties. . . . To put it mildly Dian is terribly upset. . . . Dian's responsibilities . . . are about as much as she can cope with at the moment.

As of 12:00 noon on June 4, Fossey closed down her camp and dismissed her staff. She was back to subsisting on potatoes. She had 420 francs left, which she had earmarked to provide food for her dog and her monkey.

The capriciousness of the research division of the National Geographic was inexcusable, however deep their misgivings about Fossey. Eventually the check arrived, but Campbell says that for the rest of his time at Karisoke, she was in a state of unrelenting fear about her future. Everything was touch-and-go, indefinite. Nothing could be counted on. No plans could be made. The left hand of the National Geographic—the magazine editors and the lecture staff—gave out assignments. But the right hand—the executives of the research division—took away. She never knew exactly where she stood, especially with Leakey fading. Campbell became highly indignant over the cavalier treatment of this earnest and beleaguered woman. No executive in his comfortable office in Washington had the faintest

idea of what deprivation she had to endure because of their vacilla-
tions: not one of them had ever visited her camp.

And by now Robert Hinde was all over her about Alan Goodall. To
complete his field work for his Ph.D., Goodall had to go back to
Karisoke, as originally agreed, so that he could pick up where he had
left off with Fossey's study groups. Fossey was adamant. *Goodall would
not be allowed to come back.* Hinde implied it was through her influence,
her aggressive attitude toward Africans, that Goodall had assumed it
his responsibility to shoot at poachers. Now, Hinde said, Goodall was
sorry for all that, and willing to do what he could to make amends.
Hinde said he realized now that she was perhaps resentful toward
Goodall because he was simply better trained scientifically than she.
Possibly this was the reason Goodall had been reluctant to share his
field reports with her—because of her lack of proper scientific qualifications. He said he could kick himself for not having perceived this.
He pleaded for charity toward Goodall. And finally, Hinde said, he
was acutely concerned about her own standing in the academic
community if she came to be known as someone who refused to lend
assistance to a colleague in her field.

Hinde's letter did little more than stiffen her resolve. Goodall
could not return to Karisoke, she wrote back; her camp was supported by the National Geographic Society and not by Cambridge
University. She gave another detailed list of Goodall's failures, adding
with undisguised indignation that no one was more qualified than she
to review Goodall's work, which was the main reason he had been
unwilling to make his field notes available to her.

Later, on four hours' notice, Fossey received word that Alan Goodall was coming to see her to argue his case personally. She insisted
that Campbell be present for this confrontation, and at the end of it,
she held her ground. If Goodall insisted on returning to the Virungas,
he would have to make his camp elsewhere. Her research groups
would not be made available to him.

Goodall left, for good.

•   •   •

By autumn 1971, the situation at Karisoke was dire. The Cundura affair would not die. It ricocheted from one faction to the other, from the Rwandese officials (not yet as vocal as they would become) to the research division of the National Geographic to Robert Hinde. In one way or another, all the friction, misunderstandings, and endless accusations could be traced back to an accident that should never have happened. Now even the National Geographic had sided with Hinde in favor of Goodall. Watching Fossey working herself into a state of exhaustion, Campbell decided he had had about as much as he could take. He wrote Snider at the National Geographic on November 11, straightening him out. Nine days later he wrote to Hinde at Cambridge:

Nov. 20, 1971

Having maintained a steady silence on all matters concerning the issue between Dian Fossey, Alan Goodall, and the Gorilla Research Study, I now feel compelled to write to help clarify the situation.

You must be extremely upset by this whole matter, and there are many others who have been implicated and affected one way or another. But aside from Alan Goodall himself and Dian, no one has been more deeply affected than myself. Apart from a short six week stay in 1968, I have been a near permanent resident of this camp since April 1969. I have met every person who has come here to work—in whatever capacity—and a great many others besides; from ambassadors to newspaper reporters, government officials, to people begging for work. I am aware of Dian's reaction to each and every one of them.

With a scant four-hour warning, Alan returned to this camp on the evening of November 16—and departed on the morning of the 18th. Over the evening meal of the 16th, he had a three-hour talk with Dian and myself. All the major points affecting his previous stay here came up and were discussed. . . . At no time did he try and reconcile his differences with Dian, and made it quite clear that he felt

252

he had been maligned, gossiped about, and falsely accused of various failures to comply with instructions about field reports and expenses, etc.; also—and this is a very serious matter if it is so—falsely accused of a particular shooting incident. About this I will have more to say later. I am satisfied in my own mind that Alan returned here with fixed interpretations of his obligations to Dian, interpretations which indicate in fact that his obligations are minimal. . . .

Alan was somewhat indiscreet over some of the subjects which were discussed. In spite of protestations about his respect and admiration for Dian, he quite obviously does *not* have any respect for her. He brought out the fact that he had "very revealing" discussions with people who had been to this camp, and also that he had been given access to her correspondence on himself, and quoted "extracts." He referred to what he called her "failure" to keep other people who had come to work here, implying clearly that she was responsible for the failures. He asked how many people had been allowed to work with *her* habituated gorilla groups, and suggested that all along she had not intended him to succeed here. Now on these latter points he trod on very thin ice indeed, and these sorts of questions, implications and statements could hardly have been designed to improve his relations with Dian.

First of all, the only person to "fail" here, prior to Alan's introduction, and there have been three, was Michael Burkhart, and Dian's decision to remove him was fully justified—without question. Including Alan—who was the only one to have complete freedom— five people have been allowed to work with the habituated study groups. This number includes two photographers who, as photographers, may be said to have the most disruptive influence on these particular animals, and Drs. Humphrey and Groves, both of whom received only cautionary advice and help before "working" any group. Nick Humphrey in particular was allowed a free hand—and professed complete enjoyment of the situation. Only the limited time at his disposal stopped Colin Groves enjoying the same privileges. . . . Finally, for Alan to even suggest that he felt Dian did not intend him to succeed I regard as a vindictive statement. In the nine separate

253

research and exploration camps in which I have worked, I have never seen so much care and attention lavished on a student (Ph.D. or otherwise).

Alan Goodall came to this camp in 1970 with everything going for him—a grant to cover all his expenses, financial assistance so that his wife and child could be flown out to join him in Rwanda, a fully established work camp with a staff of three to cater to his needs, transport, a house rented, cleaned and supplied with all the essentials for the comfort of his wife, and last, but by no means least, a minimum of four habituated gorilla groups with whom to work! In short, Alan had to do virtually nothing for himself. Since I was involved in all the preparations, I know just how much effort went into them, and I consider Dian exceeded all normal standards in this respect. A permanent cabin was rushed to completion so that he would not have to spend any time in a tent, and it was also arranged that I should stop my own work in order not to interfere with that of Alan's, and so that he would have a completely free hand.

I would like to end this overly long letter by mentioning again the alleged shooting incident. As you probably already know, the National Geographic Society threatened, in no uncertain terms, to withdraw their support of Dian's study when they received a report on the incident. I consider it very fortunate indeed that I flew to Washington when I did, since I was able to discuss the whole matter with the executives concerned and help to head off any hasty decisions. I was obliged to defend Alan Goodall, Dian, and the future of the study with the very minimum of "fact" at my disposal. I fully understand the severe reaction of the National Geographic and can appreciate their deep concern, and it is most unfortunate that Dian's formerly excellent relations with the Society were badly strained and there were serious after-effects. Her application for funds was passed by the Research Committee, but it was not until mid-June that she actually received them. There were also other problems which need not be detailed here. What with the worry over these strained relations, no funds to run her camp, two census workers to finance, as well as having guests in camp, I find it no surprise at all that she was extremely unhappy over this period and most dissatisfied with Alan's overall performance.

Alan has now denied that he was implicated in the shooting incident; however, I have no reason to doubt the integrity of the person who interviewed him at the time, nor the statement of the African assistant who was with him. Alan appeared to be remarkably unconcerned about the trouble caused by this matter, and now that he has decided to leave this study I hope the whole of the affair can be dropped and forgotten.

I have left a great deal unsaid and have avoided mentioning many matters that really need clarification, but I sincerely hope it will be unnecessary to go any further. . . .

Campbell's letter is of value in recounting some of the causes behind the gathering impression that there was a most erratic, if not highly neurotic, woman at work in a dangerous place on an assignment too important to entrust to someone so unstable. That this impression got no further than it did at the time was owing to Bob Campbell. Fossey had tried to explain all of it to everyone, but no one was listening to her. It took a third party, one whose credibility was unimpaired, to make her case. In late November 1971, this is what he did. And did it effectively: everybody got off her back.

Soon the money was flowing again. By the time the financial picture had eased, Fossey had received a letter from Hinde saying, quite graciously, that he considered his quickness to offer constructive criticism one of his greatest failures. He was all too aware how easy it was for her in her present isolation to feel insufficiently appreciated. He assured her that the material she had acquired would "one day soon become one of *the* great biological studies."

And so Fossey and Campbell could now return to what had become for them both an idyllic interlude. Demonstrating the effectiveness of his newfound approach technique, Campbell persuaded Fossey that both of them could move inside a group and become *accepted* by the animals, as though they belonged there. Suddenly they were seeing new things. Fossey wrote that on one occasion she was "beautifully and completely" ignored during a major interaction between Groups 4 and 5, which lasted for two days. Members of the groups were switching their allegiance, transferring from one to the other without apparent cause. Fossey and Campbell heard vocalizations they had never heard before, and at the height of the tension—when it seemed about to break into open violence—there was an ominous and inexplicable silence. They knew they were seeing and hearing things no one had witnessed before, and because Campbell's camera was *inside* the group, they were getting it all on film.

By now, all the students, census-takers, and observers had departed. Fossey's work load remained crushing, but she was alone with Campbell. The late months of 1971 were the best time she had ever known. She could move among the gorillas with ease and assurance. No one before her had done what she was doing now. From her troubled and unpromising beginnings, everything about her life seemed at last to be coming together. She was where she wanted to be, she had become the woman she had believed she could become. So much of this, she knew now, in the deepest and most secret part of her heart, was because of Bob Campbell. Though he had promised her nothing, given her no reason to believe he would stay past the time of his assignment, which now ran well into 1972, she had let herself think it possible he might want to stay there with her, for good. To help her. More than that, to take care of her. She was in love with Campbell. She was his.

The problem was, he was not hers.

Campbell was getting tired of slogging through wet mountains hauling equipment on his back, tired of living for months on end in the wild. He was exhausted. He needed a break, not just from the mountains but from the gorillas, too. He had a good start on the footage he had been assigned to film. Now he wouldn't mind working a few months on something else, even though it was understood by everyone that he had at least five or six more months of shooting at Karisoke. (There was talk now of adapting some of the more spectacular lecture footage into a television special.)

He simply didn't want to go into all this with Fossey—he knew it would upset her—and as it stood, they would still be working together until his assignment was completed. But he did want a few weeks at home in Nairobi, and so he arranged to drive back in his Land Rover early in December. He planned to return on January 20. Fossey would work on her thesis while he was gone.

Toward the end of November, Fossey told Campbell that she wanted to see a doctor the next time they left the mountain. "My notes show that she and I left Visoke on the twenty-ninth of November to go to Gisenyi for supplies," he recalls. "I recollect that Dian went off to see, I think, Alyette. I know I did not take Dian to Roz Carr's. I had no idea what was going on. Back in camp, she began hemorrhaging. She avoided any mention of what had caused the problem. I was about to return to Kenya. This was the ninth of December. Dian acknowledged that she was worried and asked me to take a letter to Dr. Weiss [at the Ruhengeri hospital]. Weiss told me nothing of what Dian had written, and indicated she would have to come to Ruhengeri herself. So, on the day I left, Dian came down with me—on a litter so as to avoid aggravating her problem. After establishing her in the hospital and being reassured she was all right, I set out on the journey to Nairobi."

In Nairobi, Campbell ran into his old friend Richard Leakey, who had just received exciting news: he had been funded by the National Geographic for a major expedition into Koobi Fora, to begin late in the following spring. He had to have Campbell along to photograph. It was going to be one of his most important expeditions (and did, indeed, prove to be so. Leakey found at Koobi Fora in the summer of 1972 the skull known as KNM ER1470, dating back 2.6 million years, a greater discovery than any made by either his mother or father). Campbell agreed. He could film gorillas until May and then join Richard at East Lake Rudolf. It was an assignment he wasn't about to miss.

To confirm this, Joanne Hess sent Campbell a letter at Karisoke, officially requesting that he suspend his gorilla filming in order to film the Leakey expedition.

Unbeknownst to Campbell, Fossey's hemorrhaging had been caused by her second abortion, a bloody back-alley operation performed by a Zairian from Goma. She had almost died, but finally returned to Karisoke in December to recover. When she saw Hess's letter awaiting Campbell, she couldn't help herself. She opened it. And that was how she learned she was about to lose Bob Campbell forever.

Before Campbell left Karisoke, Dr. Pierre Weiss—the French doctor at Ruhengeri, one of the very few doctors in Rwanda—had assured him that Fossey would be all right. Since she had made no further reference to the bleeding episode in her letters, Campbell assumed he would find her back in camp, going all out, upon his return on January 20, 1972. Fossey was a mixture of fragility and steel; her physical condition was always a problem in one way or another, but she simply ignored it, or joked about it. It was almost as if survival in the face of calamity was another accomplishment she had set for herself. Of her second abortion, she said nothing.

And so Campbell had thought no more about her bleeding. He resumed his filming as she worked in her cabin on her thesis, her maturation tables, her weight-loss tables, and the endless charts and measurements which she hated but endured. Their personal relations remained calm and decorous. But for Campbell, they started to grow a bit sticky. Though she sometimes hinted at feelings for him, she had been careful not to press the point. (Once, from Cambridge, she had written "I love you" at the bottom of one of her letters, and Heather Campbell had seen it. Heather clipped it off the letter and gave it to him; and he kept it, tucking it away among his letters.) Professional always, she had kept her emotions to herself, doubtless because she knew that was what he expected of her. He knew *she* knew very well that he was not going to divorce his wife, and that when his assignment was over, he was going home.

He recalls his surprise when, at the end of January, she began to press him a bit. There were little hints and implications: "Do you like it up here?" she would say, or "We get along pretty well as a team. Wouldn't it be nice if you could stay on up here?" But Campbell, knowing that his schedule for the coming year had changed rather drastically (he was still not aware that she knew), simply stepped up his time in the field, averaging three days of observations to one of hers, moving in ever closer to the animals, obtaining what he thought were fantastic shots. During the day he consolidated his friendship with Digit, and in the evening he made a full report of all he had seen to Fossey so that her field observations remained up to date. If, aside from her hints, her demeanor had changed, he was unaware of it.

Campbell, after two and a half years, had not become a very astute judge of the deeper sensibilities of Dian Fossey, and the truth was—however successfully she managed to conceal it—she was about to implode. Soon Campbell would be gone. Every move she would make over the next three months would be motivated by desperation—by fear of an inadmissible loss, a rejection beyond bearing.

She knew she was incapable of coping with this alone. She needed someone to talk with, to advise her, and the only person in the world whom she could trust was Alan Root. On January 29, she wrote and asked if he could spare half a day to talk with her about a matter too personal to entrust to the mails. She would fly to Nairobi. On February 3, she wrote Joanne Hess, Campbell's supervisor at the National Geographic, offering to pay the costs of keeping him there from her own pocket. On February 9, not having heard from Root, she cabled him; and four days after that, still awaiting his reply, she decided that maybe she was all wrong in the way she was going about this. The

259

sensible thing to do was to sit down over a nice dinner, with wine, and talk frankly and openly with Campbell about it.

But somehow it got away from her. She immediately accused Campbell of running out on their project, abandoning Karisoke for Richard Leakey's expedition. "I told her that I had set my mind on the Leakey expedition," Campbell says, "and that would mean a break of three or four months before I could come back to Karisoke. But I would come back and we would finish it. That was all right, and the little dinner got along fine until she got back onto it. She tried to force me to say some things I couldn't say without hurting her feelings. I was keen to continue the study and not upset her—we were getting these incredible breakthroughs, and I fully intended returning after the Leakey expedition.

"But she would have none of it. Really, she thought I could make a break of it and have a different sort of career altogether, that I would stay there with her for good. The Leakeys had become a factor, too. She had by now a rather harsh view of them. Richard had upset her, and Louis had done so often enough for her to say that she didn't want me to go rushing off dealing with the Leakey family.

"I explained to her that I enjoyed working with Richard Leakey, that that was part of what I do. I told her again I wanted to come back and complete our assignment, but not until I had covered Richard's expedition.

" 'Well,' she said, 'if that's what you want to do with your friends the Leakeys, go do it. But don't come back.' "

"I finally burst out of the cabin. I picked up one of those nice wine bottles and smashed it all over her doorstep and stormed off in a rage."

Afterward, living apart enabled them to get on with their work, and even to project a schedule of sorts based on these new circumstances. Campbell had been asked both by the National Geographic and by Richard Leakey to come to Koobi Fora, along with his wife, for ten days in March. They would join the Roots there to serve as hosts for a short visit by Prince Philip to Leakey's digs. Then Campbell would return to Karisoke to get as much film coverage as possible. (Whether he would come back or not was something Fossey chose not to think about.) Meanwhile, Fossey decided to spend some time visiting Joan and Alan Root in Nairobi.

In 1963, just before independence, land in Kenya was going for pennies. Fully expecting the Kenyatta government to expropriate all private holdings, the colonialists were getting rid of what they could before they got out. Joan and Alan Root scraped up a few thousand pounds to buy an old estate (some eighty acres) fronting on Lake Naivasha. When the Kenyans, unlike most other black African nations, decided to retain the white infrastructure and leave some of the large property holdings in white hands, the Roots found themselves with one of the most desirable homes on the lakeshore.

This magnificent house, surrounded by duikers, bushbucks, dik-diks, leopards, aardvarks, hyenas, and even pythons, is where Dian Fossey came for advice and comfort. Joan Root kept a calendar of those days: "Dian came to stay with us on the 25th of February for ten days. Because she was so depressed, we tried to show her a good time. On the first night, we stayed in Karen, and then on the 26th, we went to Naivasha. On the 27th, we flew her over to Nakuru to see the flamingos. On the 28th we went to Nairobi and then back to Naivasha. Then, on the next day, we flew down to Serengeti to our camp overlooking the lake at Ndutu. For four days we were at Seronera, where we saw cheetahs and some killings; and we flew over Natron and Lake Magadi, where we saw incredible windstorms beneath us."

During their time together, Fossey confided in both the Roots. "She poured her heart out to us," Joan says. "But, though I was involved, it was really Alan's sympathy she was seeking." Dian was very open with the Roots; her guard had finally came down, and she told them how much she wanted a man—if not Campbell, then someone.

"She desperately wanted someone to love," Joan says, "and she was a very hard person to be a friend to. No one filled the need for Dian that Bob Campbell did. You see, going back to Alan's first trip, he was a man, and it was easier for him to cope with those Africans. He was a local, he knew how to deal with them. He sort of helped her knock things into shape. She desperately needed someone to do that for her. And then Bob came, and over the years was a tremendous help to her, a companion—just everything to her."

Joan Root makes it clear that Bob and Heather Campbell were not "separated" (except geographically) during Campbell's long affair with Fossey. She emphasizes that, in her opinion, Bob's commitment to Heather never wavered. "Bob doesn't like to overexert himself," she says. "He likes things to go smoothly. Heather is a gourmet cook, a good orchid-grower, very good at what she does, and Bob likes their life. It is social, and Bob enjoys going back for his dinner parties and things like that."

In the course of their talks at Serengeti, it came out that Fossey believed she was, once again, pregnant. Then, "about a month after her time with us," Joan continues, "Alan was at Lake Rudolf with Bob for the visit of Prince Philip. Bob and Alan went off for a long walk along the lake, talking it all out for hours."

Back in Karisoke, Fossey wrote the Roots that she wasn't pregnant after all. But Campbell was acting strangely. On their first evening back together, she said, they were invited to a home in Kigali where there was a new baby. Campbell, she said, had cried out: "Why don't you hate me? Why don't you hate me?" His role, she said, was not an easy one, and she left it at that.

She was still looking for another way out. She told the Roots that on the day she said good-bye to them, she had seen a man who seemed perfect for her on the streets of Nairobi. She wasn't certain of his name—"Foggen," she thought—but he was exactly right for her: six foot four, blue eyes, sandy blond hair, thin, tan, obviously born and raised in Kenya. He wore no wedding ring. She had approached him and asked if they hadn't met before. No, he had said, he didn't believe so. She was anxious to find out anything the Roots might know about him.

Alan Root did everything it was possible to do for Fossey—which was more than anyone else could or would do. On April 3, he wrote three letters: one to Joanne Hess, Campbell's supervisor at the National Geographic (whom he knew well enough to trust); one to Fossey; and one to Campbell.

To Hess he explained the problem and how it had evolved. Campbell had assumed an ever more important role in Fossey's life over the years they worked together, and she had come to believe that their relationship would be permanent. When she learned from him that it would not continue, she went to pieces. She had come to see Root about it in Nairobi, and Campbell had sought him out at Lake Rudolf. "As you know," Root pointed out, "Dian almost never leaves Rwanda, and Bob is very reticent. So these were major initiatives." Fossey's letter to Hess, offering to pay to keep him, was an effort on her part to make him stay. But now she realized that couldn't possibly work, and so she had decided that, after May, she did not want him back. And he did not want to come back. Root warned Hess that she would ultimately have to solve the problem. Neither Fossey nor Campbell was able to say what the outcome ought to be. Fossey wanted the photo coverage of her study to continue. Campbell was in a spot, because he didn't want to displease the National Geographic. Root said he was certain that Hess would act in accordance with everyone's best interests.

To Fossey, he wrote of his twenty-mile walk with Campbell around the shores of Lake Rudolf. Campbell told Root he had never said he would marry her. When Root had asked him if he would now, he had said no, he could not and would not. "He knows that you feel that you have been used but equally he feels used in that you have expected far more from the relationship than he was prepared or free to give—i.e., you expected it to be permanent. Naturally, as the abortions were not mentioned, his case seemed much more reasonable—just a lonely woman making a big thing out of a passing, and almost enforced, relationship. I do not sympathize with him, though, as I feel that if he had no intention of marrying you, he should have been responsible enough to ensure that you didn't get pregnant. However, for all I know, you insisted that you were safely on the pill and he needn't take any precautions."

Root urged Fossey to consider the affair over. Nothing further could come of it but damage to them both. She should make it clear both to the National Geographic and to Campbell that she expected him to stay six weeks more to complete their filming, and then he should leave. "You may be tempted to say that more coverage is needed in the hope that Bob will be sent back and you will perhaps be able to win him over—please resist this, it can only lead to more heartbreak for you. Everyone will be relieved by this decision, including the National Geographic, which is as scared of scandal as everyone else."

What she should do was close down her camp for a month and come with the Roots to the Serengeti, where, at the Serengeti Research Institute, they would happily bring to her door every bachelor passing through. They would find her a husband. In the meantime, forget the guy she had seen in Nairobi. "Sorry," Root wrote, "he's married and has a family."

Finally, Root wrote to Campbell: "It seems the only solution is that you finish the film as quickly as possible, in this last six-week stay. If Dian is convinced she cannot change your mind, she will accept the inevitable."

In an awkward bit of timing, Campbell returned to camp on April 12, carrying Alan Root's letter to her of April 3. She sat down and read it right away. Then she wrote back; she wanted to reassure Root of some things. She said she knew Campbell wouldn't marry her, and she had no intention of trying to persuade him otherwise. She had assured the National Geographic that the coverage could be completed before Campbell left and that there was no need for him to return. She had also told Campbell this. After all he had given her, she had no desire to harm or hurt him in any way. Her only plans now were to make each day more perfect than the day before.

This time, she was as good as her word. She minded her own business, staying off in her cabin, working on her thesis and noting Campbell's observations—until, almost at the very end, in the last week of shooting, they slipped, almost without noticing, into an episode they had spent three years working around, the culminating moment they had never quite dared to hope for. Slowly they worked their way inside Group 4, and after some time—but almost casually, as though the impulse had been there all along—Digit moved toward Fossey. Kelly Stewart would later remark that it was a strange thing about Dian Fossey that she always looked exactly as she felt. It was so this day: she felt the intensity of Digit's closeness, and of what was about to happen to her; and through Campbell's lens, she looked radiantly beautiful.

Compared to Peanuts's movement to her two years earlier, what was about to happen was a different order of magnitude. In a sequence which seemed never to end, one experience more meaningful than the next, Digit became *involved* with Fossey. He didn't just touch her and then run away. First he took her glove in his hand and sniffed it, and then her pencil, and then he put that down and picked up her notebook and put it back down. Then, nestling in beside her, he rolled over and went to sleep.

Both Fossey and Campbell instantly realized what they had captured. Without prompting, without encouragement, a wild mountain gorilla had proved what Fossey had been trying to show the rest of

265

the world. He had demonstrated the gentleness and empathy of his species. He had shown his kinship to human beings. In 1973, this strip of film would be the centerpiece of a National Geographic television special. The special, *The Search for the Great Apes,* would ultimately be shown on television screens around the world, seen by tens of millions of people who were startled and beguiled as for the first time they saw what they had never imagined possible.

This short sequence, filmed by her departing lover, would become famous and would immortalize Digit—and Dian Fossey.

But it did not keep Bob Campbell in Karisoke.

He continued filming until just a few days before he was to leave. It wasn't until he began packing up that she seemed to realize he was really going.

"And then," he says, "she could see with her own eyes that I was packing everything that I'd laid on up there, that it was all going away with me. It took thirty-five porters to carry everything I'd accumulated. And the fact of them arriving on the next morning—really, she hadn't thought it was going to happen.

"She wouldn't come out of her cabin to say good-bye. She was just overwhelmed by it all. Until the sight of all my packing and the porters, she had retained a normal sort of composure. But then on that last day, she just broke down and she wouldn't come out of her cabin.

"I had to go back inside, and she was in her bed still. So I went to her and said, 'I'll come back anytime you're in trouble, if you like.'

"She just broke down and said, 'I don't know what to say or what to do.'

"I said, 'I have to go.'"

They saw each other only once after that.

"She came through Nairobi some years later," Campbell says. "She rang up in the middle of the night, obviously very distressed. And I said to Heather, I just had to go see her. She sounded very upset. She was staying at the Hilton. She said, 'Why don't you give it up and come marry me and stay up there with me? I know it'll work perfectly.' I said, 'Dian, it won't work. It can't work. It would be a working relationship and not what you would expect or like to happen.' And then I never saw her again."

20

....

SOLITUDE

Like Dian Fossey, Rosamond Carr was less than lucky in love. At an early age, she had married an older man and followed him halfway across the world from Asheville, North Carolina, to a mica plantation in the Belgian Congo. She knew very little about Kenneth Carr, not even his age. But he knew about Africa, and his stories of his life there drew her into the romance of the place. He had run a coffee plantation and had mined tin and gold. He had been a white hunter and had once led Prince William of Sweden into the Congo to bag fourteen gorillas for the Stockholm Museum. The idea of sharing her life with a man like that in a place like that was irresistible. Like Fossey, she left everything she knew behind her—and never looked back.

Eight years into her marriage, Carr caught a glance of her husband's passport. Her eyes fell on the year of his birth. He was twenty-four years older than she—too old, she decided. So she divorced him. But she stayed in Africa. She loved the land. Like Fossey, she stayed on alone in the place she had come to for romance.

According to Carr, after Campbell left Karisoke, Fossey stayed busy, traveling back and forth to Cambridge to finish her doctorate. She spent half of each year in England and half at Karisoke with the British and American zoologists and anthropologists who had come there to study. In England, Fossey longed for the gorillas. Some people wondered if there were any people she missed as much. Carr says she knew better.

"Dian was the most uncompromising person I've known in my life, and the most dedicated," she says. "But the stories that she was a hermit and didn't like people are a complete fabrication. She loved her friends, and there were a lot of us, usually the people at the embassy. The American Embassy had to take a great interest in Dian. For one thing, she was always getting into trouble with the Rwandan government. So they had to sell her to the Rwandans. Of course, she had lots of friends in America who adored her, too. To her friends Dian was generous to the point of absurdity. She had a genius for finding things. She would go home for a three-week lecture tour and come back with things I'd never seen in America before. Brand-new fantastic things. She did that for everybody."

It is true that Fossey made periodic trips back to the United States and that she corresponded with a multitude of people. But it is also true that the end of her affair with Campbell in 1972 also marked the close of some of her other important relationships.

By 1972 she had abandoned her friendship with Father Raymond without apparent regret. She had already jettisoned his Church, which had been so important to her in Louisville. Several years before, she had told Father Raymond that she was leaving the Church; she could not tolerate a religion that meekly accepted the horrifying murders of her young friends at Rumangabo as God's will. Campbell's departure from her life may have further shaken her faith, alienating her not only from the Church but from the friends she associated with it.

In early 1972, Fossey flew to California after receiving some terrible news: her Aunt Flossie had died, and her Uncle Bert was dying. Her mother had apparently broken her hip. There is no record of how Fossey reacted to the death of Bert (one of the few men she loved without complications) or how she treated her mother and aunt. But her behavior with other friends was mysterious. During a visit to her college roommate Patty Hjelm and her husband Bud (both Catholics), Fossey announced she had left the Church because she had fallen in love with a married man. Then, abruptly, without explanation or apology, she told the Hjelms that they should never expect to see her again. Then she left.

Old friends seemed to have no place in the life of Dian Fossey. She was no longer Kitty Price's shy daughter or Gaynee Henry's eager-to-please protégée. Rwanda was her only home now. There was no reason to think she could ever return to either of her former lives. One by one, she had burned the bridges connecting her to the past.

Back in Rwanda, she wrote the Roots that she had finally made her peace with the end of the Campbell affair. While she still loved him as deeply as she had, she said she now understood that it was giving love, not receiving it, that was most important. She did not expect to see him again.

But, despite her stoic facade, the loss of Bob Campbell left a deep wound.

Campbell is certain that Fossey was not drinking heavily at the time he left Karisoke. But according to Kelly Stewart, a researcher at Karisoke at the time, by the spring of 1974 she was drinking a case of whiskey a week. Stewart believes that Campbell's departure and her two abortions broke her spirit completely.

From this point on, reports from Karisoke confirmed that Fossey's behavior—always unconventional, always mercurial—was becoming more and more bizarre. On the mountain she was aloof, drunk, and unavailable. But down below she behaved like a normal, healthy woman. Rosamond Carr insists that she and Fossey could spend as long as three weeks together without Fossey taking as much as one glass of wine. Other friends spoke of her as charming, beguiling, and captivating.

Robert Fritts, U.S. Ambassador to Rwanda from 1974 to 1976, was one of the few people to really see both sides of Fossey's complicated nature. By the time he came to Rwanda he knew that she had a reputation for being a thorn in the sides of a lot of people. His experience quickly confirmed this. Fritts recalls her as "difficult, crusty and obsessed." (Fossey was apparently not especially fond of him; according to another ambassador's wife, she referred to him as "Cold Fish Fritts.") But Fritts also knew that no one but Dian Fossey really cared what happened to the mountain gorillas. He understood that she considered them doomed and would employ whatever means, fair or foul, to try to save them.

Fossey's methods were becoming a matter of concern to more and more people. "I was getting information from behind the scenes that some people in Kigali wanted to convince the authorities to rout her out," Fritts says. "So I went up the mountain and talked with her. I told her she ought to try and improve her image, that she ought to come down and meet with the government in the interest of creating a better understanding on their part as to the value of the animals. I told her I thought I could guarantee the appearance of the president."

Working carefully, trying to smooth the situation from both sides, Fritts invited Fossey to meet the president and his cabinet for drinks at one of their weekly informal gatherings at the Cinque Juelle hotel. She said she would come, but Fritts had no idea whether she would actually show; she had ignored similar invitations several times before.

"I sent my vehicle to make it as easy as possible for her," Fritts says. "She arrived wearing boots, jeans, and a down jacket, and we put her up for the evening at the embassy. The event was supposed to start at 7:00 P.M. Suddenly, she disappeared into the bathroom.

When she came out she was wearing a pure white gown that flowed to the floor. Her hair was soft and wispy. She had on earrings. She was *beautiful*. It was as though she was about to attend a ball. My wife and I literally dropped our jaws.

"We walked into the Cinque Juelle, greeted the president and the cabinet, and she proceeded to work the room, acting as though she attended a formal reception every night of the week. When the time came for her presentation, a lecture and a screening of the National Geographic film of her study, she spoke sometimes in English, sometimes in her rudimentary Swahili. Gesturing, eyes sparkling, she was superb. She really brought home to those officials what she was doing up there. I am certain she completely changed their image of this crazy woman on the mountain into someone who was an interesting and sincere Westerner, the epitome of knowledgeability and sophistication."

Fritts has another story—a more personal one—about the two sides of Dian Fossey.

On one occasion, Fossey extended an invitation to Fritts, his wife, and their two daughters, ages seven and ten, to come to Karisoke to see the gorillas. They were delighted to accept. They would be her guests on the mountain for three days.

"When it came time to move out to see the animals," Fritts says, "Dian in her very forceful way said that the two girls would go with her. My wife and I were to visit another gorilla group with a student researcher." The Frittses were disturbed by what seemed a peremptory decision, and they asked why.

" 'Frankly, I cannot trust parents,' " Fritts says Fossey told them. " 'When you have contact with the group you have to remember that we are all primates. Parents get protective of their children. The animals sense it, and the human parents react as primate parents do. Which is to become defensive and aggressive—protective of their young. It's happened to me before.' " She insisted that for their safety *she* would take the children. Fritts and his wife realized there was no use arguing about it.

"We didn't see them again until the evening. To this day, our children have a much better impression of Dian as a human being than do my wife and I. Apparently she dropped the sort of defensiveness she had with officials—American, Rwandan, or anybody else—and was sweet and gentle with them."

But it was more than that. Fossey had given the ambassador's daughters a magical experience, the kind of experience that few people have had before or since.

Fossey and the two girls had stopped for a rest. They had walked a long way and the girls were tired. So Fossey sat them down on a log, one on each side of her. "Just sit there and keep looking forward," she whispered suddenly. *"Don't turn around.* Digit is near here."

"Both my kids had long blond hair," Fritts says. "All of a sudden they saw out of the corners of their eyes these huge black hands coming around them. Gently, they took up our daughters' blond hair and rubbed it. And then they saw this face come around and smell the hair. Later, Dian said she was convinced the gorillas could tell color, and this was the first time one of them had seen blond hair on a human."

Fossey's hospitality to the Frittses paid off. Like the ambassadors who followed him, Fritts found himself standing up for her, arguing her case with both the U.S. State Department and the Rwandan officials. As time went on the Rwandans were becoming more and more fed up with the American woman and her behavior on the mountain, which she seemed to regard as her own property. The Rwandans had never seen a woman like Dian Fossey.

In a country where women were subservient to men, this giant female *mzungu*—looming over the pint-sized Hutu and Batwa—was subservient to no one. Not only poachers (it was not a question of racism, Bob Campbell says; if she had found a white man poaching she would have shot at him just the same), but *any* African who tried to take advantage of her was in trouble, including any of her staff she suspected of crossing her.

Just before Fritts arrived in Kigali, she had personally shot more of the local cattle and had kidnapped another child, the son of a poacher (the only prisoner, she wrote to a friend, small enough for her to catch).

Fossey saw the Africans surrounding and encroaching onto the park only as despoilers, as enemies of her beloved gorillas. As for the bloodthirsty poachers, she told *GEO* magazine in an interview that poachers got high on hashish and then "have to kill. A poacher has to kill. It's in him." Feeling as she did, she made no attempt to interact with the locals, or to see their problems, or to try to find some possible solutions. She only wanted to frighten them to keep them out.

"I had the extraordinary experience of going to a Batwa village with Dian," recalls Frank Crigler, the U.S. Ambassador who succeeded Fritts. "And 'village' is not the appropriate word. It resembled nothing so much as a gorilla nest. Their dwellings had the most primitive sort of banana-leaf roofs, more like umbrellas over the top. Dirt and scrubs were heaped up around the edge like walls. The women had nothing on above the waist. They were carrying their tiny little babies, trying to nurse them, or sitting in the dark inside their little huts, or nests, which were filled with smoke. They were just the most primitive people you can imagine, and they were absolutely terrified of her when she came in. She was looking at the time for poachers, but the men had taken off. They were a fragile, frail, frightened people. They wailed and wailed, 'Please go away. Please leave us alone.' "

So effective were her techniques of terrorizing the Africans that some members of her staff believed she had supernatural powers. One day, a tracker brought the body of a small child into her camp. He asked her to cure it, to bring the child back to life. He had no doubt that the white witch could do this. Dian had no idea how to respond. When she told the Roots about this incident, she said it broke her heart. She realized she had gone further than she intended. To the

274

Africans who surrounded her, Dian Fossey was not an ordinary woman. This may have helped her fend off the poachers and keep the trackers in line, but it could only increase her isolation and distrust.

Still, her outrageous behavior toward the Africans continued. Even some of her colleagues were amazed that the government of Rwanda allowed her to stay on. Alexander Harcourt, one of her researchers at the time, says that the general consensus among the others at Karisoke was "that if she were doing what she did in another country, she would have been in prison or kicked out of the country and never allowed to return. But the Rwandans are extremely pleasant, friendly people, who don't like to cause trouble. That's all I can put it down to."

In 1970, a year before Harcourt's arrival, a National Geographic crew had come up to film the scenes intended to accompany Campbell's documentary footage on the gorillas—setups of the camp, with Fossey at her cabin, with Cindy her dog and Kima her monkey, and with Rwelekana, her tracker, playing on his hand-carved flute. Fossey had appalled the crew with her irascible behavior. Her cooperation was minimal, and she made it clear she didn't care what they thought of her. Consequently, they thought her odd at best, mad at worst.

"Dian is turning out to be a very difficult individual to deal with," Christine Wiser, the film's California producer, wrote in her journal. "She's extremely strict with the Africans, never smiles and is always giving orders. When the porters were loading up at the base of the mountain, she beat four of them with her walking stick. Lovely."

She was becoming more violent—anyone, not just the poachers, could become the victim of her rage. Stories circulated about how the madwoman on the mountain was abusing her African staff. Kelly Stewart had seen Fossey hit Rwelekana with a flashlight, and there were other incidents. Once, after a bitter argument, Fossey had refused to pay Rwelekana his wages. Finally, he decided to go along with her; he needed his pay. He thought that if he gave up and apologized she would reconsider. It wasn't quite so easy. Stewart says that Fossey made Rwelekana kneel before her and beg her forgiveness. Each time he offered his apologies, Dian—looming over him—would demand, "What did you say, Rwelekana?" "I said I'm sorry, Madame," he repeated again and again. "Say it louder. What did you say, Rwelekana?"

"It was just awful," Stewart recalls.

People who knew Dian Fossey over time are often at a loss to explain what changed her from the shy girl who loved animals and children into a woman capable of such rage and violence.

Diana McMeekin, vice president of the African Wildlife Foundation, who had a great deal of contact with Fossey over her last six years, observed: "Perfectly balanced people don't choose to go live on a mountain in Rwanda. Dian was very wounded long before she went to Rwanda and what she brought with her couldn't endure the isolation."

But if isolation did in the fragile spirit, in Fossey's case the isolation was something she actively sought. Even when there were people around, she insisted on remaining apart. She ate her meals alone, didn't talk with the researchers that came there. That was even the pattern with her lover Bob Campbell.

Another primatologist, who insists on anonymity, says that Fossey was not so unusual. While out in the field, she felt very much like Fossey. "I didn't like humans," she says. "The monkeys allowed me to opt out, to get my need for social interaction and social closeness, so I didn't have to pay the price of human interaction."

But, like Fossey, she did pay a price, suffering a nervous breakdown upon her return to civilization. She says it took years of therapy before she was able to sleep without dreaming of the monkeys she had abandoned.

Others with far less psychological baggage than Dian Fossey have reported unsettling reactions to prolonged isolation. Robert Hinde, who has studied the effect of isolation on all kinds of field workers, reports that nearly all experience such problems as personal difficulties with co-workers (including tensions and jealousies over similar

276

research subjects), loneliness, feelings of lack of privacy, and mistrust of local people.

One of Hinde's respondents wrote: "After my first six months, when a new researcher arrived I shook his hand. It was the first person I had touched since the week I'd arrived, and I had become acutely aware of this, so much so that I felt afraid to approach anyone in case they showed signs of rejecting me." Another wrote: "One of the most potentially dangerous aspects of spending long periods more or less alone is that small and unimportant things can be magnified out of proportion with their real significance, and lead to behavior or writing of letters which have long-term repercussions." On the basis of his study, Hinde has reached one overriding conclusion: "I am absolutely sure," he says, "that the crucial issue is having somebody with whom you can talk about this wonderful experience that happened to you. . . . Since I've moved away from monkeys now and I work with people, I've come to feel that one of the most important things about close relationships is the ability to share experience. And that's what really matters."

After Bob Campbell, there was no one Dian Fossey cared to share her experiences with. It had taken her time to trust Campbell and that had led to more pain, more disillusionment. Better no trust than trust betrayed. Even her closest colleagues were shut out.

Like Campbell, Harcourt and Stewart were devoted to the gorillas, but Hinde believes that Fossey felt they were more interested in finishing their graduate work than in saving the animals. She believed herself to be the only one who really cared. "And so," Hinde says, "there was always a sort of barrier in her own mind, between her and these other people." Sooner or later, she would accuse everyone who got close to her of betrayal.

"Dian always thought everybody betrayed her trust," says Stewart. "People would stab her in the back, say bad things about her behind her back, not always give her their full love, and that's why she liked animals and children. Especially animals. They took the place of humans, because Dian couldn't deal with humans. Dian liked animals because they were completely vulnerable and could never hurt her or betray her."

Anita McClellan postulates that Fossey's fear of betrayal and her expectations of hurt from other people were rooted in a childhood trauma. If this was true, Fossey never made reference to any specific event or turning point. It was only one of the things she never told anyone.

The mistrust certainly was already there when she sought so removed a place as Louisville for her work and then settled in an old cottage in the woods. She brought the mistrust with her to Africa. And in her years in the Congo and Rwanda, through the brutalities she survived, the hardships she endured, and the isolation she imposed on herself, the mistrust of people grew until it assumed pathological proportions.

21

HER WAR WITH THE STUDENTS

"Working for her *was* impossible," admits the loyal Rosamond Carr. "She expected the same dedication from young twenty-five-year-old students that she had given herself. And she couldn't believe these young men or women who had come up there would want to go to Gisenyi or Ruhengeri to see other young people. They should have forgotten everything but the privilege of being there among the gorillas.

"I remember when Dian brought Alexander Harcourt back to her camp for the first time, and they stopped here. He was sitting in the back of her kombi, and I said to Dian, 'Ask him in.' Dian said, 'No, he doesn't want to come in. He's just a student. He wants to stay out there.' The door of the kombi happened to be open. I looked through, and it was extraordinary how handsome he was. Rosy red cheeks, blond hair. A beautiful young man! I said, 'Dian, what are you going to do about a very attractive young man like that and the problem of his finding girls?'

"Dian said, 'Oh, he's not interested in anything like that. All he's interested in is gorillas.'

"Then when Dian was gone for six months and Kelly Stewart and Harcourt were there together, she came back and wrote me: 'Guess what? They've shacked up!' That was when her illusions about what census workers wanted were shattered."

Fossey's relations with the students who came to work with her (there were students at Karisoke more or less continually from 1970 to 1985) were rocky. Working for Fossey *was* impossible for many complex reasons.

Fossey looked on the students (census workers, researchers, Ph.D. candidates) as just a notch above the Africans. She referred to them as *mtoto,* the Swahili word for children. Despite this condescending attitude, she expected them to deliver everything they were capable of—all the time. And even that wasn't enough to please her. She had problems with even her brightest, most industrious students.

After Campbell left, there was no satisfying her. Nothing was good enough; nothing was done as she thought it should be. She fired more than a few of her students, including some of the best she had. Two of them, Alan Goodall and Alexander Harcourt, later wrote books that contributed significantly to the slim shelf of field research on the mountain gorilla. Harcourt is looked upon today as the leading authority in the world on gorillas. But to Fossey, they were all *mtoto.*

Not that Dian Fossey was any less compromising about what she saw it her duty to accomplish. For example: she had enlisted sixteen students to produce, over six years, a scientifically valid census of the mountain gorilla population. To accomplish this, she and the students covered 85 percent of the Virungas parklands, a survey far more thorough than Schaller's in 1960. In 1973, when the results were tabulated and it was confirmed that more than a hundred gorillas had disappeared since Schaller's time, Fossey blamed herself. There were only 270 mountain gorillas left on earth, and it was her fault, her failure. She hadn't protected them well enough.

Some of her distrust of the students was not unwarranted. Keeping track of them was a constant headache. In the summer of 1973 she expected six, but only one showed up on schedule. Then, after working for her for three months, two left without even telling her they were going. Another student came and went in only four days. Not all of these departures can be attributed to Fossey's behavior.

Some of the students ran into trouble without causing it. Two were attacked by water buffalo, two were bitten by silverbacks, quite a few got lost, and one was speared in the wrist by a poacher. At Jane Goodall's camp, an American girl had died in a horrifying fall from a cliff, and the possibility this could happen to one of her charges terrified Fossey. But all Fossey's students survived, a fact that can be credited, at least partially, to her rigid supervision and tough training.

From the students' side, the problem was not always the stress of Fossey's expectations or the incredible work load. Very often, the problems could be traced to her manner. The students expected a camaraderie that never developed. They expected to get to know her, but she never broke out of her role as leader, as the toughest soldier in the troop.

Most of them were young—meek and mild, not used to challenging authority. When they left Karisoke they were happy to wash their hands of Dian Fossey. But there were a few others who would become deeply committed to the cause of the mountain gorilla. And if Fossey threw them off the mountain—as she was wont to do—they would not just disappear. One of those was the young man whom Rosamond Carr had found so appealing when she first saw him sitting in Fossey's car.

Alexander "Sandy" Harcourt spent the summer of 1971 at Karisoke and then went back to Cambridge to complete his undergraduate studies. He returned for a three-year stint of field research which he needed to complete the Ph.D. he was doing under the supervision of Robert Hinde.

281

Harcourt won't talk about those years anymore. But Kelly Stewart—who eventually married Harcourt—and Graeme Groom, another Cambridge undergraduate at the time, and Harcourt's best friend, offer revealing testimony.

After attending one of her lectures on gorilla behavior, Harcourt and Groom had approached Dian to ask if they could work a summer for her in the Virungas. Both were clean-cut young men, lean and fit, somewhat anachronistic to their times. After attending public school together at Wellington, they had gone on to study natural history at Cambridge. They were proficient in languages—Harcourt had lived in Kenya the first years of his life, and Groom knew both French and Swahili. During their summers off, Harcourt had gone to arctic Norway and Uganda, and Groom to Russia and the Sudan. Both considered it something of a challenge to discover, in Groom's words, extraordinary things in bizarre places.

Fossey expressed an immediate interest in them but made it clear that she wanted people who were willing to do things *her* way. She was anxious to complete the census of the gorilla population and was very particular about the methodology. Harcourt and Groom expressed their willingness to do whatever she might want. Fossey signed them up. They would have to pay for their transportation (the Fauna and Flora Preservation Society came through with that), but the National Geographic would take care of the rest.

During their first days at Karisoke, Groom and Harcourt were more than impressed by Fossey. Tall, tough, blunt, here was a woman pursuing her life's work in a setting as extraordinary as anyone might ask for. Before she sent them out for the first time, she cooked them a meal. After that they were on their own for three months, each armed with a rucksack, a typewriter, and a copy of Schaller's book.

They lived on the mountain the whole summer, counting gorillas, seeing little of each other and even less of Fossey, whom they saw only once. "You'd spend eight hours *wet,* certainly, from the waist up and often all over," Groom remembers. "You'd be carrying your equipment, trying to trek the camera, the binoculars, and you'd be writing notes as you went. You'd move from nest site to nest site, and by the time you'd finally reached one of them, you were *really* miserable. You'd search and you'd go *on* searching until you'd found *everything.*" So the summer passed. It was tough but satisfying.

The day before Groom and Harcourt left to return to school, Fossey took them into Kigali for a farewell breakfast. She was unusually open and talkative. She told them how she came by her acrophobia (the only students she ever told about the car going over the cliff). Then, as Groom recounts, as they were finishing their eggs and bacon, "she just suddenly turned without change of inflection and told us about having been raped by Congolese mercenaries." She didn't elaborate. Groom came away with two impressions: she was egocentric in her single-minded commitment to the gorillas, and she wanted both of her new field workers back. She had decided that he and Harcourt "were her golden-haired boys."

In the summer of 1972, Groom returned to oversee two new census workers she had recruited, and Harcourt to do his Ph.D. field work. For three years Harcourt worked at Karisoke on research for his thesis, and also serving as Fossey's factotum in much the same way Campbell had—chasing poachers, building cabins, and observing the animals.

Groom left at the end of the summer. He had decided to enter medical school. When Fossey asked him back again in 1973 to oversee the completion of the census, he told her he could not work without pay. He needed to make money for his medical education. By now, Fossey's funding sources had expanded. She promised him ten dollars a day; Groom had become invaluable. He agreed. He had become fond of the rugged Virungas, and the $600 salary would justify his time. Fossey had hired four new students to work under him (those from the previous year wanted no part of coming back), and Groom set out once again for the mountain.

•　　•　　•

Groom's impressions of Dian Fossey up to this point were based on very little experience. During his previous summers at Karisoke, he had seen her only rarely. He had, he says, always thought of her as a woman of extraordinary courage and endurance. But when he returned in 1973, he had the sense that something had gone terribly awry. Fossey was clearly deranged.

Three of the four students she had hired for the summer quit outright. They just took off down the mountain, not bothering to tell her they were leaving. When Groom carried the word to Fossey, her response was to weep on his shoulder. This was followed by an ill-disguised attempt to seduce him. He didn't know how to handle it. Bewildered—like Harcourt, he had initially seen her as a mother hen—he eased out of her range and fled the camp. (He does not know whether she also tried to seduce Harcourt; he could never bring himself to ask.)

Preparing to leave for home, he turned in his final census count of 278, and his bill for $600. Fossey disputed the count. She said it should be 270, and she refused to pay him what she had promised. Groom, who would later receive credit from other researchers (he receives no credit in Fossey's book), left on schedule but continued to write her from England. He said he simply had to have the money for his school fees, and she had promised to pay. He says that her response was to tell him that they had agreed he would forfeit a salary if the census work went badly. "I thought at the time, this was characteristic of her capacity for self-deception," he says. She later sent him $200.

Kelly Stewart, a Stanford graduate in paleontology, met Dian Fossey through Bob Campbell, with whom she had spent three summers at Koobi Fora.

Stewart, who would spend a total of four years at Karisoke, arrived in Rwanda in July 1973 while Groom was winding up the census and

Harcourt was about to leave for two months in England. For a long time, she was alone with Fossey in camp and came to know her as well as anyone on the mountain.

When Stewart arrived, Fossey met her at the foot of the mountain and the two proceeded alone to Karisoke. They took to each other immediately. Overweight and myopic, Stewart had trouble with the climb. Then her boots felt too tight, so she took them off and continued climbing barefoot. By the time she was halfway up the mountain, her feet were bleeding. For the next two weeks she suffered altitude sickness. But through everything she kept going, without complaint. She clearly impressed Fossey, and despite their great age difference the two women became close friends.

"She really took me under her wing," Stewart says. "She made me feel like I was the only friend she had, and I was very flattered I was somebody she could talk with and laugh with." Fossey told her things she hadn't told anyone else, although she didn't tell her everything. When Stewart pressed, Fossey tended to turn tart. "Mind your own business," she would say. Yes, she had been raped in the Congo, but that was all she was going to say about that.

One of the things they did talk about (a subject Fossey didn't broach with even Bob Campbell) was religion. It came up when three large boxes of Fossey's possessions arrived from Louisville, one of them filled with religious books and tracts. Fossey told Stewart that she had been Catholic at one time, but no longer. When Stewart asked her why, she said it was because she had "screwed a priest." She said nothing about Father Raymond or Gaynee Henry, her surrogate mother, who had died that year from a cerebral hemorrhage.

Another box contained paintings Fossey had done during her solitary evenings at the Washhouse. "She was quite artistic," Stewart says. "There was this incredible painting that she had done of herself. It was very schizophrenic. One half of the face was normal, the other was dark and brooding."

Stewart would learn that this painting was a truer representation of its subject than she imagined. But, at that time, her feelings about Fossey were uncomplicated. "I adored her," she says. "I just looked up to her so much. She had this ability of making her praise such a prize. Her praise was such a sought-after gold nugget you would put up with the bad times."

Stewart gave something in return—stories of her life with her family, which Fossey relished. She seemed as attracted to the family rituals of the Stewarts of Beverly Hills as she was to the warm playfulness of the gorilla groups. "She asked me all sorts of things about my sister and my brother, not just my parents," Stewart says. "I think it was because we were all so close and we liked each other so much. She loved hearing about how we had all grown up and what my brother and sister were doing back home. And of course I missed my family and I liked talking about them. So Dian and I would have long friendly chats over beer and some whiskey. But Dian made no bones about her dislike of her own parents."

When asked, in an interview some years later, what gorilla characteristics she considered most significant, Fossey said kinship. She loved to point out the fact that gorillas formed close-knit family groups. "They'd give their lives for one another," she said, "and when one is injured or sick, the whole group will slow down so it can keep up. It's just that their bond, their kinship bond, is so strong."

In the late fall of 1973, Fossey left for the U.S. on a lecture tour, followed by another term at Cambridge. During this time Stewart and Harcourt found themselves alone at Karisoke. But they went their own ways, Stewart says, living in separate cabins. There was nothing between them at this point.

A different idea had taken root in Fossey's mind. While away, she became convinced, with no good reason, that Harcourt and Stewart were conspiring against her. They wanted to take over Karisoke. She began writing excoriating letters to Stewart. "Suddenly, I began to get these letters from Dian sounding as though she despised me," Stewart says. "I had no idea why. She said Sandy and I were sleeping together and were taking over the camp. But we weren't sleeping together. Nothing had happened between us yet." But Fossey was so positive of her suspicions that upon her return to Rwanda she stayed at the base of the mountain for several days, unwilling to come back to camp.

Her eventual return marked the beginning of a grotesque chain of events. First of all, she broke her leg falling into a ditch. Dr. Pierre Weiss, at the Ruhengeri hospital, apparently believed an Ace bandage was all she needed to recover, and she hobbled around on it for three weeks, drinking heavily to blunt the pain. The enforced idleness, the drinking, the accusations hanging in the air: tensions were running high; there was a sense that anything could happen.

Even the gorillas were restless—in a most peculiar way. For the first time, a female took charge of one of the groups; a cranky old matriarch pushed aside the silverback, Uncle Bert. Later, after Uncle Bert had reestablished his dominance, an infant daughter of a silverback named Rafifi was found dead. It seemed that the infant had been killed by another gorilla!

Fossey examined the bites on the skull of the infant in disbelief. But she and her workers were unable to come to any other conclusion. This discovery supported one of Fossey's suspicions, one of her darkest fears about the species she so admired: a silverback will kill the infants of another male to enhance his opportunity of adding the female to his own group. She was upset and disappointed, more dubious than ever about the survival of the species. There were only 270 mountain gorillas left. How could this band of rare animals survive the hunters, the zoo people, the farmers—and themselves?

By the time Fossey returned to Karisoke, her high regard for Harcourt had turned to pure contempt, and vice versa.

In addition to her suspicions about Harcourt's relationship with Kelly Stewart, she was very angry about his criticism of her observational techniques. While she still preferred the anecdotal approach in describing what she saw, Harcourt favored statistical quantification. He used time charts and behavior charts and documented his conclusions with graphs and numbers. He suggested she do the same, but Fossey wouldn't hear of it. She was using well-established methods, and she was the world authority on gorillas.

By 1974, their differences were irreconcilable. Discussions deteriorated into screaming matches, accusations, and bitter suspicions. Finally, Fossey ordered Harcourt out of her camp.

But before he left, a young graduate from Syracuse by the name of Richard Rombach arrived. Rombach had tried for three years to get a job as Fossey's assistant, and had finally arranged it through Robert Hinde. Rombach knew little about primates, but he was willing to do whatever was asked of him.

Fossey's apprehensions about this inexperienced young worker were endless and they were compounded by her resentment and jealousy toward both Harcourt and Stewart. "He came at a terrible time," says Stewart. "She was the worst I ever saw her. She was in terrible pain because of her leg. But she blamed everything on that. She made it an excuse for the way she behaved. She went through a terrible thing with Sandy and me. She really felt I had abandoned and betrayed her."

By that time, Stewart concedes, the romance between her and Harcourt had actually begun. Fossey was livid about it. She accused them of unprofessional behavior; she raged at Harcourt and said that she should never have trusted him. She said that Stewart and Harcourt had lied to her.

During the course of one bad night, Rombach wandered off into the foggy woods and disappeared. In the middle of the night, Fossey, drunk, was so terrified that he might fall off a cliff and die (like Jane Goodall's student) that she set off on her own to search for him. But she went in the wrong direction.

Stewart and Harcourt went after her. "I got there as she threw down her lamp and broke it," Stewart says. "She was sitting in the mud, covered all in mud, in the dripping forest. And she was a sight in the halo of light from the lamp.

"Sandy said to me, 'I'm going back to find Richard. You can stay here if you want, or you can come back and help me.' And he turned around and left. And Dian said to me in a guttural snarl, 'Go on. Follow your white bwana. Leave me in the forest to die of a broken leg.'

"Well, Dian saw this was the big moment for me to choose between her and Sandy. I wasn't going to prolong this—and I turned around and went back. She never forgave me for that. Afterwards she brought that up as the night I betrayed her."

Then a terrible accident happened. Harcourt was gored by a water buffalo and nearly killed.

Feeling it wasn't safe to move him, even on a stretcher, Fossey nursed him for three days, keeping the wound drained. Finally, she took him to the hospital in Ruhengeri, and from there he was flown by private plane back to England.

To the extent that they spoke of their enmity at all, Harcourt contended that Fossey hated him because of his superior scientific knowledge. She contended that Harcourt hated her because she saved his life.

Their feelings toward each other might not have mattered in the least. But once Harcourt began to publish his research, he slowly established himself in scientific circles as more of an authority on the mountain gorilla than his mentor. As the years passed, Fossey found herself pitted against her former student and the substantial forces at his command.

22

THE OTHER SIDE OF THE LINE

In 1974, after Harcourt and Stewart went home, Richard Rombach—his sense of direction unimproved—got lost again. This time, however, there was a different ending: he fell down a ravine and was badly injured. When he was finally discovered by Rwelekana and the trackers, Rombach seemed at the point of death. Fossey nursed him, as she had Harcourt, until he was well enough to be moved to the Ruhengeri hospital.

By this time, Dr. Pierre Weiss at Ruhengeri knew a lot about Dian Fossey. He had treated her for bleeding after her botched second abortion and tended her long list of maladies, including her broken leg. He had been impressed by the way she treated Sandy Harcourt's wounds after he was gored by the buffalo. Weiss's respect was not insignificant. He was considered an extraordinary doctor. Patients bypassed Kigali to seek treatment at Ruhengeri. He was a fine physician, not easily impressed.

Weiss was past sixty, and shorter than Fossey, but he had Continental manners and piercing, cornflower-blue eyes that other women had described as "incredible." He was no "great white hunter" like Alan Root or Bob Campbell, but he had style, intelligence, and social position. Many people were surprised when he began making frequent climbs up the mountain to court Dian Fossey.

"He would always arrive at the camp really early, under darkness, and leave in the dark," recalls Kelly Stewart, who had returned to Karisoke, without Sandy Harcourt, to finish her dissertation. Few of the residents of Karisoke got to know him, she says. To most he remained an enigma.

Fossey, guarded as usual, said little about her visitor. She was fanatical about her privacy. But as the courtship progressed, she began to loosen up. She told people that Dr. Weiss had proposed marriage. She was considering it, but there was a problem. Weiss wanted her to live in Ruhengeri, but she was adamant about remaining on her mountain with the gorillas. There were other complications, too.

Weiss lived with his three children by a mistress who had died. Also part of the household was the children's nanny, an African woman named Fina, and her three children. Fina and Weiss had at one time been lovers, and Fina wasn't about to be displaced in the doctor's home by Dian Fossey.

"All I know about this came from Dian," says Stewart, "but Fina apparently felt that Dian was moving in on her territory. When Dian went down to talk to Weiss she used to put Mace in her purse to protect herself against Fina. She said, 'Fina is a crazy, crazy, wild woman.'" One day when she came back from visiting Weiss, she found her car window smashed. She said Fina had done it.

Weiss eventually asked Fina and her children to move out of his house, and he and Fossey actually came close to marrying, to the point of posting banns—a Catholic announcement of an impending marriage—at the French Embassy in Kigali.

Rosamond Carr confirms this and makes it clear that the relationship with Weiss was not a figment of Fossey's imagination. "He just couldn't stop smiling," she says. "He was walking on air. I saw him quite a lot because he was the only surgeon we had at that time, and he was absolutely great, really a very talented doctor. Then all of a sudden it came to an end. But it ended because somebody had told Dian that he was once again seeing Fina sometimes."

Stewart was at Karisoke when it ended. She says that one evening she noticed that Fossey, cooking dinner for a guest at camp, seemed very upset and nervous. When she asked her what was wrong, Fossey said, "It's finished. It's over."

Stewart had the impression that it was Fossey who had broken it off. She seemed relieved, Stewart says. "I don't think Dian really wanted to go through with it." But despite this, Fossey made the breakup of the affair into another hurt, another rejection.

Sometime later, Weiss married Fina and left for France. Fossey's grieving intensified and her mood darkened again. Even if she had decided not to marry Weiss, she had a desperate need to be wanted and loved. For Dian Fossey, Pierre Weiss became yet another human being who had betrayed her.

Only the gorillas stayed true. As those who spent time near her repeatedly observed, for Dian Fossey gorillas were surrogate humans. But there is great danger for a primatologist who is that emotionally involved; it becomes impossible to maintain the objectivity needed for scientific study.

Fossey no longer treated the gorillas as subjects of study. "She treated them as friends," Harcourt says. "She played with them, she groomed them, she cuddled them, and almost treated them as pets, except that they were wild roaming animals. It's easy to see from her book that she became extremely personally involved with some of them, and certainly, judging from what she said to people about them, she had personal likes and dislikes of the individual animals. The difficulty with this is that her personal likes and dislikes affected her interpretation of their behavior."

Many scientists take a less circumspect view of anthropomorphism than Harcourt. These experts say that the projection of the observer's attributes and emotions onto the study animal is not necessarily bad. They believe that anthropomorphism can be a useful tool. Frans de Waal, the author of *Chimpanzee Politics,* does not apologize for his anthropomorphic bias. There's no other way, he says, to look at these animals, they're so close to humans.

Kelly Stewart agrees, explaining that anthropomorphism has given her a lot of insights into gorilla behavior. She says that thinking in an anthropomorphic way can help scientists understand the gorilla's motivation.

The trick, Stewart says, is to maintain the distance between observer and subject: "Always say *as if*—the animal acted *as if* he were jealous. Dian got to the point where she was saying 'This animal *was* jealous.' She attributed to them emotional responses that were very personal, that were the result of *her* feelings for them."

By 1976, Fossey had finished her thesis and was working on articles and her book (which would appear in 1983). She had all but abandoned any pretense to scientific objectivity. Now when she went out to the field, she still took her camera, but it was as if she were going to visit friends and take snapshots. For hours at a time, she sat among the gorillas, coaxing the infants onto her lap, cuddling and tickling them as if they were children. The adult gorillas were unconcerned. By now, they were completely receptive to her presence in the group. (Today, visitors to Karisoke must deal with the disconcerting and sometimes dangerous behavior of adult gorillas, now weighing more than three hundred pounds, who want to play the games that Dian Fossey taught them. They still want to sit in a human lap and be tickled.)

Fossey often wrote her friends that it was only among the gorillas that her troubles would lift. She described her magical encounters with them, particularly with Group 4—Uncle Bert's group.

There was the time when the gorillas, having eaten their morning meal, went to rest in their day nests. While the others napped, tiny Kweli, the year-old son of Uncle Bert and Macho, came over, touched Dian curiously, and fell asleep on her foot.

Another time, after watching the gorillas for many hours, Fossey, feeling despondent and soaked to the skin after a downpour, started back for her cabin. Suddenly, Digit appeared in front of her. His soft brown eyes seemed to take in her anguish, her misery, her loneliness. He had a stalk of the wild celery that gorillas love, and shyly laid the offering at her feet. Before she could react, he disappeared.

There were many such encounters. Some were funny and happy, as when she showed Puck the pictures of himself in *National Geographic.* Laughing to herself, she photographed him as he examined the magazine in puzzlement. Other times, like an incident she described in *Gorillas in the Mist,* were even more satisfying. After a day of observation, Fossey—thinking the gorillas gone—stood up to determine their direction for the next day's contact. "Suddenly," she wrote, "I heard a noise in the foliage by my side and looked directly into the beautifully trusting face of Macho, who stood gazing up at me. She had left her group to come to me. On perceiving the softness, tranquility, and trust conveyed by Macho's eyes, I was overwhelmed by the extraordinary depth of our rapport. The poignancy of her gift will never diminish."

The gorillas seemed to embody many of the qualities Fossey perceived in herself—the essential tenderness and vulnerability—and the gifts they gave her were a respite from her loneliness. With them, she felt trusted, welcomed, loved. "Dian really believed that the gorillas loved her," says Kelly Stewart. And she would do anything to save them. Already she had publicly stated (at the 1974 Wenner-Grenn conference in Vienna) that she would protect the gorillas with her life. Hinde says she said similar things to him on many occasions. She certainly "did feel that the preservation of the mountain gorilla was more important than the interests of the Rwandadese," he says. "She didn't mind if the gorilla moved out and raided the crops and did damage outside the forest. *Nothing* should come in the way of the gorilla being preserved."

By this time it was clear to many people that Fossey's feelings toward the gorillas had gone far beyond professional dedication to their survival. The preservation of the gorillas had become her obsession, the expression of all Fossey's deepest emotions and fears.

She seemed possessed—by love and inexhaustible rage. The romance of Dian Fossey, the American woman who came to Africa and stayed, was turning dark.

Ian Redmond, whom Fossey affectionately nicknamed her "worm boy," came to Karisoke to study the intestinal parasites that plague the apes. He was one of the few students she did not turn against. He stayed from 1976 through the end of 1978—the longest uninterrupted time of any of the students. He seems to have survived by keeping to himself and doing what he was told. Usually he was spared her wrath, possibly because he helped see her through the most traumatic events she had experienced on the mountain. To this day, Redmond has remained loyal to Fossey, writing about her after her death with admiration and affection.

Redmond is reluctant to describe some of her more bizarre behavior. He seems to have had a sixth sense for avoiding it; generally, when poachers were caught and brought into the camp, he kept to his cabin. Once, however, about six months after his arrival, he saw Fossey at the height of her anger. It was a sight he would not forget. He saw Dian Fossey order a captured poacher stripped and whipped about the genitals.

"The thing I remember the most about that incident is the intensity of the feeling in Dian's expression," he says. "It can only be described as hatred. That's the only word for it." When Redmond tried to calm her down, she screamed that he was stupid. The poacher had killed many of her gorillas. She had the proof from informers. He had been brought to her by a park guard.

Captured poachers were delivered to Fossey by park guards. "The reason they did so," Redmond says, "was because she encouraged them—partly to reward them, and partly so that she could interrogate the poachers. This was largely done through interpreters because the poachers didn't necessarily know Swahili. She would ask them names, places, dates, and try to get information out of them in the hope that the park authorities would use that. She would keep records of it. I think she always felt that one day these people would be prosecuted and all this evidence that she had accumulated would be useful. She also tried to make them feel like a piece of dirt, and she would do that by spitting at them and insulting them in any way she could think of. She was trying to stop these people from coming in the forest and killing gorillas.

"She kept building up the larger-than-life image so that they believed she was someone with strange powers. She really played on this. She knew the importance of black magic in Africa and she knew that if somebody put a spell on one of her staff, he would start to waste away." But the elaborate spells that Fossey used to psychologically torture the poachers weren't her only methods. "She would use any means available to her to discourage or humiliate or frighten the poachers," Redmond says. "But she obviously didn't want to be kicked out of the country. She didn't leave a mark on them. She kept a tight control on herself and she always insisted on not being left alone with them. There were always witnesses—this way no one could accuse her of having gone off alone with a poacher and done unmentionable things to him, or killed him."

On the night that Redmond watched Fossey torture the poacher, there were half a dozen park guards present. There was also a Rwandan student and the usual African staff of three or four men. Fossey watched as the witnesses encircled the prisoner, who was being held by two of the guards. "She had the snares that the poachers used put on his wrists to hold him," Redmond says. "It was partly so that he wouldn't run away and partly out of a sense of poetic justice."

The next phase of the torture began with Fossey smearing the poacher with gorilla dung. "Again, this was to humiliate him and to maximize the psychological effect," Redmond says. All during the brutal ritual, Fossey shouted obscenities at the prisoner, "a mixture of words that came into her head—English, French, German, Swahili," communicating "a feeling of absolute outrage."

While she ranted, one of her African staff whipped the poacher's genitals with stinging nettles. "He didn't cry out, as I recall," Redmond says, "and it wasn't a case of pinning him down and slowly and maliciously tormenting him. It was all part of a tirade of physical and verbal abuse."

Then Fossey asked him questions about other poachers, incidents, locations of snares, and so forth. After half an hour the man was released.

"He wasn't the first poacher to be taken up to camp and interrogated and humiliated," says Redmond. "I think *humiliated* is the important word to remember. I don't think Dian was trying to wreak physical revenge for the gorillas they had killed. I think she was just trying to scare the shit out of them and prevent them from coming back."

Having said all that, Redmond wants to set the record straight on some overblown rumors. "She did not pistol-whip poachers, and she did not interfere with their testicles with pliers. The pliers were just tools in the camp. She would approach the poacher, holding pliers or machete, looking at that part of their anatomy and threatening them."

Nor, says Redmond, did Fossey ever set fire to a poacher's hut, as some have claimed. But he does admit that she set fire to a mattress. He says that she did not shoot at tourists—she fired over their heads. He says that she did not shoot forty head of cattle—she shot one cow and held the others hostage. It wasn't as bad as some people have made things out to be, says Ian Redmond.

But it was bad enough.

23

THE DEATH OF DIGIT

"Digit was two and a half years old when I first met him in September, 1967, on the slopes of Mount Visoke within the Parc des Volcans of Rwanda," Dian Fossey wrote in an essay entitled "His Name Was Digit." "He was then a playful little ball of disorganized black fluff from which protruded two button-like velvet brown eyes full of mischief and curiosity."

Fossey observed Digit for over ten years. She came to see him as nearly human. He was gentle, a quality she admired above all others—in man, where she seemed to rarely find it, and gorilla, where it always seemed close to the surface.

As she watched Digit grow up, she saw the first sparks of inquisitiveness and the first inklings of trust. She saw him as a shy, childish wallflower, gradually coming out of his shell and making friends. She loved to tell of his first awkward sexual encounter—at the age of six. She wept when he suffered wounds in a fight with a rival male. She worried when, at age eleven, Digit himself became a silverback. She found it sad to watch the young playful animal endure the transition from "childhood" to a new role in the group. As one of the "watchdogs," Digit's job was to stay on the periphery of the group, assisting the dominant silverback in the protection of the other animals.

It is not difficult to imagine Fossey's devastation on December 31, 1977, when Digit, holding off six poachers and their dogs, took six spear wounds to his body. Thanks to his valor, the rest of the group were able to flee to safety. Digit was able to kill one of the poachers' dogs before dying alone. "I cannot allow myself to think of his anguish, his pain, and the total comprehension he suffered of knowing what humans were doing to him," Fossey wrote.

When Ian Redmond found Digit's body, the carcass had been mutilated. His head and hands were chopped off. No tragedy on the mountain—and there had been so many—had a greater impact than this one. No hurt had penetrated Dian Fossey so deeply.

Digit, the star of the National Geographic television special, was the most famous of all the mountain gorillas. Fossey's photo of him examining her pencil and notebook had become something of a classic gorilla portrait. Another photo had been used for a Rwandan travel poster. Digit's serene countenance had been seen all over the world.

When she learned of Digit's death, Fossey did not rant and rave. She was composed, Redmond says, and the two of them stayed up all night discussing what to do next. They talked of distributing a poster, identical to the travel poster, but with Digit's head cruelly hacked off. They talked of starting a fund to hire proper patrols to protect the gorillas. Digit could not die in vain, Fossey insisted. She was forming a plan.

The next day, Fossey's African staff caught a man with a blood-stained bow and five arrows. He was tortured—Fossey admitted as much, bragged about it even, in a letter she wrote a week later to Ambassador Crigler. During the course of his torture, the man confessed to killing Digit and named his accomplices. Fossey turned him over to the park guards.

"I was only some 10 or 20 minutes alone with him," Fossey wrote to Bob Campbell. "I could not trust myself with that thing; for Digit's sake I couldn't kill him."

Fossey buried Digit in the cemetery she had established for gorillas behind her cabin, close to where she herself would be buried eight years later. "There are times when one cannot accept facts for fear of shattering one's own being," she wrote. "From that moment on, I came to live within an insulated part of myself."

Dian Fossey declared war against any person or institution that would bring harm to her animals—deliberately or accidentally. In the days following Digit's death, she wrote to the president of Rwanda, Juvénal Habyalimana, and to just about every person she could think of. She begged for punishment of the poachers. Her letter to Crigler said she wanted President Habyalimana to grant her the authority to kill poachers. She wrote Robinson McIlvaine, head of the African Wildlife Leadership Foundation, her backer in the early days, that she wanted "complete revenge" for Digit's death. She admitted to him that she had come close to killing the poacher responsible for the gorilla's death.

Perhaps the most poignant was the letter Fossey wrote to Bettie Crigler, the wife of the ambassador, in which she wrote that she wished she could have died in Digit's place.

In the first two weeks of 1978, Fossey was battling pneumonia and a fever of 104 degrees, but she managed to write twenty letters. The results were impressive. The *New York Times* reported Digit's death; Walter Cronkite reported it on his evening broadcast; the story made international news. The British Flora and Fauna Preservation Society offered to help. The world turned its attention to the plight of the mountain gorillas in Rwanda. A Digit Fund was established to collect the contributions that began pouring in.

In the wake of Digit's death, Fossey became increasingly identified around the world as the gorillas' champion. There was nothing self-serving or opportunistic in her response to her increasing fame. She allowed herself to become a celebrity because she realized that world-wide attention was necessary to keep the remaining gorillas alive.

But publicity wasn't Fossey's only outlet; there were more inter-rogations and more whippings. By May, her behavior had become so outrageous that the Rwandan government fined her $600 for tortur-ing a suspect named Munyarukiko, whom she considered the ring-leader. Fossey said she happily paid the money in order to be allowed to stay in the country.

Meanwhile, cables were flashing between the U.S. Embassy in Kigali and the State Department. "Dian Fossey is near hysterical," Crigler reported.

No one could decide what to do about Dian Fossey.

Fossey was very ill at times and, some days, was barely able to move around. After more than a decade of pushing herself beyond endurance, she was still driven. But by this time revenge was her sole motivation. For years, her love for the gorillas had sparked her effort. Now the only emotion driving her was hate.

The hate blinded her to everything around her. And while she railed against the poachers who had killed thirteen of her gorillas between 1976 and 1978, she drank herself into oblivion. Then the unspeakable happened: two researchers accused Fossey of causing the death of a baby gorilla while in a drunken stupor.

The researchers, Amy Vedder and Bill Weber, say that this in-cident caused them to turn against Dian Fossey. As workers for the New York Zoological Society, they had come to Karisoke shortly after Digit's death. In February 1978, they traveled to Zaire to pick up a baby gorilla being held by park officials there. When they brought the sick, half-starved infant back to Karisoke, Fossey, uncharacteris-tically, didn't allow herself to get involved. She kept her distance and told Vedder and Weber to nurse it. They agreed, sensing that Fossey

301

could not handle another emotional attachment to an animal that was likely to die. She gave them careful instructions. But she stayed away.

Under their care the gorilla seemed to be coming around; its condition seemed to be improving. Then one night Fossey, very, very drunk, came to check up on them. They weren't feeding the gorilla right, she accused them—she would show them how it should be done. Swaying on her feet, barely able to stand, she insisted, despite outcries from the others, on pouring liquid medicine down the gorilla's throat. The animal began to choke. When it passed out, Vedder and Weber managed to revive it, but too much liquid had got into the infant's lungs. It died shortly thereafter.

After that, Vedder and Weber were willing to believe the worst of Dian Fossey. For her part, Fossey added their names to the long list of people who were conspiring against her.

The deaths of Digit and the infant gorilla were the first of more deaths to come.

On July 24, a student named David Watts found the body of Uncle Bert, the patriarch of Group 4, Digit's old group. He had been shot, and his head chopped off. Then, just after Fossey left camp to chase the poachers, Vedder and Weber found another body. Macho, the female whose quiet gaze had once comforted Fossey, had also been shot, and her side sliced open. Kweli, the child of Macho and Uncle Bert, had been wounded by gunshots but was still alive. He managed to live until October 25.

It was determined after an investigation that the gorillas had been surprised by the killers while they were still asleep in their night nests. They stood no chance against the attackers.

The park officials reacted swiftly to the horror, arresting numerous suspects. But it couldn't escape anyone's notice that it was as if Group 4—Fossey's favorite—had been specifically selected for destruction. The gorillas were not killed by trapping or baiting. They had been slaughtered intentionally, for a reason—perhaps to send a message to the woman who loved them.

Fossey cabled Ian Redmond, who was back in England nursing a badly infected wrist wound, and he returned immediately to help her organize additional patrols. When he sized up the situation Redmond concluded that the killings were not a planned retaliation against Fossey. "A lot has been said about that," he says, "but I was the one who had found Digit and the reason that I found him was that I was following a trap line, a line of snares. We'd cut several snares. There had been a lot of poacher activity seen in the area by a tracker who went out to find Group 4. When I found Digit's body it was evident from the line of the traps that we'd been following, and the direction of the footprints, that the poachers came across the gorillas, or they heard them ahead."

At the time of the killings seven months later, "Group 4 had moved to the Zaire border section of the park and there had been no reason for the poachers to know particularly that they were the gorillas of Dian Fossey," Redmond says.

Amy Vedder agrees that Digit's killing was probably not planned. But she believes that the killings of the other three gorillas happened under very different circumstances and for very different reasons.

"The poachers," Vedder says, "had camped the night before in close proximity to Group 4. There were no trap lines around, and it looked very much like they came specifically to hunt gorillas and to hunt that group. It was done very early in the morning before David Watts would get out there. He was out there every day with that group. So, it looks like they knew much more about what they were doing, and had planned it quite well. So the circumstances surrounding that killing are quite different than the killing of Digit. And there's the possibility that it was done in retaliation for what had gone on between the death of Digit and the end of July. It was during that time that a lot of these illegal acts had been committed by Dian."

Fossey suspected that Digit had been killed for his skull—there was a well-established European market for gorilla skulls at the time. And she believed that the Rwandan park guards were responsible for the subsequent killings. The publicity surrounding Digit's murder had generated foreign aid to help protect the remaining gorillas, and she believed that the guards wanted to make sure the money kept coming in.

Unlike the gorillas killed earlier, Uncle Bert, Macho, and Kweli had been shot. But few of the impoverished people who lived around the park could afford a rifle. "The evidence suggests," says Redmond, "that it was a bolt-action medium-velocity rifle, the sort that the park guards use. I'm not saying it *was* a park guard," he adds, pointing out that poachers often bribe guards for the use of their weapons or simply steal them.

With the exception of Redmond, the other researchers at Karisoke, the primatologists involved with the issue, and Rwandan and U.S. officials were unanimous in their opinion: the gorillas were killed as revenge against Fossey's tortures and humiliations. Had she not been so brutal with the poachers, they said, the gorillas wouldn't have died.

Frank Crigler cabled the State Department that the government of Rwanda believed the gorillas had been killed as part of a vendetta against Fossey. He warned that she might be expelled from the country.

Fossey would never admit that the killings of the Group 4 members were a vendetta against her. She would simply not consider the possibility—not in conversation, not in her letters, not in her diary. Instead, she became even more vicious toward the poachers.

While Fossey continued to argue for the protection of the gorillas with armed patrols authorized to kill, the Mountain Gorilla Project, a group organized by Alexander Harcourt and underwritten by the

British Fauna and Flora Preservation Society, came up with a plan for saving the gorillas based on long-term conservation principles.

Clearly not intended to win Fossey's approval, Harcourt's proposal completely ignored her or any of her contributions to gorilla observation, habituation, or protection. It was not surprising that she dismissed the proposal out of hand.

A lot of influential people, however, saw a great deal of sense in the plan. For the first time since the Parc des Volcans was created by white colonialists, Harcourt's proposal made allowances for the concerns of the Rwandan government and the local people.

The basic stance of the Mountain Gorilla Project could be summarized as follows:

The fewer than three hundred mountain gorillas left on earth survive in a little patch of wilderness, surrounded by a densely populated area—600 people per square mile—and these people are very poor and hungry. They are told not to cross an invisible boundary beyond which is a virtual grocery store stocked to the rafters with fresh antelope and buffalo meat, and beyond which are rich grazing fields for their skinny cows. The only thing that keeps them from overrunning the park are the rantings and ravings of a white woman who cares more about gorillas than people. Fighting the locals is a losing battle. What you have to do is manipulate them somehow into wanting to preserve the park and the gorillas. What they want is food and money, and what will bring both into the area is foreign tourists. Tourists—wanting to see the gorillas up close—will spend hard currency in Rwanda. The government of Rwanda will thus take a more active role. Tourists will create jobs for the locals in hotels and restaurants. Tourists will need drivers, guides, porters, suppliers of equipment. Make it as easy as possible for the tourists to visit the gorillas in their natural setting and you've won the battle.

The Mountain Gorilla Project intended to send primatologists into the park to habituate a couple of new groups of gorillas specifically for tourists. With the new groups, the groups that had been under study for years would not suffer from overexposure to people, and scientists

could peacefully continue to record their behavior. The newly habituated gorillas wouldn't flee from people, and the people would have
the thrill of seeing the animals up close.

Fossey reacted to this plan as if someone had proposed a development of high-rise apartments in the heart of the wilderness. The
gorillas *must* be left alone. She was trying to keep people *out* of the
park, not bring them in. Tourists would cause trouble. They would
bring disease—and gorillas were highly susceptible to human germs.
The money, she said, should be spent on *protecting* the gorillas; patrols
were needed to cover every inch of the Virungas. If any funds were
left over, then they could think about long-term conservation. She
used every argument imaginable, but it was not a battle that she could
win.

"I was hearing stories that Rwandans were getting annoyed at her
and might push her out any day," says Robinson McIlvaine of the
African Wildlife Leadership Foundation. "It was all over the anti-
poaching. I said, I want to get you out of that business, to train people
to do that work. She agreed. But very quickly I discovered that she
didn't want to give up her anti-poaching patrols after all. She was
getting to the point where, because of her emphysema, she was no
longer able to follow the animals around and do her research. So the
anti-poaching had become her big thing."

To try to patch things up, McIlvaine and the Criglers went up to
Karisoke to see Fossey. McIlvaine remembers the visit well: "She said
a very revealing thing: 'All of you have family, a marriage and kids. I
don't have any family. Those gorillas are my family and that hut is my
home.' She was feeling very poorly, she wanted to die there. In the
end she managed it."

Even as she tried to rally her energies against the Mountain Gorilla
Project, Dian Fossey was slowly giving up. Little by little, she was
turning away from everything and everybody, even the gorillas.

Looking back on their final memories of Fossey, Amy Vedder and

Bill Weber cite Christmas Day, 1978, when members of Group 5 came within four hundred yards of her cabin.

"I said, 'Group Five has brought you a Christmas present. They're right here!' " Vedder recalls. "Dian didn't want to go and see them. I thought it would be something that would give her some kind of spark and a reason for being. There they were—on Christmas Day!"

But Fossey, despondent and defeated, stayed in her cabin.

24

EXILE

The concentrated effort to eject Dian Fossey from Rwanda began in 1978, shortly after the July killings in Group 4. According to Ambassador Crigler, she had become a "liability" in everyone's eyes.

Frank Crigler encouraged her in a letter to go off somewhere and finally finish her book. Fossey's response was filled with venom and paranoia. No, she said, she could never leave the gorillas unprotected. She said she suspected the park officials of killing the gorillas, and added that her book, when it appeared, would have to be titled "And Then There Were None."

She was under enormous pressure; everyone wanted her to leave. Both the Leakey Foundation and the National Geographic had threatened to withhold their subsidies. The Leakey people had even asked her point-blank to go away for at least six months—until things quieted down.

The State Department seemed the most anxious to arrange her

departure, but they tried to work in a diplomatic manner. One confidential State Department memo reported that delicate negotiations were under way to avoid an international fiasco. The Rwandan officials were adamant about Fossey's departure. They wanted her out, and the sooner the better; her latest offense had been to fire a gun in response to an unannounced visit by a tourist group from Chicago. Attempting to ease the situation, U.S. officials pointed out that Fossey was world-famous. They said that when anyone in Europe thought of Rwanda they thought of gorillas and Dian Fossey. They promised Rwanda that she would go soon and stay out of their hair for two years. But please, they begged, allow her to leave of her own volition.

Even Secretary of State Cyrus Vance got involved, cabling Frank Crigler the news that the plan for Fossey's departure had been worked out with the National Geographic. They had promised to provide the money to operate Karisoke while she was gone.

Peter Veit, Fossey's research assistant during this time, remembers the pressure well. "When I was there, the Rwandans were constantly trying to get rid of the research station and Dian. And it made good sense. There were seven wonderful cabins up there. They could charge three hundred dollars a night. The tourists who come will pay whatever it costs. And you're in walking distance of Group Five, which is wonderful to see.

"Before the Mountain Gorilla Project started we were having a lot of renegade guides who would bring tourists up from the bottom of the mountain. They would interrupt our research. We would try to scare them by threatening to report them. But they weren't about to turn around and go back, having hiked four hours to get there. The tourists were obnoxious, too. 'Forget it, man,' they'd say. 'I paid my fifteen dollars to see those gorillas, I'm going to *see* them.' This would happen during the summer every day. That all changed after the Mountain Gorilla Project took over. They've kept tourists in line and traffic flow to a minimum."

About that time, Fossey's cabin was broken into. "The cabin's tin sheeting had been cut with cutters, and they'd gone in and ransacked the cabin," Veit recalls. "We estimated about $10,000 worth of stuff. It was apparent that they knew where to go in and where things were in Dian's cabin." Veit, inside his cabin at the time, heard nothing. Fossey, luckily, was away for the night.

The pressure was reaching a breaking point. The tension showed. Fossey had definitely slowed down, but at this point no amount of rest could relieve the burden of her long sacrifice. She had emphysema; she suspected she had cancer. But she didn't stop smoking or cut her alcohol consumption. She did slow down her pursuit of the poachers—as a result of the problems of the previous year.

Suddenly, with the Mountain Gorilla Project parked at the bottom of her mountain, there were people around all the time. The idea of strangers on her mountain, invading her territory, may have been the final straw. More than any government plea or warning, it was what convinced her to leave Karisoke.

Once she decided to go, the arrangements were complicated; the problem of who would run Karisoke seemed insurmountable. Initially, she agreed—very grudgingly—that Sandy Harcourt was the best-qualified candidate. However, she withdrew her approval of him when she learned that he intended to bring Bill Weber and Amy Vedder along to habituate new gorilla groups for the Mountain Gorilla Project. Weber and Vedder had replaced Harcourt and Stewart as her most despised enemies.

The negotiations might have gone on forever were it not for a Cornell professor, Glenn Hausfater, who came to see Fossey at Karisoke in August 1979 and offered to arrange a visiting professorship at his university. She accepted.

In the letter to Bettie Crigler informing her of the decision, Fossey didn't linger over the details of her appointment; she had other news: Munyarukiko, the worst of the poachers, was dead. He "somehow met with an accident in the forest," she wrote. "Isn't that a shame!" But her sadness came through in a letter to Jim Doherty of *International Wildlife* magazine. She feared that the anti-poacher patrols would be abandoned in her absence. She said she had agreed to leave only because she was so ill.

After what seemed like endless deliberation, Fossey agreed that Harcourt and Stewart should run Karisoke in her absence. After weeks of fighting like hell about it, she had finally capitulated and, ever mercurial, seemed to completely reverse her feelings. She told people she was enthusiastic about Harcourt and Stewart taking over—and she seemed sincere.

"There were still problems," Stewart recalls, "but they weren't very big. A lot of it was just countless little problems. Problems with the National Geographic making us sign away our rights to photographs, but not paying us any salary, or anything. It was pretty niggling. In fact, it was actually the best relationship Sandy had with Dian in a long time."

Ian Redmond, temporarily employed by the Mountain Gorilla Project, saw her off. He remembers her departure as a sad one: "She was packing up to live in Ithaca and do an associate professorship and she had come back to camp [after a three-month absence while making arrangements] and found that her monkey was dead, and that her dog was in bad shape. Dian had ideas that people had tormented the dog, and that the Africans hadn't fed it. She felt that the camp was falling apart, too, and that all she had worked for looked like it was in danger of falling apart or being used for a tourist camp.

"I stayed at the camp that last night and helped Dian do her packing, and the next day porters came down with her dog Cindy. I've got some photographs of the truck that she hired with all the Africans in the back and all the stuff and her inside. It was a very tearful farewell because a lot of these guys had been working for Dian for years. It may not have been a bosom friendship, but it was like any long employer-employee relationship."

After saying good-bye to her, Redmond realized that she had no intention of coming back. "This appeared to be it," he says. "She'd packed her house and it wasn't a case of going away for six months or three months. It appeared that this was it."

The shock of life in a busy college town after nearly sixteen years of isolation in the African rain forest is hard to imagine. Fossey's living conditions at the university, recalls Anita McClellan, her closest friend during this period, were unspeakable. "She lived in this really terrible student-type housing, really cheesy," McClellan says. "I remember being horrified that a famous primatologist was living in a kind of apartment that I personally would hate to live in. And the people next door to her were having rock parties on Saturdays."

During the day, Fossey lectured—unforgettably. Her presentations, which drew people from all over, were vivid and extremely moving. She drew her listeners into the world of Karisoke with an irresistible force—and an almost unbearable sadness.

At night, often alone in her room, she wrote letters compulsively, deep into the small hours. She wrote back to everyone who wrote to her. McClellan recalls a letter from a third-grader in Wisconsin who wanted to know what the insects in the forest looked like. Fossey spent hours drafting a reply. She wanted to make sure children understood her explanations, giving their letters the kind of careful attention few busy adults could match.

Karisoke, however, was never far from her mind. Africa still held her, and the mountain gorillas, the dead and the survivors, lived in her thoughts. Before she could grow too anxious about what she had left, long letters arrived from Kelly Stewart and Sandy Harcourt. "We'd write her about the gorillas," says Stewart, "and she would write very friendly letters thanking us. I was under the impression that it all actually worked out quite well."

Besides her lectures and correspondence, Fossey tried to work on revisions of her book. Stacey Coil, her secretary at the time, recalls that she got pneumonia while working on it. "She sat in her apartment with the doors wide open in the dead of winter so that the dogs and cats and birds and everybody could come say hello," Stacey says. "She missed the big fireplace from camp, so she went and bought a fake fireplace. She had a mattress on the floor for Cindy, she had her little typewriter and an African table. She'd sit there with her coat on, typing, with the door open, freezing. It was ridiculous. She got a staph infection in her foot. It was very swollen right up to the anklebone, black, horrible. She wouldn't go to the doctor. I'd have to drag her each time."

The book wasn't going well. McClellan was starting to worry about whether it would ever be finished. She had bought the rights to the book years before, when an agent sent her Fossey's outline, "a very rough thing that she had banged out in the forest." Then the waiting had begun. McClellan sent Fossey frequent letters and notes of encouragement, but she saw little evidence of real progress.

The book was something like six years overdue by the time Fossey arrived at Cornell. At this time, McClellan read a draft for the first time. It was a mess, she recalls. "She had a manuscript that was written chronologically and that had basically something like 275 gorillas running around loose in it. I couldn't keep it straight. And there was almost nothing of Dian in it. Just a little, little bit."

McClellan knew that Houghton Mifflin was not interested in publishing a dull, dry scientific text. The company wanted a book for the popular market, and Dian Fossey was a gold mine of riveting copy, if only it could be prised out. This woman had, after all, gone into the jungle, untrained, on her own. She was the first human to be touched by a gorilla, the first human to play with them. McClellan's problem was how to get Fossey to produce a best-selling book.

When the two women visited the National Geographic Society in Washington to look at possible illustrations for the book, McClellan was still thinking hard about how to infuse some emotion into the work. Fossey was so tough, so guarded. But sitting in the photo archive, sifting through pictures taken over the past twelve or thirteen years, Fossey changed before McClellan's eyes. "She looked at herself in pictures and she looked at herself with gorillas that had been murdered or that had died and gorillas that hadn't grown up to have offspring yet. She just relived all of those experiences minute by minute and with such a depth of emotion and purity of reaction that I felt almost embarrassed to be there. This love of the gorillas was very, very much a part of who she was. That was the Dian that I knew."

Those moments began a strong emotional connection between Fossey and McClellan, a bond that resulted in *Gorillas in the Mist*. Because of the trust Fossey had started to show in her, McClellan was able to convince her that she needed to rewrite the book in a way that would make gorillas come alive for people who knew nothing about them. Fossey eagerly responded to the idea.

McClellan suggested first off that they reorganize the manuscript. "So," she says, "we took the manuscript and cut the thing up." The fragments were tossed into dishes from Fossey's kitchen according to category. "We had a 'silverback' dish and a big bowl of 'infants,' and so forth. And then it got hot in the apartment, and we opened the sliding glass doors and a gust of wind came and all those little paragraphs went flying. It was a nightmare."

All that effort came to naught, however. "She rewrote the book according to the scheme that we had with the dishes, and it didn't work at all because it was still dry as toast. So she had to do it all over again."

McClellan was beside herself. The book she envisioned would never get written at Cornell, with the rock music blaring next door. She felt her "best talent" deserved better, and she proposed, for the summer of 1981, to relocate Fossey to a cabin in Maine. She thought that the book would receive the author's best attention there in the quiet woods.

This proved the ideal solution. The setting reminded Fossey of her

Karisoke home. "The climate was ideal," recalls McClellan, "because it was misty and wet, but it wasn't freezing cold, and there was a big stone fireplace exactly like in her cabin. And there was a little kitchen; it was the perfect setting for us, because she started to get right into the environment of what she was writing about."

That summer, the two women talked for hours about what should be in the book. Sometimes the talks grew very emotional. Fossey was drinking a lot, and could be extremely difficult at times. But McClellan's respect and admiration for her never diminished. "She was writing about her life and these were very hard chapters to write," McClellan says. "This was stuff that was difficult for her to even talk about, much less write about. But she wanted to write about it well. And she wanted to write about it honestly. She also wanted the book to get the gorillas visibility and not have her be in the forefront. So we had many complicated goals to achieve, and of course it had to be scientific." Fossey—cognizant of the opinions of Sandy Harcourt and others—was concerned about accusations of anthropomorphism that could discredit the book, but McClellan helped her overcome her fears.

In the end, the book did get written. Fossey bounced around a number of titles—"Gorillas of the Mountain Mists," "Mountain Gorillas of the Mist," "Misted Mountain Gorillas"—before deciding on the final "Gorillas in the Mist." The Houghton Mifflin people didn't much like it, but she stuck with it.

Published in 1983, the book was a huge popular success, accomplishing Fossey's goal of reaching many of the people who were in a position to do something about the gorillas' survival. But, as she had feared, the scientific community received it coolly. Peter Veit, reviewing it in *Natural History* magazine, summed up the general feeling: "It is not a scientific exercise professionals will likely cite."

As soon as the book was finished, and long before it was published, Fossey, having also finished her lecture commitment at Cornell, began to talk about returning to Karisoke.

315

She saw plenty of urgent reasons for her return. For one thing, Harcourt had announced he intended to leave, and the station would be without a strong leader. Fossey's reaction to the news of Harcourt's departure was mixed. She was both distressed and relieved. She wrote Rosamond Carr that she had no one to replace Harcourt, but "a snake might do." After an exhaustive review of the possibilities, she finally settled on Richard Barnes, a Madingley Ph.D. who had studied hyenas in Kenya.

Uppermost in Fossey's mind was the fact that during her absence the gorilla population had suffered further decimation. The culprits, of course, were the poachers. By 1983, the price of a gorilla skull had risen to $500. This was a fortune to an impoverished Rwandan. But the most shocking news was the report that another zoo—the Antwerp Zoo in Belgium—had placed an order for an infant mountain gorilla. The African Wildlife Foundation (formerly the African Wildlife Leadership Foundation) estimated that at least ten adult mountain gorillas were killed (in November and December 1982) before an infant (as it later turned out, not even a mountain gorilla) was delivered. Fossey knew that the Antwerp purchase actually cost even more gorilla lives than that: *two other* infant mountain gorillas had been seized before they could be smuggled out of the country; they had clearly been captured by poachers who had heard of the Antwerp offer. Since Belgium never ratified the 1975 international treaty making such an act illegal, the conservation community could do little more than protest.

Convinced that her methods were the only ones that worked, Fossey packed her bags and returned to Karisoke in June 1983.

25

....

NYIRMACHABELLI

Climbing up to Karisoke with an oxygen booster in tow, Fossey was overwhelmed by the old magic of the place. But more than anything, she was overwhelmed by the welcome of her old friends. In a letter to Stacey Coil, she described her first encounter with Group 5. The gorillas approached her without hesitation, touching her, cuddling her. "I could have died right then," she wrote, "and wished for nothing more on earth simply because they remembered." She knew she had done the right thing by coming back.

Then she found the research center in what she considered abominable shape. No sooner had she put her bags down than accusatory letters began to fly.

It didn't take long for the members of the Mountain Gorilla Project consortium to get worried about the trouble she might cause. She was a "time bomb," one of them said. But, surprisingly, the government of Rwanda welcomed Fossey back with open arms. John Blane, the

317

U.S. Ambassador who had replaced Crigler, explained to the State Department that those in power in Rwanda were aware of her attitude toward Africans but also realized that she had made a great contribution to science, and to Rwanda. Blane said he found Fossey "perfectly rational" upon her return and added that she had agreed to curb her "freewheeling" a bit.

At first, she was on her best behavior. She appeared more rational and seemed healthier. She welcomed the procession of journalists who had come to Karisoke to record her return—the Garsts came to make a film for *Wild Kingdom,* Kevin McKean came to do the same for *Discover,* and Ron Hollander came to do an article for *Town & Country.* She charmed them all; she had never lost that gift.

But as soon as the journalists departed, the old Dian Fossey emerged.

Richard Barnes, in place by now as director of Karisoke Research Centre, was surprised. He thought she had returned for a short stay, but it was almost immediately apparent that she was back for good. Soon, he and another researcher, Karen Jensen, realized that if Fossey stayed, they would have to leave.

"We were disturbed by her racial attitudes," says Barnes. Fossey screamed at the African staff, insulting and humiliating them. The Africans "were frightened of her and carried themselves like beaten dogs," he recalls. Then Barnes witnessed his first poacher interrogation. He was scandalized.

"She sat with a lamp beneath her, asking the poacher simple questions at first, trying to find out who his companion had been," Barnes says. "He pretended he didn't understand. She snarled at him. When he refused to talk she struck him across the knees with a ballpoint pen, like a schoolteacher. She became increasingly aggressive. She discovered he had no identity card. She said, 'You have no identity card, so you could disappear. We could kill you and nobody would know.' He still didn't answer. She took a rope from a snare and

318

knotted it into a noose and put it round his neck and threw it over a beam. She said, 'I'm going to kill you,' and she started pulling on it as if she was going to hang him. By this time I was becoming disturbed. I said, 'I hope you're not going to go any farther.' I knew she wasn't, I knew she had no intention of hanging him, but all the same I wanted it to come to an end then. She said no, and stopped."

Six months after Fossey's return, Barnes wrote to the National Geographic (which had paid his salary) to explain why he was leaving his post. "I have some experience of life in the bush and I have worked before with an eccentric recluse in the bush. However, Dian Fossey . . . seems unable to perceive the world as others see it, and one suspects that she may not be able to distinguish between right and wrong."

But as had so often been true, Dian Fossey could appear as different as night and day. It all depended on who was around. When McClellan came to see her (she stayed for about a month, through New Year's of 1984), she was entranced by Karisoke—and her hostess.

Fossey took McClellan out to see the animals. "It was a huge physical exercise for her to do that," McClellan says. "She tried not to let on to me. We went together maybe three or four times. And it was extremely moving."

One of the gorillas they saw was Tiger, who represented an unusual phenomenon—a silverback living alone, without a group. "She was totally at home in the forest," McClellan says, "totally in her element. She knew where Tiger was. And when she made gorilla sounds he came out."

He recognized Fossey; there was no question in McClellan's mind. "He touched her. And it was so intimate, I started to cry. I was so moved by it that tears were streaming down my face. I felt like an intruder, it was such an intimate, personal greeting. It was almost like Anatoly Sharansky meeting his wife again after eighteen years of solitary confinement."

• • •

By 1984, the National Geographic Society had completely cut off Fossey's support. But, with her last burst of energy, she rallied again, using contributions to the Digit Fund and proceeds from her book to step up the poacher patrols. Her report for the first quarter of 1984 stated that 582 traps had been cut and 67 poachers had been spotted.

The only thing slowing her down was her health, which she had all but ignored. In April she had to be brought down on a stretcher to the Ruhengeri hospital. She thought she'd had a heart attack, but the problem—as before—was her emphysema.

The people who knew her well believed she was dying of cancer. Stacey Coil thought so. She had become certain of it when she learned in Ithaca that Fossey was making out her will. "I'm sure it was terminal," Coil says. "Nothing else would have made her write a will without telling me."

Ambassador Blane thought she was dying, and the last time Frank Crigler had seen her—about a year before she was killed—she appeared weak and listless. He never learned exactly what her medical problem was, but he, too, was persuaded she was dying, and his first thought was that she would commit suicide.

On Crigler's last night at Karisoke, Fossey had taken him outside her cabin and pointed across the meadow. In the darkness, the eyes of all the creatures of the meadow were visible. "Wasn't this wonderful," she said to him.

Mrs. Carr, her loyal friend, tells of the last days of Dian Fossey: "Every two months she had to renew her visa application, and she had to get down the mountain to do that. First of all, her porters had to see that a taxi of some kind, some kind of a vehicle, arrived at the foot of the mountain. Then, after a two-hour ride, when she got to Ruhengeri, she would get another taxi filled with Africans to take her to Kigali. And she had to do that every two months until December 1985.

"And not only that, she would arrive in Kigali and would have to get a letter from the Director of Tourism for the immigration people. And she would wait for that letter, and she would go back sometimes three days in a row before he gave it to her. And then finally she would get a paper saying that she could have a two-month visa. And then, to her utter amazement, she was given a two-*year* visa. It was about—I don't know the exact day, probably the fourth or sixth of December. And she was so overjoyed that she went all over Kigali— into stores, everywhere, telling people, hugging people and saying 'Now I can go back and stay at the mountain, I don't have to come down every two months. Oh, it's so wonderful, I'm so happy.' And three weeks later she was killed."

The murder of Dian Fossey made headlines around the world. Tributes poured in. Scenes of Fossey playing with Digit flashed from TV news broadcasts. In Rwanda, the investigation of her murder began.

Six months later, the Rwandans charged Rwelekana, her tracker, and Wayne McGuire, the only white person present in the camp, with her murder. The charges against Rwelekana were dropped after he allegedly hanged himself in his cell. McGuire, fearing the worst and proclaiming his innocence, fled the country.

The government of Rwanda made no attempt to seek McGuire's extradition from the United States. Instead, after a forty-minute trial, he was convicted in absentia and sentenced to death by hanging. The motive ascribed to him by the investigators was theft. They said he killed Fossey in order to steal her research notes.

But that made no sense to anyone who knew anything about Dian Fossey and her research. There was really nothing there to steal. And why would McGuire peel away the side of her hut, when he could have walked in through the front door? Much was made of the fact that the hair in Fossey's hand was not African hair; there were suspicions it belonged to McGuire. But it proved on analysis to be hair from Fossey's own head.

For months, Fossey's students and acquaintances continued to speculate about the circumstances surrounding her death.

"My immediate reaction was that somebody had taken revenge on her," says Harcourt. "And that, as far as I know, was the immediate reaction of almost everyone. And the other immediate reaction of almost everybody was that they weren't the slightest bit surprised—because we'd all been wondering for a very, very long time when this was going to happen. You just can't treat other people in the way that she did, without at least wondering whether somebody is going to take revenge, if not necessarily expecting it. She expected revenge herself."

Dian Fossey's final resting place is the yard behind her cabin at Karisoke among the graves of her beloved gorillas. Engraved on her tombstone, is her African nickname, Nyirmachabelli.

When she learned that this was what the Africans called her, she said she wanted it on her tombstone. She said it meant "the woman who lives alone on the mountain."

NYIRMACHABELLI
Dian Fossey
1932–1985
No one loved gorillas more
Rest in peace, dear friend
Eternally protected
In this sacred ground
For you are home
Where you belong

POSTSCRIPT

The words on her tombstone are not the last words on Dian Fossey. Her epitaph continues to be written.

"It is her monument, her epitaph, that there are more gorillas than ever in the Parc National des Volcans," says Diana McMeekin of the African Wildlife Foundation. "For this alone she deserves veneration. There are now 310 gorillas—ninety more than Dian Fossey's lowest tally—and their number is growing, not diminishing."

Since Fossey's death, only one gorilla has fallen victim to the poachers' snares. Thanks to the efforts of the government of Rwanda and generous public contributions to the Digit Fund, now sponsored by the Morris Animal Foundation of Englewood, Colorado, and to the Mountain Gorilla Project, sponsored by the African Wildlife Foundation, the Fauna and Flora Preservation Society of Great Britain, and the World Wide Fund for Nature, there are daily patrols which monitor the health and safety of the gorillas. The patrols also remove snares intended to capture game, which can cause fatal wounds to gorillas.

Six gorillas have died of diseases shared with humans—one of them from measles. McMeekin speculates that a local tourist guide or woodcutter could have brought the disease into the park. There was an epidemic of measles among the Rwandans at the time.

Fossey's research station at Karisoke continues to function. And tourists are flocking to Rwanda. These new visitors are discouraged from making physical contact with the gorillas, but sometimes this is impossible to avoid. Having read Fossey's book and seen the popular film it spawned, the tourists want to reach out to them, and the gorillas seem to welcome it. McMeekin says that even though every one of the gorillas has witnessed some atrocity perpetrated on their own kind by human beings, all are still willing to give humans the benefit of the doubt.

It is not hard to imagine what Dian Fossey would have to say about tourists on *her* mountain. But the woman who made the long trip from Louisville to see the gorillas, the woman who feared that the entire species was destined for almost immediate extinction, would undoubtedly be happy to know that Digit's ancestors still live in the meadows of the Virungas where she found her home.

BIBLIOGRAPHY

Abrams, Meyer et al. *The Norton Anthology of English Literature,* 3rd ed. New York: W.W. Norton, 1975.

Abramson, Howard S. *National Geographic: Behind America's Lens on the World.* New York: Crown, 1987.

Adamson, George. *Bwana Game.* London: Collins & Harvill, 1968.

Africa Review 1986. Essex: World of Information, 1986.

Ajayi, J.F., and Michael Crowder, eds. *Historical Atlas of Africa.* Burnt Mill, England: Longman House, 1985.

Akeley, Carl. *In Brightest Africa.* New York: Garden City, 1925.

Allen, Philip, and Aaron Segal. *The Traveler's Africa.* New York: Hopkinson and Blake, 1973.

Andrews, Wayne, and J.G.E. Hopkins, eds. *Dictionary of American History: 1940–1960.* New York: Charles Scribner's Sons, 1961.

Aman, David. *Apes: Monster of the Movies.* London: Lorrimer, 1975.

Audrey, Robert. *African Genesis.* New York: Dell, 1961.

Bailey, J.R.A., ed. *Profiles in Africa.* Nairobi: Drum Publications, 1985.

Baumgartel, Walter. *Among the Mountain Gorillas.* New York: Hawthorn Books, 1976.

Bayly, Joseph. *Congo Crisis.* Grand Rapids: Zondervan, 1966.

Beard, Peter, ed. *Longing for Darkness: Kamante's Tales.* New York: Harcourt Brace Jovanovich, 1975.

Bibliography

Benirschke, Kurt, ed. *Primates: The Road to Self-Sustaining Populations.* New York: Springer-Verlag, 1986.

Bourne, Geoffrey. *The Ape People.* New York: G.P. Putnam's Sons, 1971.

Brown, Dale, and Edmund White. *The First Men: The Emergence of Man.* New York: Time-Life Books, 1973.

Brown, Leslie. *Africa: A Natural History.* New York: Random House, 1965.

Cohen, John. *Africa Addio.* New York: Ballantine Books, 1966.

Cole, Sonia. *Leakey's Luck.* New York: Harcourt Brace Jovanovich, 1975.

Conrad, Joseph. *Three Great Tales.* New York: Vintage Books, 1958.

———. *Congo Diary.* New York: Doubleday, 1978.

Craig, Hugh. *Great African Travelers.* London: George Routledge and Sons, 1890.

Crewdson, John. *By Silence Betrayed.* Boston: Little, Brown, 1988.

Crichton, Michael. *Congo.* New York: Alfred A. Knopf, 1980.

Croegaert, Luc. *Premières Afriques.* Brussels: Didier Hatier, 1985.

Crowther, Geoff. *Africa on a Shoestring.* South Yarra, Australia: Lonely Planet Publications, 1977.

———. *East Africa: A Travel Survival Kit.* South Yarra, Australia: Lonely Planet Publications, 1987.

Curtis, Arnold, and Elspeth Huxley, eds. *Pioneers' Scrapbook: Reminiscences of Kenya 1890 to 1968.* London: Evans Brothers, 1980.

Dart, Raymond. *Adventures with the Missing Link.* Philadelphia: The Institutes Press, 1959.

Dasmann, Raymond. *The Conservation Alternative.* New York: John Wiley & Sons, 1975.

De Gramont, Sanche. *The Strong Brown God.* Boston: Houghton Mifflin, 1977.

Desmond, Adrian J. *The Ape's Reflexion.* New York: The Dial Press/James Wade, 1979.

Devore, Ivan, ed. *Primate Behavior: Field Studies of Monkeys and Apes.* New York: Holt, Rinehart and Winston, 1965.

De Waal, Frans. *Chimpanzee Politics: Power and Sex among Apes.* Baltimore: Johns Hopkins, 1989.

———. *Peacemaking among Primates.* Cambridge: Harvard University Press, 1989.

Dewsbury, Donald, ed. *Leaders in the Study of Animal Behavior.* London: Associated University Presses, 1985.

Dinesen, Isak. *Isak Dinesen's Africa.* San Francisco: Sierra Club Books, 1985.

Dixson, A.F. *The Natural History of the Gorilla.* London: Weidenfeld & Nicolson, 1981.

Evans, Bergan, and Cornelia Evans. *A Dictionary of Contemporary American Usage.* New York: Galahad Books, 1957.

Fage, J.D. *A History of Africa.* New York: Alfred A. Knopf, 1978.

Fagg, William, ed. *The Living Arts of Nigeria.* New York: Macmillan, 1972.

Fetner, P. Jay. *The African Safari: The Ultimate Guide to Photography, Wildlife, and Adventure.* New York: St. Martin's Press, 1987.

Forbath, Peter. *The River Congo.* New York: E.P. Dutton, 1979.

Fordham, Paul. *The Geography of African Affairs.* Harmondsworth: Penguin, 1965.

Fosbrooke, Henry. *Ngorongoro: The Eighth Wonder.* London: Andre Deutsch, 1972.

Fossey, Dian. *Gorillas in the Mist.* Boston: Houghton Mifflin, 1983.

———. "Infanticide in Mountain Gorillas with Comparative Notes on Chimpanzees."

Bibliography

Glenn Hausfater and Sarah B. Hrdy, eds. *Infanticide: Comparative and Evolutionary Perspectives*. Hawthorne, N.Y.: Aldine, 1984.

Garrat, John, and Peter Gay, eds. *The Columbia History of the World*. New York: Harper & Row, 1972.

Garver, Richard, ed. *Research Priorities for East Africa*. Nairobi: East African Institute of Social and Cultural Affairs, 1966.

Gatti, Attilio. *Here Is Africa*. New York: Charles Scribner's Sons, 1943.

Gide, André. *Travels in the Congo*. Harmondsworth: Penguin, 1986.

Goodall, Alan. *The Wandering Gorillas*. London: William Collins Sons, 1979.

Goodall, Jane. *In the Shadow of Man*. Boston: Houghton Mifflin, 1971.

————. *The Chimpanzees of Gombe*. Cambridge, Mass.: Belknap Press of Harvard University Press, 1986.

Graham, Alistair. *The Gardeners of Eden*. London: George Allen & Unwin, 1973.

Griffin, Donald. *Animal Thinking*. Cambridge, Mass.: Harvard University Press, 1984.

Grzimek, Bernhard, ed. *Grzimek's Animal Life Encyclopedia,* vol. 10. *Mammals Pt. 1*. New York: Van Nostrand Reinhold, 1968.

————. *Encyclopedia of Ecology*. New York: Van Nostrand Reinhold, 1976.

————. *Encyclopedia of Evolution*. New York: Van Nostrand Reinhold, 1976.

————. *Encyclopedia of Ethology*. New York: Van Nostrand Reinhold, 1977.

Hahn, Emily. *Eve and the Apes*. New York: Weidenfeld & Nicolson, 1988.

Hamburg, David, and Elizabeth McCown, eds. *The Great Apes*. Menlo Park: Benjamin/Cummings, 1979.

Hatch, John. *Africa Emergent*. Chicago: Henry Regnery, 1974.

Hausfater, Glenn, and Sarah Blaffer Hrdy. "Comparative and Evolutionary Perspectives on Infanticide: Introduction and Overview." *Infanticide: Comparative and Evolutionary Perspectives*. Hawthorne. N.Y.: Aldine, 1984.

Hayes, Harold T.P. *The Last Place on Earth*. New York: Stein and Day, 1983.

Hemingway, John. *No Man's Land: The Last of White Africa*. New York: E.P. Dutton, 1983.

Hennessy, Maurice. *The Congo*. New York: Frederick A. Praeger, 1961.

Hibbert, Christopher. *Africa Explored: Europeans in the Dark Continent 1769–1889*. New York: W.W. Norton, 1982.

Hinde, Robert A. *Ethology*. Oxford: Fontana Paperbacks, 1982.

————. "Can Nonhuman Primates Help Us Understand Human Behavior?" in Barbara B. Smats et al. *Primate Societies*. Chicago: University of Chicago Press, 1986.

Hofer, Angelika, and Gunter Ziesler. *Safari: East African Diaries of a Wildlife Photographer*. New York: Facts on File Publications, 1984.

Hoff, Michael, and Terry Maple. *Gorilla Behavior*. New York: Van Nostrand Reinhold, 1982.

Hrdy, Sarah Blaffer. *The Woman That Never Evolved*. Cambridge, Mass.: Harvard University Press, 1981.

Huet, Michel. *The Dance, Art and Ritual of Africa*. New York: Pantheon Books, 1978.

Jackson, Henry F. *From the Congo to Soweto: U.S. Foreign Policy Toward Africa Since 1960*. New York: Quill, 1984.

Bibliography

Jolly, Alison. *The Evolution of Primate Behavior.* New York: Macmillan, 1985.

Kane, Robert. *Africa A to Z.* rev. ed., New York: Doubleday, 1972.

Kanza, Thomas. *Conflict in the Congo.* Harmondsworth: Penguin, 1972.

Kaplan, Marion. *Focus Africa.* New York: Doubleday, 1982.

Kevles, Bettyann. *Watching the Wild Apes: The Primate Studies of Goodall, Fossey, and Galdikas.* New York: E.P. Dutton, 1976.

————. *Thinking Gorillas: Testing and Teaching the Greatest Apes.* New York: E.P. Dutton, 1980.

Kingdon, Jonathan. *East African Mammals,* vols. IIA, III, IIIA. New York: Academic Press, 1974, 1977, 1979.

Lamb, David. *The Africans.* New York: Random House, 1982.

Leakey, L.S.B. *By the Evidence.* New York: Harcourt Brace Jovanovich, 1974.

Leakey, Mary. *Disclosing the Past.* New York: Doubleday, 1984.

Leakey, Richard, and Roger Lewin. *Origins.* New York: E.P. Dutton, 1977.

Legum, Colin, ed. *Africa: A Handbook to the Continent.* rev. ed., New York: Frederick A. Praeger, 1966.

Lemarchand, Rene. *Rwanda and Burundi.* London: Pall Mall Press, 1970.

Lewin, Roger. *Bones of Contention.* New York: Simon & Schuster, 1987.

Lewis, David Levering. *The Race to Fashoda.* New York: Weidenfeld & Nicolson, 1987.

Lewis, John, and Bernard Towers. *Naked Ape or Homo Sapiens?* New York: Humanities Press, 1969.

Linden, Eugene, and Francine Patterson. *The Education of Koko.* New York: Holt, Rinehart and Winston, 1981.

Linden, Eugene. *Silent Partners: The Legacy of the Ape Language Experiments.* New York: Times Books, 1986.

Littell, Blaine, and Eric Robins. *Africa: Images and Realities.* New York: Praeger Publishers, 1971.

Lopez, Barry. *Of Wolves and Men.* New York: Charles Scribner's Sons, 1978.

Manyeto, Rex, ed. *The ABC of Modern Africa.* Los Angeles: African American Trading Company, 1979.

Marais, Eugene. *The Soul of the Ape.* New York: Atheneum, 1969.

Mazrui, Ali. *The Africans: A Triple History.* Boston: Little, Brown, 1986.

McEvedy, Colin. *The Penguin Atlas of African History.* Harmondsworth: Penguin, 1980.

McEwan, P.J.M., ed. *Twentieth-Century Africa.* New York: Oxford University Press, 1968.

Monti, Nicolas, ed. *Africa Then: Photographs 1840–1918.* Alfred A. Knopf, 1987.

Moorehead, Alan. *No Room in the Ark.* Harmondsworth: Penguin, 1962.

Morris, Desmond. *The Naked Ape.* New York: McGraw-Hill, 1967.

Morris, Ramona, and Desmond Morris. *Men and Apes.* New York: McGraw-Hill, 1966.

Mowat, Farley. *Woman in the Mists.* New York: Warner Books, 1987.

Munger, Ned. *Touched by Africa.* Pasadena: Castle Press, 1983.

Murray, Jocelyn, ed. *Cultural Atlas of Africa.* New York: Facts on File Publications, 1981.

Naipaul, V.S. *A Bend in the River.* New York: Vintage Books, 1980.

328

Bibliography

Nyamweru, Celia. *Rifts and Volcanoes: A Study of the East African Rift System.* Nairobi: Thomas Nelson and Sons, 1980.

Odhiambo, E.S. et al. *A History of East Africa.* Burnt Mill, England: Longman, 1977.

Passmore, John. *Man's Responsibility for Nature.* London: Gerald Duckworth, 1974.

Perrin, Alwyn, ed. *The Explorer's Ltd. Source Book.* New York: Harper & Row, 1973.

Perrin, Porter. *Writer's Guide and Index to English.* 3rd ed., Chicago: Scott, Foresman, 1959.

Pictorial Rhodesia. Salisbury: Rhodesia National Tourist Board, no date.

Reed, David. *111 Days in Stanleyville.* New York: Harper & Row, 1965.

Regan, Tom. *The Case for Animal Rights.* Berkeley: University of California Press, 1983.

Renard, Jules. *Natural Histories.* New York: Horizon Press, 1966.

Reuter, Henry, ed. *Official Touring Guide to East Africa.* Nairobi: News Publishers, 1970 and 1973.

Rimanoczy, Richard, and Leighton Wilkie. *The Principles of American Prosperity.* Old Greenwich, CT: Winona Press, 1975.

Rumbaugh, D., ed. *Language Learning by a Chimpanzee: The Lana Project.* New York: Academic Press, 1977.

Rwanda: A Country Study. Washington, D.C.: The American University, 1974.

Schaller, George B. *The Year of the Gorilla.* Chicago: University of Chicago Press, 1964.

————. *The Serengeti Lion.* Chicago: University of Chicago Press, 1972.

————. *Serengeti: A Kingdom of Predators.* New York: Alfred A. Knopf, 1972.

————. *Gorilla: Struggle for Survival in the Virungas.* New York: Aperture Foundation, 1989.

Seton, Ernest Thomson. *Wild Animals I Have Known.* New York: Penguin, 1987.

Severin, Timothy. *The African Adventure.* New York: E.P. Dutton, 1973.

Shoumatoff, Alex. *In Southern Light: Trekking through Zaire and the Amazon.* New York: Simon & Schuster, 1986.

Strum, Shirley C. *Almost Human: A Journey into the World of Baboons.* New York: Random House, 1987.

Taylor, Jane, and Leah Taylor. *Fielding's African Safaris.* New York: Fielding Travel Books, 1987.

Tongren, Sally. *To Keep Them Alive.* New York: Dembner Books, 1985.

Traveller's Guide to the Belgian Congo and Ruanda-Urandi. Brussels: Tourist Bureau for the Belgian Congo, 1951.

Traveller's Guide to Central and Southern Africa. London: IC Publications, 1986.

Traveller's Guide to West Africa. London: IC Publication, 1986.

Treager, James. *The People's Chronology.* New York: Holt, Rinehart and Winston, 1979.

Turnbull, Colin. *The Forest People: A Study of the Pygmies of the Congo.* New York: Simon & Schuster, 1962.

Turner, Kay. *Serengeti Home.* New York: The Dial Press, 1977.

Turner, Myles. *My Serengeti Years.* London: Elm Tree Books, 1987.

Turner, Thomas, and Crawford Young. *The Rise and Decline of the Zairian State.* Madison: University of Wisconsin Press, 1985.

Bibliography

Van Lawick, Hugo. *Among Predators and Prey.* San Francisco: Sierra Club Books, 1986.
Vienne, Gérard, and Guy Vienne. *Akagera.* Paris: Flammarion, 1980.
Wannenburgh, Alf. *The Bushmen.* Secaucus, N.J.: Chartwell Books, 1979.
West, Richard. *Congo.* New York: Holt, Rinehart and Winston, 1972.
Williams, J.G. *A Field Guide to the National Parks of East Africa.* London: William Collins Sons, 1967.
Winternitz, Helen. *East Along the Equator: A Journey up the Congo and into Zaire.* New York: Atlantic Monthly Press, 1987.
Wood, Michael. *Go an Extra Mile: The Adventures and Reflections of a Flying Doctor.* London: William Collins Sons, 1978.
Woodcock, P.G., ed. *Dictionary of Ancient History.* New York: Philosophical Library, 1955.
Young, Crawford. *Politics in the Congo.* Princeton: Princeton University Press, 1965.

Magazine/Journal Articles

Butynski, Thomas, and Jan Kalina. "The Impenetrable Forest." *Animal Kingdom,* 89:50–58, 1986.
Dart, A. "The Heart of Africa." *South African Journal of Science,* 54:49–51, 1958.
Donisthorpe, J.H. "A Pilot Study of the Mountain Gorilla in Southwest Uganda." *South African Journal of Science,* 54:52–73, 1958.
Fossey, Dian. "Making Friends with Mountain Gorillas," *National Geographic,* 137:48–67, 1970.
————. "More Years with Mountain Gorillas," *National Geographic,* 140:574–85, 1971.
————. "The Imperiled Mountain Gorilla." *National Geographic,* 159:501–23, 1981.
Hayes, Harold T.P. "Animal Kindom . . . or Animal Farm?" *Life,* 5:116–30, 1982.
————. "Living Relics of Our Past." *International Wildlife,* 13:4–13, 1983.
————. "The Dark Romance of Dian Fossey." *Life,* 9:64–70, 1986.
Hemingway, Ernest. "African Journal." *Sports Illustrated,* (dates unknown).
Leakey, Richard, and Alan Walker. "Homo Erectus Unearthed." *National Geographic,* 168:624–29, 1985.
Munger, Edward. "Conflict in the Congo: An Inquiry into Rape Charges." *American Universities Field Staff Reports,* 3:187–201, 1960.
Veit, Peter. "Gorilla Society." *Natural History,* 91:48–59, 1982.

Thesis and Lectures

Fossey, Dian. The Behaviour of the Mountain Gorilla. Darwin College, Cambridge University, April 1976.
Galdikas, Birute. Orangutan Adaptation at Tanjung Puting Reserve, Central Borneo. University of California, Los Angeles, 1978.

Bibliography

Lecture series by Dian Fossey, Fall, 1980

No. 1 Evolution and Classification of Primates

No. 2 Classification of Social Structures and Definitions of the Age-Sex Classes of the
Three Great Apes

No. 3 Relationships of Differential Physical Characteristics to the Respective Environ-
ments

No. 5 Physical and Behavioral Development of the Infant and Juvenile Stages of the
Three Great Apes.

No. 8 Methods of Communication

No. 9 Antagonistic and Affinitive Behavior

No. 10 Sexual Behavior

No. 11 Untitled

No. 12 Infanticide and Other Aberrant Behavior

Taped Interviews

Alexander, Cynthia 1/13/87
Alexander, John 7/87
Alexander, John (Baumgartel letter)
Attenborough, David
Barnes, Richard & Karen Jensen I
Barnes, Richard & Karen Jensen II
Belville, Norma 5/9/87
Brenan, Martin 11/12/86
Brown, Gordon 12/2/86
Burkhart, Michael
Caldwell, Tita I 10/21/86
Caldwell, Tita II 10/28/86
Caldwell, Tita III
Campbell, Bob I, II 1/27/87
Campbell, Bob III, IV 1/27/87
Campbell, Bob V, VI 1/87
Campbell, Bob (Mowat's version)
Campbell, Bob
Campbell, Bob 3/88
Caro, Tim 3/18/87
Carr, Rosamond (Roz) 1986
Carr, Rosamond I, II 1/87
Carr, Rosamond III 1/87
Clay, Peter 3/87
Coil, Stacey I
Coil, Stacey 3/16/87

Bibliography

Cox, Victor (on Fossey)
Coy, Dr. Fred & Welch, Dr. Richard (Kosair)
Crigler, Bettie I
Crigler, Bettie II
Crigler, Bettie 3/19/87
Crigler, Frank
Crigler, Frank (on mercenaries) 7/87
Croegaert, Fr. Luc 1/31/87
Cyr, Leo
D'Arcy, William, 3/25/87
Devore, Ivan
De Waal, Franz
DuBray, Sally
DuBray, Sally 4/8/86
DuBray, Sally
Ende, Sally & William
Flanagan, Kevin 8/28/87
Flanagan, Mary
Forrester, Alexander
Fossey-Cornell Conference
Fossey-Cornell Conference
Fossey, Galdikas (on Leakey)
Fossey (for GEO)
Fossey (memorial service I)
Fossey (memorial service II)
Fossey & Rowe
Fossey, Harry
Fossey (on gorillas)
Foster, James 4/88
Fowler, John 10/18/86
Fritts, Robert 8/86
Galdikas, Birute I 5/4/87
Galdikas, Birute II, 5/4/87
Galdikas, Birute I, II 1988
Galdikas, Birute III 1988
Garst, Warren 11/16/86
GEO/AWF 10/27/83
GEO/Serengeti 10/27/83
Sister Gerald (Weiss letter) 6/6/87
Goodall, Alan (dinner mtg.)
Gould, Root, McMeekin 4/87
Grobmyer, Mary White 3/17/87
Grobmyer, Mary White 5/30/87
Grobmyer, Mary White I

Bibliography

Grobmyer Mary White II
Grobmyer, Mary White (on Alene) 9/28/87
Grobmyer, Mary White 7/31/87
Groom, Graeme 1/16/87
Hamberger, Bob & Sonia
Hamberger, Lisa I
Hamberger, Lisa II
Hamburg, David
Harcourt, Alexander I
Harcourt, Alexander II
Harcourt, Alexander & Kelly Stewart 1/13/87
Hinde, Robert 1/87
Hinde, Robert II
Hjelm, Harold
Hoffman
Huber, Kathleen
Huges, Nancy 12/2/86
Humphrey, Nick 1/87
Imvaho
Jackman, Brian
Kalter, Sy 11/20/86
Kevles, Bettyann
Klein, Dr. Harold 11/23/86
Kitlhewer
Kotok 6/30/88
Krause, Patricia 7/27/87
Krause, Patricia 8/1/87
Leakey, Richard 6/24/87
Leakey Symposium I
Leakey Symposium II
Leakey Symposium III
Leakey Symposium IV
Lema, Benda
Levin, Rachel
Lewis & Hancock 5/18/87
Louprey (primatologist)
Maple, Terry 11/1/86
Martin, Bradley 6/23/87
McClellan, Anita I 12/6/86
McClellan, Anita II 12/6/86
McClellan, Anita III
McClellan, Anita 3/87
McClellan, Anita 8/6/87
McGinnis 5/10/87

Bibliography

McGreal, Shirley 11/15/86
McGuire, Michael I
McGuire, Michael II
McGuire, Michael 12/12/86
McGuire, Michael 2/25/87
McIlvaine, Robinson
McMeekin, Diana 3/88
Melone, Bob 8/5/86
Monfort, Alan & Nicole
Morgan, Barbara 6/16/87
Munger, Edwin
Murray, Dan 3/9/87
Nadler, Ronald 11/7/86
Nichols, Nick
Nichols, Nick 4/20/88
Nixon, Bob 11/25/86
NPR on Fossey
NPR on Fossey
O'Brien, Helen 6/8/86
Osmondson, Lita 10/20/86
Perlmeter, Stuart I
Perlmeter, Stuart II 6/12/86
Peckness, Mary 6/13/86
Phillips, Caroline 2/26/87
Pilbreay, David
Pierce, Ann 1/2/87
Pierce, Ann
Pierce, Ann 3/16/87
Price, Harold 11/18/86
Price, Harold 2/26/87
Rafert, Jan 11/7/86
Raine, Jacqueline 4/14/88
Ramsey 4/27/88
Father M. Raymond 7/16
Father M. Raymond 3/28/87
Redmond, Ian 1/87
Redmond, Ian 1/87
Redmond, Ian
Redmond, Ian
Rhine, Ray 9/6/86
Rombach, Richard I, II 3/19/87
Rombach, Richard III, IV 3/21/87
Rombach, Richard V 3/22/87
Root, Alan 10/7/88

Bibliography

Root, David 11/6/87
Root, Joan 6/21/87
Rust, Katherine I 5/19/87
Rust, Katherine II 5/19/87
S. F. Memorial I 5/1/86
S. F. Memorial II 5/1/86
Schaller, George 8/20/87
Schaller, George 11/19/87
Schwartzel, Betty 10/8/86
Schwartzel, Betty II
Schwartzel, Betty, Doppleman, Enrich
Shalley, Craig
Smith, Bob 10/11/86
Smith, M.G. 8/6/86
Snider 8/7/86
Stewart, Kelly 1/6/87
Stewart, Kelly 10/23/87
Stewart, Kelly 10/23/87
Stewart, Kelly (gorillas)
Strum, Shirley 6/14/86
Strum, Shirley
Talbot, Lee I
Talbot, Lee II
Taylor, Christopher
Tolbert/Lanford
Tompel, Barbara 5/27/86
Turner, Thomas & Newbury, David 1/88
Veit, Peter I 6/1/86
Veit, Peter II 6/1/86
Voelmayer, Gloria
Washburn, Sherwood 11/14/86
Watts, David I, II 1/22/87
Watts, David III
Watts, David IV, V
Watts, David (on McGuire) 2/10/87
Weber, Bill & Vedder, Amy I, II 1/25/87
Weber, Bill & Vedder, Amy III, IV 1/25/87
Weber, Bill V, VI 1/31/87
Weber, Bill VII, VIII 3/1/87
Weber, Bill & Vedder, Amy 3/28/87
Weber, Bill
Wenner-Grenn 7/22
Wenner-Grenn 7/23–25
Wenner-Grenn (Fossey)

Bibliography

Wenner-Grenn (Conclusion)
White, Tim I 7/5/86
White, Tim II 7/5/86
White, Tim 11/86
Wilkie, Leighton 6/21/86
Will Settlement 1/14/88
Wiser, Christine
Wrangham, Richard I 10/13/86
Wrangham, Richard II

INDEX

337

340

343

348

San Diego State University, 212, 219
San Francisco Chronicle, 56
San Jose State College, 38–39, 57, 58
Sanweckwe (tracker), 99, 131, 141,
    143, 149, 155, 157
  Fossey's relationship with, 147–48,
    151–52, 153
  poachers encountered by, 95, 144
Saturday Evening Post, 112
Schaller, George, 72, 80, 84, 118, 127,
    131, 134–41, 146, 147, 171,
    186, 198
  anthropomorphism issue and, 140
  background of, 138, 145
  base camp of, 90, 143
  books by, 118, 145, 282
  census conducted by, 90, 138, 206,
    280
  concerned for survival of mountain
    gorillas, 141, 149
  extraordinary career of, 137–38
  findings of, 134–37, 139–40
  hours of observation accumulated by,
    90, 150, 151, 189
  L. Leakey's desire to expand on work
    of, 113, 121–22
  lions of Serengeti studied by, 123, 150
  tracking and observation methods of,
    89–90, 138–39, 145, 199
  trouble in Congo and, 90, 137, 197
Schaller, Kay, 138, 143
Schwartzel, Betty Henry, 53, 54, 103,
    105, 120, 164
Scott, Jonathan, 203
Scott, Peter, 212
Search for the Great Apes, The, 257, 266,
    272, 275, 299
Serengeti Plain, 78, 79, 83–84, 90, 123,
    150
Serengeti Research Institute, 264
Serengeti Shall Not Die, 195
Shackford (candidate for assistantship),
    209, 210, 211, 212
silverbacks, 135, 136, 137
  infants killed by, 287
Simbas, 129, 158
Smith, Marshall, 237, 241, 249
Snider, Ed, 160, 250, 252
Staley, Tom, 161

Stanford Center for Intellectual Studies,
    137
State Department, U.S., 178, 179, 273,
    301, 304, 318
  in effort to eject Fossey from
    Rwanda, 308–9
  trouble in Congo and, 159–60, 162
Stewart, Kelly, 164, 265, 270, 282,
    284–87, 294, 310
  on anthropomorphism issue, 293
  on Fossey's abuse of African staff,
    275–76
  Fossey's accusations against, 286–87,
    288–89
  Fossey's friendship with, 285–86
  on Fossey's mistrust of humans, 277–
    278
  on Fossey/Weiss affair, 291, 292
  Harcourt's romance with, 280, 287,
    288
  Karisoke run by, during Fossey's
    absence, 311, 312

Taung Baby, 64–65, 71
Thomas Aquinas, Saint, 111
Thorpe, Edmund, 91
Thorpe, W. H., 127–28, 194
Tiger (mountain gorilla), 319
Tinbergen, Niko, 194
tools and tool making, 65, 71, 121
tourism, 92, 323–24
  Mountain Gorilla Project and, 305–6,
    309
Town & Country, 318
Traveller's Rest, 50, 86, 128–30, 163
  bought by Baumgartel, 39–40, 42
  de Munck boys' execution and, 174,
    175, 177
  Fossey's escape to, 165
  Fossey's first stay at, 86, 88–91
  Fossey's return to, 128–30
  guests entertained with gorilla lore
    at, 66–67, 88–89
  as place to see mountain gorillas,
    51–52, 66, 67–68
  refugees from Congo at, 129
Tsavo, 78, 79
Turner, Thomas, 175
Tutsis, *see* Watutsis

349

PHOTO CREDITS

1–3. Courtesy of Mrs. Betty Schwartzel

4. The Louis Leakey Foundation/National Geographic Society

5. Dian Fossey, courtesy of Joan and Alan Root

6. Alan Root/National Geographic Society

7–15. R. I. M. Campbell

16. Evelyn Gallardo

17. A. H. Harcourt

18. K. J. Stewart

19. Linda Flynn

20. Ian Redmond

21–22. Y. Arthus Bertrand, Peter Arnold, Inc.

23–24. Brenton Kelly

ABOUT THE AUTHOR

HAROLD T. P. HAYES was editor-in-chief of *Esquire* and *California* magazines. In addition to many articles, he was the author of *The Last Place on Earth, Three Levels of Time,* and *Smiling Through the Apocalypse: Esquire's History of the 60s.* He lived in Los Angeles and died on April 5, 1989.